ACTIVITY-BASED COST MANAGEMENT IN GOVERNMENT

Second Edition

ACTIVITY-BASED COST MANAGEMENT IN GOVERNMENT

Second Edition

Gary Cokins

MANAGEMENTCONCEPTS
Vienna, Virginia

ɭɭɭ
MANAGEMENTCONCEPTS
8230 Leesburg Pike, Suite 800
Vienna, VA 22182
(703) 790-9595
Fax: (703) 790-1371
www.managementconcepts.com

Printed in the United States of America

Library of Congress Cataloging-in-Publication Data

Cokins, Gary.
  Activity-based cost management in government / Gary Cokins.
— 2nd ed.
    p. cm.
  Includes bibliographical references and index.
  ISBN 1-56726-181-7
  1. Finance, Public—United States—Accounting. 2. Activity-based costing—United States. I. Title.

HJ9750 .C65 2006
352.4'4—dc22   2006046229

This book is dedicated
to the late

Robert A. Bonsack,

a friend, a mentor, and a craftsman
in the field of
advanced cost management.

About the Author

GARY COKINS is an internationally recognized expert, speaker, and author in advanced cost management and performance improvement systems. He received a BS in Industrial Engineering/Operations Research from Cornell University and an MBA from Northwestern University's Kellogg School of Management.

Gary began his career as a strategic planner with FMC Corporation developing business simulation models. With FMC's Link-Belt Division he served as Financial Controller and then Production Manager, which exposed Gary to the linkages among cost information, operations, performance measurements, and results.

In 1981, Gary began his management consulting career, first with Deloitte, where he focused on designing and implementing performance improvement systems. Next, with KPMG Peat Marwick (which became Bearing Point), Gary implemented integrated business systems and ultimately focused on cost management systems, including activity-based costing (ABC). At KPMG Peat Marwick, Gary was trained in ABC by Professor Robert S. Kaplan of the Harvard Business School and by Professor Robin Cooper. In 1992, Gary became the director of the National Cost Management Consulting Services for Electronic Data Systems (EDS), which merged with A.T. Kearney. In 1996, Gary joined ABC Technologies, Inc., then the global leader in activity-based cost management software, which was acquired in 2003 by SAS Institute Inc. (www.sas.com), where Gary serves in a thought-leadership role. SAS is a global leader in business intelligence, predictive analytics, and performance management software solutions.

Some of Gary's public sector clients have included Parks Canada, Los Angeles Power & Water, the Tennessee Valley Authority, the Chicago Housing Authority, the World Bank, the U.S. Marine Corps, the U.S. Air Force, and the U.S. Army.

In 1993, Gary received CAM-I's Robert A. Bonsack Award for Distinguished Contributions in Advanced Cost Management.

Gary was the lead author of the acclaimed *An ABC Manager's Primer* (ISBN 0-86641-220-4), sponsored by the Institute of Management Accountants (IMA) and the Consortium for Advanced Manufacturers-International (CAM-I). His *Activity-Based Cost Management: An Executive's Guide* (ISBN 0-471-44328-X) has ranked as the best-selling book of 151 titles on the topic. His other books include *Activity-Based Cost Management: Making it Work* (ISBN 0-7863-0740-4) and his latest work, *Performance Management: Finding the Missing Pieces to Close the Intelligence Gap* (ISBN 0-471-57690-5).

Gary is member of the *Journal of Cost Management* Editorial Advisory Board, a columnist for www.DMreview.com, and is Certified in Production and Inventory Management (CPIM) by APICS (The Association for Operations Management). He serves on numerous professional society committees, including the American Society for Quality's quality cost committee and the Supply Chain Council's supply chain operations reference (SCOR) framework cost metrics committee. He was the co-editor of CAM-I's *2001 Glossary of ABC/M Terms*.

Gary welcomes e-mail at: garyfarms@aol.com.

Table of Contents

Risk Management in the Departments of Defense and
Homeland Security 250
Filling the Risk Management Gap 251
The Integration of ABC/M and Performance Measures
in Risk Management 253

CHAPTER 9 **Implementing ABC/M through Rapid Prototyping** 255
ABC/M Is Perfectly Obvious—After the Fact 256
Rapid Prototyping: Eighteen Holes of Golf on a
Polo Horse 258
Building the First ABC/M Model—Tap Dance Now,
Waltz Later 260
Cost Object Profiling: A Key to Getting
Desired Results 262
Teach Them to Fish, and They Can Fish Forever 263
Constructing and Populating ABC/M Model #0—
The Starting Point 265
Analyzing Model #0 to Get Buy-In 268
Securing and Propagating the Learning:
A Communication Plan 269
ABC/M Model Design and Architecture for
Special Cases 270
Building the ABC/M System: Basic Factors 271
Right-Sizing the System 272
Time-Phasing ABC into ABM 272

CHAPTER 10 **Examples of ABC/M in the Public Sector** 275
An Introduction to Public Sector Case Studies 276
Case Studies 277
Parks Canada 277
U.S. Office of Rural Economic and Community
Development 280
U.S. Army, Fort Riley 281
City of Philadelphia Department of Streets 284
U.S. Navy, NAVAIR 286
U.S. Veterans Benefits Administration 291
U.S. Forest Service 295

Foreword

N THEIR PIONEERING BOOK *Relevance Lost: The Rise and Fall of Management Accounting,* Robert S. Kaplan and H. Thomas Johnson said that managerial cost accounting fell out of favor as industry paid more attention to financial accounting and reporting for external compliance rather than to managerial information for internal planning and control. One might say that financial accounting came to loom so large in the minds of business executives and stockholders that they lost sight of the meat-and-potatoes cost accounting that helps managers make daily decisions. When the top executives no longer cared about cost accounting, its value diminished in the eyes of managers.

The situation is no different in federal, state, and municipal governments, where fund accounting has long eclipsed any other method of determining how taxpayer money will be spent. As with financial accounting, using fund accounting for accurate cost estimation is difficult and often impossible. However, fund accounting is all that most legislators, political appointees, and career civil service executives appear to know. Only in the past few years have government leaders started to require the use of managerial cost accounting, but as yet not many at the very top know how to use it. If they do, they are not sufficiently skilled to use it effectively. As a result, progress has been slow in implementing activity-based cost management (ABC/M), a widely accepted cost accounting method in the commercial sector. However, now, during the 21st century's first decade, things are picking up. New uses for ABC/M, such as performance-based budgeting, have increased demand for this accounting approach. This bodes well for a future government that is

ACTIVITY-BASED COST MANAGEMENT IN GOVERNMENT

more cost-conscious and capable of delivering cost-effective services to citizens.

ABC and the Nature of the Federal Government

Before discussing activity-based cost management (ABC/M) in the federal government, readers who are not in the public service need some context regarding the size and structure of departments and agencies and the way they are funded on ABC/M's introduction and use. With nearly two million civilian employees (excluding the Postal Service) and more than 1.4 million in the active Army, Navy, Marine Corps and Air Force, the federal government is the largest employer in the U.S. The government's employees work in 15 major departments with dependent agencies, plus another 60 independent agencies. Each department, and often agencies within departments, may be viewed as quasi-autonomous subsidiaries of a massive holding company. As Chief Executive, the President presides over most of these entities, while a few report directly to the U.S. Congress. However, money for all federal entities comes through appropriations by legislators, so departments and entities tend to have two masters: Congress and the President. A staggeringly large and loosely organized entity with dual leadership, the federal government takes time to absorb changes such as activity-based costing. Similar comments apply to state and local governments.

The U.S. Congress allocates resources to departments and agencies through line item funding, most of the time with strictures on the use of the money. As a result, federal managers have less flexibility than their private sector counterparts in shifting resources to improve operations. Indeed, in 2005 one major federal entity was investigated by the U.S. Government Accountability Office (GAO), Congress' auditor and watchdog, for using funds allocated for certain operations to do cost studies of parts of those operations. Congress had forbidden the entity from applying funds in this way, yet had refused to provide money for any cost studies. Lacking flexibility with resources, federal managers have less reason to use managerial cost accounting. Yet, despite these obstacles, many departments, agencies, and individual federal managers have made substantial progress in introducing ABC/M to the federal government. This is because of regulations requiring managerial cost accounting in some form, continued pressure from the executive branch of government, competition from the private sector, and a general desire on the part of federal managers to provide better service to citizens.

Legal Background of Laws and Regulations Supporting ABC/M

Like many government management practices, ABC/M and managerial cost accounting in general have a legal background of laws and regulations. At the federal level of for the U.S. government, the first of these is the Chief Financial Officers Act of 1990 (the CFO Act), which gave rise to the Federal Accounting Standards Advisory Board (FASAB), which promulgates generally accepted accounting principles (GAAP) for federal entities. In the past 20 years, no single pronouncement by the FASAB has had more potential for improving government operations than that issued in July 1995 concerning managerial cost accounting. Formally, the pronouncement is called Statement Number 4 of the Statements of Federal Financial Accounting Standards (SFFAS No. 4), *Managerial Cost Accounting Concepts & Standards*. SFFAS No. 4 mandated the use of managerial cost accounting by federal entities and stated that the federal approach to cost accounting should:

- Regularly accumulate and report costs of activities to be used for management decisions
- Establish responsibility segments that link costs to outputs
- Determine full costs of government goods and services
- Recognize costs of goods and services supplied by one federal entity to another
- Use suitable costing methods to accumulate and assign costs to outputs

ABC/M is one of several forms of managerial cost accounting mentioned in SSFAS No. 4, and the FASAB "...encourages government entities to study its potential within their own operations." Over the years, ABC/M has become the most frequently used formal managerial cost accounting method in the federal government.

Other laws and guidance, such as the Joint Financial Management Improvement Program's *Framework for Federal Financial Management Systems* and the Federal Financial Management Improvement Act of 1996 (FFMIA) added requirements related to accounting standards and information systems. In addition, the U.S. Office of Management and Budget (OMB) directs two initiatives—the President's Management Agenda and the Program Assessment Rating Tool (PART)—which have spurred departments and agencies to adopt better cost and performance measurement, including managerial cost accounting such as ABC/M.

In addition, federal entities are required to compete with the private commercial sector for the privilege of providing internal support services of a commercial nature, such as payroll, accounting, travel, vehicle maintenance and other activities. The legal requirement for this is found in Office of Management Circular A-76, *Performance of Commercial Activities*. Many federal entities use ABC/M to determine the true cost of internal delivery of commercial-type services for which they are now competing with private contractors. This facilitates apples-to-apples comparisons of the prices and costs bid by the private contractors who want to do the work.

Early Use of ABC/M in the Federal Government

In the U.S. federal government, projects involving activity-based cost management started in the early 1990s and focused mainly on operations improvement and restructuring organizations. The U.S. Internal Revenue Service (IRS) was among the earlier adopters of ABC/M in the federal government, starting in 1991 as a result of an audit recommendation to develop a cost accounting system. The IRS' approach, based on ABC/M, included understanding program user needs and integrating the approach with solving problems related to tax administration. The IRS used the Private Sector Council for pro bono advisory services and Professor Robert S. Kaplan of the Harvard Business School, one of the pioneers of ABC/M, provided expert advice and support. The development of the IRS's initial approach to managerial cost accounting included completing 30 process evaluation projects that yielded more $30 million in potential cost and efficiency savings. This early effort was the springboard for how the IRS costs some of its services related to user fees, like installment agreements, to help determine where and how to make up funding shortfalls and for configuring costing and formulation modules for the Service's enterprise resource planning (ERP) system. Another pioneering user of ABC was the U.S. Navy, which, as it started reducing the number of active shipyards it owns, applied process mapping and ABC/M to determine the nature, size, and cost of shipyard operations. Among civilian agencies, the U.S. Department of Energy experimented with the same approach used by the Navy when it was closing down nuclear weapons facilities.

More Recent Application of ABC/M in Government

By the mid to late 1990s, some defense organizations, such as the U.S. Army Force Command (FORSCOM), started to use ABC/M as an ongoing managerial cost accounting system at major military installations. Civilian agencies such as the Forest Service and the Bureau of Land Management, started to do the same. In the 2000s, entities such as the Federal Bureau of Investigation's Criminal Justice Information Services Division used ABC to determine fees to charge for services, such as fingerprint identification. An increase in applications of ABC/M has resulted from a directive from the Office of Management and Budget (OMB) Circular A-76 on competitive sourcing. Other departments and agencies, including several discussed in this book, have adopted ABC/M as their in-house cost accounting system, although the primary uses of the resulting financial and process information continues to be operations improvement, fee setting. and competitive sourcing.

In 2006, defense and disaster cleanup costs are straining the federal budget, which may mean funding cuts for many agencies over the next few budget cycles. Given tighter budgets, some federal entities are turning to ABC/M to get ready for more austere operations. The old way was to make across-the-board cuts to budget and headcount. Now, using performance management and performance-based budgeting (PBB), which has an ABC/M foundation, government executives are finding it easier to establish funding scenarios that link an agency's activities to the services it delivers to the public and to outcome goals. As a result, executives can show the affect that an agency has on outcomes and, as a corollary, the impact of budget cuts on those outcomes. With better, integrated performance and budget information, a government agency can distribute its funds in ways that will maximize outcomes and overall benefit to the public.

Appreciation of Those Who Make ABC/M in Government Possible

By its nature, ABC/M is a behind-the-scenes activity, one that is rarely noticed even by those who benefit the most from the information this cost accounting method generates. Fortunately, people like Gary Cokins did take notice of the need to write comprehensive books on ABC/M and how it can be applied in the public sector. As a result of Gary's broad management consulting experiences and, in particular, his accomplishments with ABC/M implementations; Gary is arguably one of the best-known global thought leaders in the field of cost accounting and performance management. This book, *Activity-based Cost Management in Government*, provides a comprehensive approach to applying ABC/M in the just-described government environment. Gary's contributions to ABC/M in both government and industry deserve the appreciation of everyone interested in cost-effective public service.

Clifton Williams, Partner
Srikant Sastry, Partner

Grant Thornton
www.gt.com
September 2006

Preface and Acknowledgments

HAVE BEEN FORTUNATE in my professional career—a career that began in 1973 as an accountant and continued into operations management and management consulting. Without realizing it, through this series of jobs and management consulting assignments, I somehow earned a reputation as an internationally recognized expert in activity-based cost management (ABC/M). In truth, I am always learning about how to build and use managerial accounting systems. I'm not sure that any expert in ABC/M exists. I'm just fortunate to have been formally working with ABC/M since 1988. Sometimes luck beats planning.

I have already written three books about ABC/M, so why would I want to write another? Several reasons come to mind.

The growth and acceptance of ABC/M in the public sector continues to accelerate. Articles on ABC/M usually focus on applying ABC/M for commercial businesses. It seemed appropriate to publish a book about ABC/M exclusively for public sector organizations.

A great deal of progress has occurred with ABC/M. There has been a marked increase in successes with ABC/M by organizations of all sizes. As evidence, the attendance at ABC/M software user group conferences is almost exceeding the capacity of the largest hotel conference centers.

There is an increasing understanding that ABC/M provides data and information that integrate into a broad number of uses. ABC/M data in isolation are not an improvement program—they are an enabler for other improvement methodologies, including all of the many solutions that comprise what is popularly called Performance Management. In some cases, ABC/M data allow processes to be performed better and decisions to be made better. In other cases, they make decisions possible that were not possible before.

I have personally seen that the impediments that have been preventing ABC/M from exploding faster in growth and acceptance are the misconceptions about ABC/M. They range from "ABC/M is monstrously large and complicated" to "ABC/M takes forever to implement." These falsehoods must be replaced with the evidence that quickly implemented, non-complex ABC/M models ignite the best results.

Poor ABC/M model design and architecture will inevitably lead to poor results. Large ABC/M systems are sometimes flawed right from the beginning design steps. I believe that ABC/M is a craft—and I hope this book provides guidance to those with craftsman-like minds.

The advanced and more mature users of ABC/M—those who have been recalculating their ABC/M autopsy data (i.e., historical expenses) for several years—have pushed the ABC/M methodology to be applied to future time periods, for predictive accounting and activity-based budgeting and planning. These advanced organizations want to gauge the consequences of their decisions and scenarios. They want to know what will change based on pursuing alternatives available to them. This introduces predictive analytics and cost estimating, which are forms of resource capacity planning.

Finally, I am writing another book simply because I have learned a lot since my last book was published. Some readers may dismiss some writers as simply displaying ego rather than offering practical guidance. I'd like to think that my contribution to the field of managerial accounting originates more from a sense of duty than ambition. I have now seen a lot of ABC/M systems, and I have been comparing and contrasting them as my way of doing research on what contributes to designing and implementing successful and sustainable ABC/M systems. In short, I'd like to make a difference.

As you wander into my book, I'd like you to watch for one key message: Managerial accounting is transitioning into managerial economics. Many of those fuzzy questions about marginal costs and economic decisions can finally begin to be answered using valid data with credible assumptions. And software and data are no longer the inhibitors to computing results that they were in the 1990s. The technology problem has been solved. The major obstacle is not producing the cost math—it is in people's thinking. It is how they frame a problem, make assumptions, and consider what they are really trying to do.

I wrote this book to focus more of the managerial accounting community's attention on the thinking than on the math. The margin for error is continuously narrowing, so I want ABC/M data and their uses to help people and organizations make better decisions and perform better and more in alignment with their defined strategy. Governments will serve people better when they can manage their own affairs more effectively and make better decisions.

Overview of Book

The book consists of thirteen chapters and three appendices.

Chapter 1 describes why activity-based cost management has become so relevant for the public sector and government organizations.

Chapters 2, 3, and 4 describe why managerial accounting has evolved from reporting budget and spending information to calculating the costs of outputs of all forms. These chapters describe how activity-based cost systems are constructed and designed. They also provide insight into why misconceptions cause some ABC/M implementation projects to fall short of expectations.

Chapter 5 describes a bonus that comes with ABC/M: attributes. Attributes provide an additional dimension to the cost data to tag and score various types of costs. For example, the organization can view its cost structure based on where it is adding greater or less value. Another example describes how quality management efforts can be quantified in financial terms.

Chapter 6 addresses the topic of performance measurements and how ABC/M supports strategy mapping and balanced scorecard principles.

Chapter 7 advances the use of ABC/M for predictive planning purposes. Here we discuss not only reforms to budgeting, but the broader uses of predictive accounting as well.

Chapter 8 introduces the concept of risk management and why there is an increasing need to develop a comprehensive framework for balancing and integrating cost, performance, and risk management.

Chapter 9 describes how ABC/M can be implemented quickly using rapid prototyping techniques. This method is in stark contrast to the traditional approach of taking years to construct massive, detailed ABC/M systems while postponing results.

Chapter 10 presents a series of examples of public sector organizations that have implemented ABC/M.

Chapter 11 describes critical success factors for implementing ABC/M and what pitfalls to avoid.

Chapter 12 touches on information technology systems integration issues related to ABC/M.

Chapter 13 concludes the book with a crystal ball description as to where ABC/M is likely to evolve. It summarizes the book's central theme that managerial accounting will become the managerial economics for better decision making.

I would like to thank contributors to various sections of this book: Joe Clark, Steve Clyburn, Martin Croxton, Kathryn East, Alan Fabian, Srikant Sastry, Stu Schaefer, Mike Tinkler, and Clifton Williams. Finally, I am forever grateful to my wife, Pam Tower, who for the many months I was writing this book allowed me to balance my job, my family, and this book.

Gary Cokins
Garyfarms@aol.com
September 2006

Chapter 1

The Utility of ABC/M in Government: Some Opening Comments

"Printers are educated in the belief, that when men differ in opinion, both sides ought equally to have the advantage of being heard by the public; and that when truth and error have fair play, the former is always an overmatch for the latter."
— Benjamin Franklin, American scientist, diplomat, and publisher, *Apology for Printers* (1731)

"Nothing else in the world ... not all the armies ... is so powerful as an idea whose time has come."
— Victor Hugo, French novelist, *The Future of Man* (1861)

N RECENT YEARS, government organizations have begun to look to private industry for ideas on how to improve their business practices and their efficiency in resource use. Activity-based cost management (ABC/M) is one of the most important tools being introduced in the effort to achieve these ends.

ABC/M provides fact-based data. In the absence of facts, anybody's opinion is a good one. And usually the biggest opinion, which may be the opinion of your supervisor or the supervisor of your supervisor, wins. To the extent that the decision-makers are making decisions based on intuition, gut feel, or misleading data, your organization is at some risk.

Many senior managers have gotten used to making decisions without good information, so they think they do not need it. But the pressure to make better decisions and use resources more intelligently has increased. ABC/M provides valuable information that can be used to make a broad range of decisions, spanning outsourcing to operational planning and budgeting.

ABC/M has often met with a mixed response in its initial stages, despite widespread discontent with traditional accounting mechanisms and despite its proven track record elsewhere. This book is intended to lay out what ABC/M is—and what it is not—intended to do, in the hope that such enlightenment will help in applying a powerful tool to the critical problems now facing much of the public sector.

Activity-based concepts were introduced nearly two decades ago, but their development was sidetracked by the headlong gold rush of consulting and software firms clambering to sell services and products that were based on immature and incomplete ideas. The results were high-cost, limited-value solutions whose success fell far short of expectations.

Activity-based concepts are, however, the most powerful tools yet developed for creating valid economic cost models of organizations. By using the "lens of ABC (activity-based costing)," organizations of all sizes and types can develop the valid economic models required for their executives and managers to make value-creating decisions and take actions to improve their productivity and resource usage—and ultimately to better serve their constituencies.

In this opening chapter, I touch lightly on the pressures for improved cost accounting in government, misapprehensions and other sources of resistance against ABC/M, and successful applications of this system in the public sector to date. Many of the subjects introduced will be examined more closely in later chapters, most particularly those dealing with the mechanics of ABC/M itself. In the end, I hope to have convinced the reader that ABC/M in government is an idea whose time has come, if only because it makes sense.

POLITICAL PRESSURES TO HOLD DOWN COSTS

Public sector organizations at all levels and of all types are facing intense pressure to do more with less. Federal, national, state, county, municipal, and local governments in almost all the countries in the world are feeling some sort of fiscal squeeze. This includes departments, administrations, branches, foundations, and agencies.

The pressure on spending has many sources. It can come from politicians aiming to win taxpayers' approval or directly from taxpayer special-interest groups. There is pressure from the competition with other cities to attract homebuyers or with other counties, states, or nations to attract businesses. In the United States, the cities don't just compete against other cities—each city competes against its own suburbs. And the suburbs often have an advantage in attracting residents and businesses. They may offer lower taxes, better schools, and less crime. As residents and businesses relocate, the cities and towns they departed from lose a little more of their tax base. Less spending is available unless tax rates are raised.

Additional pressure may come from declining demand, regardless of the reasons. An example is rural road maintenance. In these cases, economies of scale are less easily achieved and the fixed costs become less affordable.

In the United States, the federal government is shifting some responsibilities to state and local governments, but providing only limited funding to fulfill those obligations. Regardless of where the pressure is coming from, the message is: better, faster, cheaper—hold the line on taxes, but don't let service slip.

Meeting this daunting challenge often requires:

- Determining the true and actual costs of services
- Implementing process improvements
- Evaluating outsourcing or privatization options (i.e., is it better to deliver internally or purchase outside?)
- Aligning activities to the organization's mission and its strategic plan

The solution for governments under pressure cannot be to simply uncover new sources of revenue or to raise tax rates again. Some have succumbed to these quick fixes, only to meet with a downward spiral as more businesses and families move to more economically attractive locations. Governments must get a handle on their problems. Holding the line on raising taxes will need to be more than a hollow campaign slogan; it may become an absolute requirement to retain the tax base. This restriction will create a lot more reasons to understand costs. Efficiency and performance, once reserved for the private sector, will increasingly be part of the language of the public sector.

Activity-based cost management (ABC/M) and its companion, activity-based scorecarding (i.e., performance measures), offer potential solutions to the problem. Providing meaningful, fact-based information to government officials, managers, and employee teams can be a cost-effective means of bringing about beneficial change and improved performance in government and not-for-profit environments. Intuition and political persuasion are becoming less effective as means for decisionmaking.

The pressure on the public sector is undeniable. People want government to work better and cost less. To do so, public sector managers will have to change their way of thinking about the true costs—and value—of the services they provide.

AN EXCESSIVE FOCUS ON FUNCTIONS

When a new mayor takes office in a city, he or she may be told by the city managers that the finances are reasonably healthy. Expenditures and resources are in balance; there is no fiscal deficit. But can those same managers tell the new mayor how much it costs to fill a pothole, to process a construction permit, or to plow a highway mile of snow?

The reference to the cost of outputs will repeatedly resonate throughout this book. It is inescapable. The need to consider outputs, not simply the level of manpower, equipment, and supplies, is what is forcing the awareness and acceptance of ABC/M. At a very basic level, ABC/M is simply a converter and translator of expenditures restated as outputs.

ABC/M answers fundamental questions such as "what do things cost?" and "why?" It further answers "who receives them?" and "how much costs did they each receive?" Examples of output costs are the cost per each type of processed tax statement or the cost per each type of rubbish disposal pick-up. ABC/M serves as a calculation engine that converts employee salaries, contractor fees, and supplies into outputs. The work activities are simply the mechanism that produces and delivers the outputs. The work is foundational; all organizations do work or purchase it. All work has an output. This topic of outputs will be constantly revisited. It is a critical aspect of ABC/M.

The dilemma for many not-for-profit and government agencies, branches, administrations, and departments is their fixation with determining budget levels for spending without many facts to go from. From the budget requestor's perspective, an annual budget negotiation is usually an argument to retain or increase the level of resources relative to the existing level. Regardless if this behavior is due to an ego display by ambitious or fearful managers or a lack of any better means to determine resource requirements, it is the rare manager who accepts a reduction in anything—except maybe a reduction in headaches caused by his daily problems. Defending one's budget was not the way it worked in the beginning. Let's now revisit the past and understand some history about budgets.

THE EVOLUTION OF BUDGETS

Organizations seem to go through an irreversible life cycle that leads them toward specialization and eventually to turf protection. When organizations begin, things are fairly straightforward. With the passing of time, the number and variety of their services change as well as the needs of their customers and service-recipients. This introduces complexity and results in more indirect expenses to manage the complexity.

Following an organization's initial creation, all the workers are reasonably focused on fulfilling the needs of whatever created the organization in the first place. Despite early attempts to maintain flexibility, organizations slowly evolve into functions. As the functions create their own identities and staff, they seem to become fortresses. In many of them, the work becomes the jealously guarded property of the occupants. Inside each fortress, allegiances grow and people speak their own language—an effective way to spot intruders and confuse communications.

With the passing of more time, organizations then become internally hierarchical. This structure exists even though the transactions and workflows that provide value and service to the end recipients pass across internal and artificial organizational boundaries. These now-accepted management hierarchies are often referred to, within the organization itself as well as in management literature, as "silos," "stovepipes," or "smokestacks." The structure causes managers to act in a self-serving way, placing their functional needs above those of the cross-functional processes to which each function contributes. In effect, the managers place their personal needs above the needs of their service-recipients.

At this stage in the organization's life, there is less sensitivity to the sources of demand placed on the organization from the outside and to changes in customer needs. In other words, the organization is in danger of losing sight of its *raison d'être*. The functional silos compete for resources and blame one another for any of the organization's inexplicable and continuing failures to meet the needs of their customers or service-recipients. Their arguments about the source of inefficiencies are little enlightened by the conflicting priorities involved.

By this evolution point, there is poor end-to-end visibility regarding what drives what inside the organization. Some of these organizations evolve into intransigent bureaucracies. Some functions become so embedded inside the broader organization that their work level is insensitive to changes in the number and types of external requests that were the origin of why their organization was created. They are somewhat insulated from the outside world.

As will be described throughout this book, the actual or planned spending levels reported by the general ledger or fund balance accounting system eventually emerge as the primary financial view for each of the functional managers. This has become the only way that functional managers can think about what level of spending can satisfy the needs of people relying on them for good service. Most managers are reasonably confident in the reported numbers underlying this view. They roughly know their employee salaries and benefits, have authorized most of the purchasing requests, and under-

FIGURE 1-1 The Primary View of Most Managers

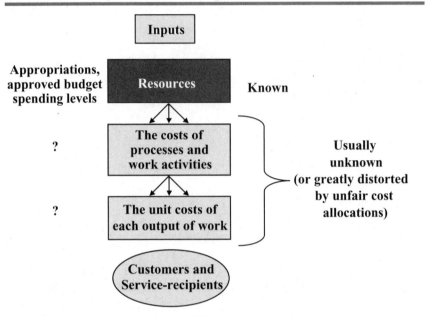

stand (but may despise) the allocation for support costs that they are charged with. That is, the managers understand the bookkeeping system, including its archaic cost-chargeback schemes. Figure 1-1 illustrates the limited view that many managers have of their fiscal condition.

The traditional accounting structure mirrors the hierarchical organizational structure. Each function is a cost center of sorts, and the accountants consolidate the functional expenses into totals with elegant roll-up procedures. But is managing a cost structure all about focusing on the supply-side of resources, which is basically the organization's capacity to serve? Or should the focus begin with reacting to the demands for work placed on the organization from service-recipients and customers? ABC/M brings visibility and understanding to the latter—fulfilling the needs of the service-recipients and customers consuming the organizational outputs.

The ABC/M view is a radical departure from the norm for governments and defense organizations. Consider how politicians campaign for votes.

They communicate in terms of *inputs*. Politicians who want to be viewed as tough on crime will propose spending more money on police forces and prisons. Those who want to be perceived as kind and generous will offer more money for social programs. This fixation with inputs does not conclude with the election. Following the politician's campaign rhetoric, press releases applaud the funding of programs as if the money going in automatically ensures that desired results will come out the other side.

In the military services, newly assigned field commanders regularly arrive at their bases sharing a single interest: they lobby for a bigger budget. They may be granted the money. But holding them accountable for the results or how efficiently they use the government's money is a separate matter.

Government employees and managers often view the annual fiscal budgeting process with cynicism. ABC/M practitioners have learned that it is better if buyers and consumers, including government buyers and procurement agents, purchase *outputs* instead of the inputs. Fortunately, the focus within the public sector has begun to shift from budget management to performance-based results measurement. Chapter 7 will discuss traditional budgeting and describe how activity-based budgeting (ABB) can leverage the ABC/M methodology and produce more credible and valid budget planning of resource needs and utilization.

REMOVING THE BLINDFOLD— OUTPUTS, NOT JUST RESOURCES/EXPENDITURES

The traditional financial accounting system has evolved in such a way that all public sector managers reasonably know what expenditures they have made in past time periods. But none of them knows what the costs were either in the aggregate or for the individual outputs. So what are the costs of outputs? What is the cost of *each* output? How does one accurately calculate these costs?

To simplify semantics, *resources* are used and *expenses* or *expenditures* are incurred when money is exchanged with third-party suppliers and with employees. *Costs* are always "calculated" costs that restate the expenses as work activities or as outputs. Expenses and costs equate in total, but are not the same things.

Figure 1-2 illustrates how management's limited view can be fruitfully extended beyond the resource/expenditure level. Traditional financial management systems focus on the expenses of labor, supplies, etc., rather than on

FIGURE 1-2 Expenses and Costs Are *Not* the Same Thing

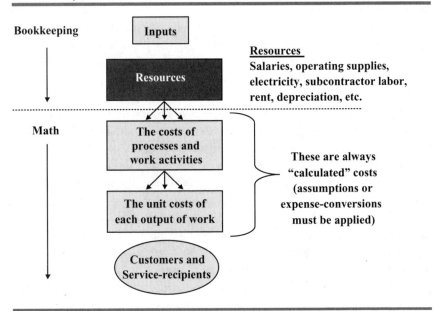

what work is performed and the outputs resulting from using these resources. ABC/M makes visible what has been missing in financial reporting.

Governments adhere to and comply with standard government accounting principles. For example, fund accounting is similar to the general ledger bookkeeping that commercial businesses use, except that fund accounting adds an extra step. In most simple terms, fund accounting first establishes a planned or budgeted spending ceiling for various funds and their accounts. (Funds are comparable to responsibility cost centers in general ledger accounting.) Approved spending often comes in the form of appropriations.

The extra step involves requisitions. Managers basically use requisitions for spending; if the spending ceiling has been reached, or if the requisition fails other tests, then the purchase is prohibited. In effect, government and not-for-profit accounting adds an extra level of spending control. However, although these extra controls deter government managers from committing fraud or stealing money, they do little to stop them from wasting it.

In many cases, the accounting system calculates overhead or support costs and allocates them to the final outputs of the organization. The basis for how the cost allocation is distributed is usually convenient for the accountants but does not reflect the unique and relative relationship between resource consumption and the final outputs, much less the work processes involved. In the end, many managers dismiss the calculated cost from their accounting system as a bunch of fictitious lies. It may accurately reconcile in total for the organization, but not in the pieces. Unfortunately these same managers have little choice but to go along with these flawed costs. They have little influence or control over the accountants. The accountants count the beans, but they are not tasked to grow the beans.

When managers and employee teams do not reliably know what the costs are for their current outputs, they have a difficult time knowing what the future costs may be for future levels of demand or for changes in requests for their outputs. Most managers consciously or subconsciously stick with the primary view of the costs they are familiar with—their spending. And the accounting system, structured to report spending this way, reinforces this view. As mentioned, no managers willingly volunteer to continue into a future year with fewer resources, so they fight for the same or (usually) more resources at budget planning time.

When managers receive their monthly responsibility center report calculating the favorable or unfavorable variance between their actual spending and their budget, what does that information really tell them? When they look at their variances, they are either happy or sad, but they are rarely any smarter! ABC/M extends the minimal information in the departmental spending reports to make managers and employee teams smarter. This extended information is then used for making decisions—better decisions than are made without the ABC/M data.

Decisions always affect the future. The past has already happened. ABC/M's strength is giving insights based on understanding past costs, not just spending, and then applying the same data to make better decisions.

Let's add some more realities to this description of government and defense organizations as service providers. Let's now include the key players—public sector workers, taxpayers, and users of the government services:

- The civil service worker or military member might simply prefer the status quo or whatever may be a little bit better for him.
- The taxpayer prefers to be taxed less.

- The user of government services desires more and higher quality service.
- The functional manager is defending the existing level of his resources and fiscal budget.

It is a no-win situation. Something has to give. The combination of these disparate interests creates tension and conflict. How does one untangle the knots? Untangling is difficult when the primary financial view that is used by management only shows spending for resources. There must also be an *equivalent* financial view of the outputs. Questions and discovery begin when the costs of outputs can be made visible and compared. A more reasonable discussion about spending levels occurs when you can *equate* the spending and what the service-recipients get for the spending.

And even if two outputs, such as the unit cost per rubbish disposal for two neighboring houses per month, appear to be the same amount, each house may have consumed different work. One may have had fewer containers but with cumbersome items, like wood blocks and metal rods, for the material handlers to deal with. The other may simply have more containers, but with standard contents. Alternatively, compare two municipal rubbish disposal services with the identical number of residential stops and identical work crew staff at similar weekly wages. All things being equal, if one crew averages seven hours per day while the other averages eight hours, the cost per house disposal is equal for each municipality, but the work material handling content is not. One has more unused capacity than the other. One has a higher disposal cost per residential home for the productive work.

By adding the financial view of the outputs to the financial view of the resources, managers and employee teams can much better understand the behavior of their cost structure. The visibility that comes from knowing the costs of outputs becomes the stimulant to understanding the cost structure. Outputs are the linkage to the external recipients as well as to the internal work activities. The distribution of workload adapts to changes in demand levels for outputs. Output costing can also benefit the cross-functional processes. An ABC/M information system gives visibility to all of these relationships (and even more with the additional capability to score or tag costs with ABC/M's attributes).

ONE CITY'S BENEFITS FROM ABC/M

The City of Indianapolis, Indiana, was one of the first major cities to embrace ABC/M. In the mid-1990s, the Indianapolis government joined forces with local business leaders to apply contemporary business improvement practices. Knowing what things cost was considered a prerequisite to focusing on what to change. They applied ABC/M in several areas. Some of the earliest results were remarkable, and in some ways amusing.

- When managers in the Department of Public Works analyzed their costs of picking up trash, they discovered that, over four years, they had spent $252,000 on repairs to a garbage truck that could be purchased new for $90,000. The city garage where the repairs were made had no reason to care how much it spent to fix the same truck. When they accumulated all the costs associated with that truck, they discovered that it was costing the taxpayers $39 per mile to operate, an obviously enormous amount when compared with other vehicle-use costs.
- An employee of Parks and Recreation bought stacks of chalk to line softball fields. He made the purchase at year's end out of fear of having his annual budget reduced if he had any money left over. (The requisitioner had exhibited classic use-it-or-lose-it spending behavior at the end of the fiscal year.) As a result, the city owned enough chalk to line all the city's softball fields for five years. Ironically, another department had independently determined that it was more economical to spray-paint the lines rather than chalk them. But it was too late to change. The chalk had already been purchased.
- The Department of Public Works was spending $2.9 million annually collecting on sewer water bills that amounted to $40 million. This equated to 7.25 cents on a dollar just to get paid. The city opened the process to competitive bidding. The local, privately owned water company that won the bid produced a 30% annual savings in expenses **and** recognized that it could identify previously unbilled or underbilled sewer users. They proposed, if given the chance, to give the city the first $500,000 in collections and then evenly split the collections beyond that. In the first two years, the city and the contractor company split $11 million.
- Before the ABC/M analysis, the city was spending $1.4 million annually to operate three printing and copying centers with more than 200

copiers. Each print center operated independently without any coordination. The operation was let to competitive bid, and annual expenses were reduced about 35%, to $900,000. The private company generated additional unexpected savings when it offered its expertise in helping the city conduct a "red tape" initiative to reduce the number of forms used by city departments.

As the printing and copying center example reveals, governments operate businesses where commercial companies perform comparable work. Despite the similarities, both business leaders and public officials often have a misconception that the services are in some way different. This is an artificial mental block. The differences are minor, and the mindset only gets in the way of improving productivity and service levels for all concerned.

One of the main messages to be gleaned from these examples is the long-known fact that competition creates innovation. By defining the problem and its scope, a new approach can lead to large magnitudes of savings and improvements, not just marginal increments.

A second message involves accountability. When various government services are reviewed and measured, including the costs of the work activities, processes, and their outputs, accountability is likely to increase. The process of writing contracts, establishing performance measures, assessing costs, and measuring results creates a level of accountability to the public well beyond what existed before.

ABC/M is decision-neutral here. ABC/M data does not take sides. It simply makes visible some facts and some cost rates that can be used to estimate reliably what the cost consequences might be for future scenarios and options. It is true that while government must ensure the provision of certain services, there is no reason why government must also produce and deliver those services. ABC/M data is, however, very work-centric. Regardless of who does the work, ABC/M measures the costs. And in the end, governments still set policy for the delivery of services to the citizenry, so important issues beyond the cost of providing services can always be addressed.

BUT OUR DEPARTMENT DOES NOT HAVE OUTPUTS

It is a bogus statement by some departments that, presumably due to the nature of their work, they have no outputs. There is no dichotomy between workers who think and plan and workers who deliver services and tangible products. Managers and workers who think, plan, and give direction conclude that since their work deals with intangibles, not things, then there is no definable output from their work. But outputs can be intangible. Many are. What is the output of a university education? Is it the diploma? Is it each professor's course? Is it the learning by each student? These may all appear to be intangible. But the financial cost for each one is measurable.

Several years ago at one of the U.S. government laboratories, where well-paid physicists wrestle with theory and advances in their field, a business-process effectiveness study was conducted. Debate surrounded how to map inputs, processes, and outputs. Some of the physicists believed their work was un-mappable. The physicists argued that one could not rigorously define the brain's thinking process when it comes to innovation. That is not the point with ABC/M.

All work has outputs. For example, when one of this same government laboratory's experiments is conducted, there is a "completed" experiment. When a research paper is written and submitted by a physicist, there is a "completed research paper." There may have been lots of thinking, preparation, typing and copying support, and so on to "finish" the research paper, but these costs can be appropriately assigned. When the report is done, the aggregate output can be described as a "completed research paper."

Moreover, all completed research papers are not equal in the time, effort, and support needed and used. There can be great diversity and variation. ABC/M measures that variation and links the costs back to what the organization spent in paying for salaries and supplies. The focus is not on who funded that spending, although there is a clear audit trail back to the source. ABC/M cares that spending did occur and went somewhere and into something for somebody.

Seeing the true cost of outputs can produce some organizational shock. To exaggerate, if a "completed report," after all the time and support is traced into it, costs let's say $325,000, that may be a surprise. If it is read by only three young advisors to a U.S. Senator, and they brief the Senator in a quick hallway conversation without any more use of that report, it makes you wonder whether the report was worth it. You cannot be sure, but at least you have a significant piece of information that you did not have before—the true cost to produce that particular report. The $325,000 price tag would clearly make some *other* government service-provider—let's say one that may be very strapped on budget and whose mission is feeding and caring for children in need—really think about whether appropriations are fairly distributed. Employment by government is not an entitlement program for its workers. Understanding the value of the contribution of work must be understood and compared among alternatives.

The purpose here is not to get emotional or political or to tug on heart-strings. ABC/M does not take sides. It just reports the facts. People can then debate their own positions about what is the value of it all. But ABC/M does provide the basis for determining cost/benefit tradeoffs and thus allows comparison with other services competing for tax dollars. This type of dialogue and discussion cannot easily occur when funding is simply stated in the form of salaries, supporting expense, and supplies. Dialogue is better stimulated when costs are stated in other terms, such as unit costs per each output, permitting comparisons to be made.

A recognized need to shift emphasis from inputs to outputs is leading some civilian and defense organizations to adopt financial funding relationships based on *pay for performance*—rather than simply disbursing cash to service providers as if they were entitled to it. As an example, one city government had historically funded one of its social service agencies based essentially on inputs. The mission of this particular social service organization was to prepare and place unemployed people into jobs as workers. Historically the agency billed the city's central funding authority based on the number of unemployed candidates interviewed and the number of hours of job training provided. Whether any of these candidates actually got a job was irrelevant to the agency getting paid. The basis for payment to the agency was events involved in the process, rather than the relevant results—successful hirings—that the city had hired the agency to produce.

The city government altered the payment arrangement to one based on the number of jobs lasting for at least six months that were secured for these former welfare recipients. This output-based solution worked. The agency recognized that it needed to customize its training according to individual needs and shortcomings. In the end, the agency benefited as well—its revenues are now increasing at a 20% annual rate.

ABC/M USES (AND SOME PITFALLS)

A significant lesson learned from previous implementations of ABC/M is the importance of working backwards with the end in mind. That is, it is to management's benefit to know in advance what it might do with the ABC/M data before the calculation effort is launched. The end determines the level of effort required.

Although ABC/M is basically just data, one of its ironic shortcomings is the wide variety of ways the data can be used. Different uses require more or less detail or accuracy. Accordingly, the system should be built with a clear idea of the types of decisions or assessments that the ABC/M data will be asked to support. Some ABC/M implementations may miss the mark by being initially designed as either overly detailed or not detailed enough.

Eventually, as the ABC/M data are applied as an enabler for multiple uses, the size of the system and level of effort to maintain it stabilizes at an appropriate level. Through using the data, the ABC/M system self-balances the tradeoff between the level of administrative effort to collect and report the data and the benefits as it meets various users' needs.

Here are examples of the more popular uses of ABC/M by governments and defense organizations:

- **Fees for service/cost-to-serve**—to calculate costs of specific outputs as a means of pricing services provided to customers and other functions/agencies.
- **Outsourcing/privatization studies**—to determine which specific costs will actually remain or go away if a third party were to replace an existing part or all of an organization. Increasingly, commercial companies are positioning themselves to perform services once viewed exclusively as a public-sector domain. Some government agencies are learning that it is better to proactively measure their costs to prevent the possibility of a poor decision by an evaluation team. For example, the team may mistakenly conclude that outsourcing makes the most sense and discover after-the-fact that more accurate data would have reversed that decision. ABC/M can also help a government organization bring its costs in line with those of a commercial provider; its governing authority may allow a grace period for doing so.
- **Competitive bidding**—Increasingly, commercial companies are positioning themselves to perform services, such as operating prisons, that were once exclusively the domain of the public sector. But the reverse is possible too. Some government departments, such as those performing road maintenance or tree trimming, may excel and compete with commercial companies.
- **Merging/diverging agencies or functions**—to identify administrative

services that could be shared or combined among multiple agencies or functions.

- **Performance measurement**—to provide some of the inputs to weighted and balanced scorecards designed to improve performance and accountability to taxpayers.
- **Process improvement/operational efficiency**—to optimize resource use and, at times, to serve as a key to an agency's survival. Some agencies are facing budget cuts (or taking on additional activities due to consolidation) and are unclear about the costs of their internal outputs. What does it cost to process a new registrant versus a renewal? Why might these two costs be so different? Do both costs per each event seem too high?
- **Budgeting**—to routinely plan for future spending not based on the current rate of spending but, more logically, on the demand volume and mix of services anticipated.
- **Aligning activities to the strategic plan**—to correct for substantial disconnects between the work and service levels that an organization is supplying and the activities required to meet the leadership's strategic goals. It can be shocking for organizations to discover to what extent they are very, very good at things they do that are deemed very, very unimportant to the strategic plan.

There are many uses for managerial accounting data. The idea here is not to start an ABC/M implementation process just because it seems to feel right or because an authority commands or dictates it. Know in advance what problems the better data will be solving.

MULTIPLE VIEWS OF COSTS ARE EMPOWERING

When senior leadership, managers, and employee teams are provided reliable views of not only their resource spending but also the costs of work activities, costs of processes involved in these activities, and the total and unit costs of the outputs deriving from the activities, they have so much more basis for making decisions. Compare all that to what they have today. They have the spending view, but no insight as to how much of that spending is or was really needed or why. Managers need to know the casual relationships. And, when employees have reliable and relevant information, managers can manage less and lead more.

An ABC/M system provides a good starting point for any non-profit or government organization to model its cost behavior. It is a solution looking for problems—and all organizations have problems. ABC/M provides a top-down look at how an organization's resources get used...and why...and by whom...and how much. This is so logical and elementary.

In your mind, divide resource spending into two categories: resources used and resources unused (i.e., idle capacity). For the first category, resources used, a cost can only be incurred if some person or piece of equipment does something. In other words, if one wants to understand your cost behavior, one must understand which activities your organization performs, which other work activities or services these activities support, what outputs derive from these activities, and the characteristics of who is requesting and using these outputs. There are linkages. An ABC/M system models these linkages and reports the results. One gains multiple views of the costs plus an understanding of the relationships.

A major benefit from ABC/M is the provision of data of varying detail and accuracy to managers and employee teams in a distributed fashion. These data allow each person to see, analyze, and manage the costs and activities that are within his control. It is at this level that real and meaningful changes in cost structure, performance measurement, and service delivery will occur. Today, this type of management data can be provided with commercially available software products that link to existing fund accounting, cost, and metric systems. And ABC/M software can flexibly deliver meaningful reports to an individual's work station—whether through integrated systems or web delivery. This is a cost-effective way of achieving performance improvement.

ABC/M can be applied in different ways to achieve different outcomes. It is a flexible and powerful methodology that has a unique ability to deliver true cost information, from which critical decisions can confidently be made. As demand pressure mounts and budget funding is reduced, the public sector and not-for-profit organizations clearly need this kind of information to achieve effective results.

DEALING WITH THE DARK SIDE: DOWNSIZING PUBLIC EMPLOYEES

Many organizations experience an illusion that if they introduce productivity improvements and streamlining actions, they will automatically save costs. But being more efficient does not equate to realized savings in expenses—as opposed to costs—unless resources are removed (or when volume increases, extra resources do not have to be acquired).

Where do cost savings come from? All things being equal, and if there are no significant changes in revenues or funding following a change in services, then the only positive impact on cash flow must come from reduced variable costs. If purchased materials and supplies are reduced a certain percentage, those costs are totally variable and consumed as needed. The financial savings are real. That is, the cost savings are truly realized as cash outlay expense savings.

But when an organization works more efficiently and manpower staffing remains constant, then basically there is a freeing up of unused capacity in the workers. These workers are more available to do other things. But as long as they continue to get paid their salary and wages, the organization realizes zero expense savings. Unlike the totally variable "as-needed" purchased materials, workers are "just-in-case" fixed costs where their full capacity is, in effect, contracted in advance of the demand for their services. If they are not totally needed all the time, the government pays for their idle capacity time as well.

As efficiencies are produced, manpower cost savings or future cost avoidance can only be realized by management in two ways:

- It can fill the freed-up worker's time with meaningful work, ideally addressing new volume of customer orders.
- It can remove the capacity. That means remove the workers to realize the savings in expense.

The issue here is that of transferring employees, demoting them, or removing them. One of the most difficult political issues stemming from privatization is the loss of public-employee jobs. This problem can be mitigated, however, if government and its private-sector partners work together to ensure the least pain and most gain for the individuals displaced. Similarly, kinder and gentler ways can be found to reduce staff when required by gains in efficiency or changes in demand level. For example, factors such as seniority should be taken into account. But in the end, the organization requires a minimum of distractions from its core role of delivering products or services efficiently.

The loss of jobs must be dealt with openly, compassionately, and comprehensively. There are several ways to accomplish this. Ideally, in an outsourcing situation, the private-sector company can rehire a portion of the existing government employees who are, after all, already experienced in the outsourced activities. The problem of inefficiency and lack of innovation is often not caused by worker incompetence but by weak processes or a heritage of poor managerial styles. Much of that changes when a new group of managers takes over.

Additional ways to address the loss of jobs is through transfer and attrition. Some employees can be placed in growth areas of the organization or elsewhere in the government as opportunities arise. In the interim, some organizations will set up a temporary "job bank" that uses the displaced workers in a meaningful way until attrition or new needs create job openings. Some employees are not totally wed to their employer, and the thought of quitting to do something else may be appealing to them. A financial incentive to quit can be just the stimulant to help them make that decision for themselves.

Ultimately, there may be no alternative but to terminate some employees. Grievances and threats of lawsuits may result, but an organization should never fear these if not guilty. Finally, remember that there are outplacement services with job training, paid for and cost-justified as part of the transition, that employees needing extra help in job relocation can use.

Not every transition to privatization goes smoothly. But people's lives are involved here and must be considered too. Good approaches to addressing the loss of jobs are opportunities to soften the impact of entering into a partnership with the public sector. Compassion exhibited here may reduce the pace of realizing cost savings, but minimizing the short-term trauma of job displacement can bring longer-term benefits.

Finally, if an organization is downsizing, do not neglect the employees who remain to operate the organization. There is an old message that these people have heard: "The good news is you are the survivors. The bad news is you are the survivors." Sometimes management removes the bodies but not the work caused by external drivers. And the old methods and old systems often remain in place. Management may have met some short-term objectives, but needs the surviving work force to operate with the long term in mind. Try to understand the processes, workload, and capacity before making radical changes.

WHY CHANGE NOW?

It is a flip phrase to say that change is the only constant, but it is so often true. The question for the public sector is whether it will drive change—or be driven by it. In the United States, large federal budget deficits and new regulations, such as the Government Performance and Results Act (GPRA), have acted as catalysts for change in the way that government units perform their functions. Competition from the private sector will place additional pressures on governments, agencies, and the military to provide good service economically.

THE UNDER SECRETARY OF DEFENSE
3010 DEFENSE PENTAGON
WASHINGTON DC 20301-3010
09 JUL 1999

MEMORANDUM FOR

SECRETARIES OF MILITARY DEPARTMENTS
CHAIRMAN, JOINT CHIEFS OF STAFF
UNDER SECRETARIES OF DEFENSE
DIRECTOR, DEFENSE RESEARCH AND ENGINEERING
ASSISTANT SECRETARIES OF DEFENSE
DIRECTOR, OPERATIONAL TEST AND EVALUATION
DIRECTORS, DEFENSE AGENCIES

SUBJECT: Defense-Wide Implementation of
             Activity Based Management

In July, 1997, as part of the National Performance Review, the Secretary of Defense established a DoD Acquisition Year Goal to:

"Define requirements and establish an implementation plan for a cost accounting system that provides routine visibility into weapon life-cycle costs through activity based costing and management. ..."

On November 23, the Department's senior Acquisition, Financial, and Logistics Executives met to decide on the course of action to be pursued. It was agreed that:

Declining resources are providing significant incentives to manage better all costs;

Activity Based Cost Management (ABC/M) is most appropriately pursued on a broad department-wide basis rather than being narrowly focused on "weapon system life-cycle costs" only;

.....

In furtherance of the above, I direct the Secretaries of the Military Departments and the Directors of the Defense Agencies to pursue aggressively ABC/M implementation in maintenance depots and everywhere else it could be expected to provide improved cost management. ...

(signature)
J.S. Gansler

Without visible, relevant, and valid data, it is difficult for organizations to stimulate ideas and evaluate what options are available—and their financial impact. ABC/M data provide fundamental information that is part of the solution. Applying ABC/M may well be critical to an organization's survival.

I believe that government is moving past the initial stage of rethinking what government does and how it does it. Restrictive funding pressures have already jump-started that. Government units are adopting a greater performance orientation and are replacing a detailed micro-management style with a more practical approach where the costs are justified by the benefits. ABC/M is now and will continue to play an important role in helping government to manage its affairs. See the preceding abbreviated version of a letter from top management in the Department of Defense promoting the implementation of ABC/M in the U.S. military. I am hoping that this book provides additional thought on how ABC/M systems can be improved and applied in the public sector as a whole.

> **"A thing is not proved because no one has ever questioned it ... Skepticism is the first step toward truth."**
> —Denis Diderot, French philosopher, *Pensees Philosophiques*, Book XXI (1746)

> **"Whoever is careless with the truth in small matters cannot be trusted with important matters."**
> —Albert Einstein; German-born Swiss-American scientist;
> *Ideas and Opinions of Albert Einstein* (1954)

Chapter 2

Understanding ABC/M:
A Few Basic Truths

"There are in fact four very significant stumbling-blocks in the way of grasping the truth, which hinder every man however learned, and scarcely allow anyone to win a clear title to wisdom; namely, the example of weak and unworthy authority, longstanding custom, the feeling of the ignorant crowd, and the hiding of our ignorance while making a display of our apparent knowledge."
—Roger Bacon, English philosopher, *Opus Major* (1266-67)

"Between truth and the search for truth, I opt for the second."
—Bernard Berenson, American art critic, *Essays in Appreciation* (1958)

A T THE FEDERAL LEVEL in the U.S., the President's Management Agenda, Office of Management and Budget (OMB), the Government Accountability Office (GAO), and Congress are demanding transparency and accountability of effectiveness of government programs. Federal agencies are required to assess and determine performance. And funding will increasingly be determined according to demonstrated results.

The purpose is to improve performance and program management by creating a focus on results. Ineffective programs are being reformed or constrained, or are facing closure. Programs deemed ineffective or with questionable results are losing budget funding and face poor publicity. Agencies find themselves defending program missions and their budgets to Congress.

Agencies at the state and local level face similar pressures. In many states, the governor, state legislature, and the public are impatient and demanding accountability and transparency of government effectiveness, as well as improved efficiency, due to state budget crises.

All government agencies are faced with the daunting challenge of determining and proving program effectiveness. In addition, they are asked to assess costs, justify budget requests with performance information, and communicate expected and tangible results. They are being held accountable for every taxpayer dollar going towards their services and programs. The need for more quantitative and fact-based financial information, a strength of ABC/M, is undeniable.

As mentioned in Chapter 1, a number of government organizations have already launched ABC/M systems and are benefiting appreciably from their application. Other government organizations are intrigued—or perhaps feeling threatened—by the prospect of adopting this new methodology. Experience has shown that eliminating some common misconceptions about ABC/M would substantially ease the path to its acceptance and use. In this chapter, I try to lay out some simple truths about the purpose of ABC/M, its scope, and its applicability to public sector enterprises as well as to private industry.

Remember that rules are many and principles are few. ABC/M is a methodology based on the principle of cause-and-effect relationships, similar to the law of physics that states every action involves an equal and opposite reaction.

Also, at the end of this chapter you'll find examples of ABC/M in action.

WHAT IS ABC/M?

First, let us look at some of the concrete benefits that accrue to an organization when it adopts ABC/M. The system serves a variety of purposes. By now, some should be obvious; others are less clear.

An Alternative to the Tyranny of Traditional Cost Allocations

Imagine that you go to a restaurant with three friends. You order a little salad or cheeseburger and they each order a great big and expensive prime rib steak or lobster. When the waiter brings the bill they all say, "Let's divide and split the check evenly." How do you feel?

That is how many product- and service-lines feel in the cost accounting system when the accountants and comptrollers bunch large indirect support and overhead expenses and *allocate* them as costs using broad averages without much (or any) logic. That is, there is minimal or no linkage between the true relative use of the expenses and their allocation to the individual products, service-lines, or end users. This is unfair. It is unfair in what is being costed, and it is unfair to people who use these data to make decisions.

Activity-based cost management is a method that gets it right. In our restaurant example, it splits the check more fairly. It creates four individual checks—you pay for only what you consume. You don't subsidize the others or receive a generous gift from the others. To many ABC/M practitioners, the word *allocation* is one they wish had never existed. It implies inequity to so many people because of past abuses in their organization's accounting practices. The word *allocation* practically means *misallocation*, since that is usually the result. ABC/M practitioners often say that they do not *allocate* expenses; instead they *trace and assign* them based on cause-and-effect relationships.

Many operations people cynically believe that accountants count what is easily counted—but not what counts. Outdated, traditional accounting blocks managers and employees from seeing much of the relevant costs that are accurately attributable to their outputs. This problem has become increasingly significant as indirect costs have ballooned relative to direct costs.

Figure 2-1 reveals that, over the last few decades, support and overhead costs have been displacing direct, recurring costs as the major share of total expenses as organizations mature. Under the traditional accounting system, the organization has a reasonably clear view of direct expenditures for front-line labor and for material purchases. It has little insight, however, into the causes of its support and overhead spending.

For example, a banking institution is experienced at monitoring the work of its tellers and other employees who perform recurring work that is closest to the products and services benefiting its customers. It uses cost rates and performance-related factors, such as labor variance reporting, to calculate *standard costs* that are output-related. Many banks consequently know their standard cost per each deposit, per each wire transfer, and so on. They do not, however, have comparable financial information for the many vice presidents working on the second floor to the top of their building! The only financial information applied for those expenses is the annual budget plan, under which spending is monitored for each department or function only to see if performance is under or over the budget.

When you ask people why, in their view, indirect and overhead expenses are displacing direct costs, they almost invariably say that it is due to technology, equipment, automation, or computers. In other words, organizations are automating what were previously manual jobs. This cause, in my view, is only a *secondary* factor. The *primary* cause for the shift reflects the gradual proliferation in products and service-lines that has occurred over the last few decades. Organizations now offer a greater variety in products and services and use more and different types of distribution channels to serve a wider variety of end-users and service-recipients. For example, 20 years ago most entry-level soldiers in the U.S. military were considered similar. But today,

FIGURE 2-1 The Need for ABC

A key to understanding ABC is to understand how cost behavior truly varies in relation to other factors

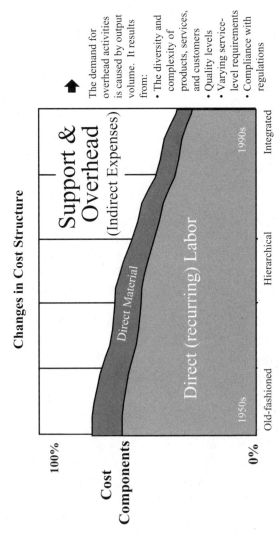

Changes in Cost Structure

100%

Cost Components

Support & Overhead (Indirect Expenses)

Direct Material

Direct (recurring) Labor

0%

Old-fashioned   Hierarchical   Integrated

Stages in the Evolution of Businesses

1950s   1990s

The demand for overhead activities is caused by output volume. It results from:

• The diversity and complexity of products, services, and customers
• Quality levels
• Varying service-level requirements
• Compliance with regulations

not only are extra costs associated with corps composition (e.g., the influx of women), but there are many more functions for which entry-level soldiers must be trained.

Greater variation and diversity (i.e., heterogeneity) create complexity and, in turn, more indirect and overhead expenses to manage the complexity. Thus, a larger overhead component of expense does not automatically mean that an organization is becoming inefficient or bureaucratic. It may simply mean that it is offering more variety to a broader array of recipients. For those who may not be convinced by this explanation, I ask you to interview a long-time employee who is about to retire. Ask him or her "How thick was our 'product catalogue' when you joined the organization, and how thick is it now? What types of citizens or government agencies did the organization serve at its creation, and how many more types does it serve now?" I think the real reason for increasing overhead will become evident.

Whatever the derivation of indirect support and overhead costs, it is clear that traditional accounting methods have failed to meet the challenge. What ABC/M can do is extend the visibility now pertaining to direct spending to illuminate what has for many organizations become the lion's share of spending. It then becomes an organization-wide method of understanding true work-activity costs and thus provides a reliable basis for predicting the outcome of decisions affecting the future.

A Better Gauge than Benchmarking with Blinders

Some governments and government organizations fool themselves into thinking that they are efficient when they benchmark their activities against similar activities performed by other governments or organizations. Their consulting firms sometimes even maintain benchmarking databases that are restricted to government agencies. The cost rates may be unfavorable relative to private sector companies, but without such comparisons, government agencies relying on benchmarked data may unknowingly continue to believe there is little room for improvement.

As an example, the City of Indianapolis decided to look for cost-savings opportunities in its wastewater treatment plants even though these plants were already considered among the best run in the United States and had won numerous awards. It engaged a prestigious consulting firm to do a benchmarking study. Using their vast database, the consultants confirmed that the plants were among the most efficient government-operated plants in the nation. But, having discovered that European countries relied more on private companies for wastewater treatment, the City of Indianapolis decided to seek outside proposals. In the end, a French firm was brought in to create a consortium that is well on its way to realizing a 44% reduction in operating costs. Had the city allowed "good enough for government work" to be its standard, Indianapolis would have lost millions of dollars in savings and technical improvements to its wastewater treatment operations.

ABC/M can be used effectively either as an alternative to benchmarking or as a means of improving benchmarking as an informative tool. Alone, it gives management a true picture of cost/benefit relationships and thus a firm basis for effecting beneficial change. It also can serve as an essential adjunct to accurate and useful benchmarking.

Help in Improving Requests for Proposals

The role and purpose of requests for proposals (RFPs) could use some fresh thinking. ABC/M can help in delineating an organization's problem areas and defining the scope of the outside assistance that should be sought. Sometimes just better thinking is what it takes to get better results.

When governments consider outsourcing or privatization ventures, effective results occur if the private companies are allowed to bring their expertise to bear on the real problem. Successful commercial companies thrive on innovation, and they can offer new ideas rather than perform the same old tasks that the government performed—with only nominally improved efficiency. When companies are limited to complying to tightly worded RFPs, they are restricted in bringing improvements. An RFP that is more broadly and appropriately defined allows private companies to go beyond doing government pretty much the same old way and to propose how the job can be done better.

The City of Indianapolis has an anecdote for the results often experienced under RFPs as they are currently designed. Its city planning department had hired a private engineering firm to speed up the process of issuing construction permits. The engineering firm was given control over the slowest part of the process. After a year with the firm involved, permit turnaround times had improved only slightly, and the city complained about performance. In return the city got an earful. The engineering firm pointed out that the city had outsourced a bad system under guidelines that provided little or no opportunity for creativity. When the RFP was reworded to allow redesigning the entire system for issuing permits, the engineering firm reduced total costs by 40%, despite a 25% increase in volume, and average turnaround time from about four weeks to three or four days.

Acquiring accurate information about costs is one of the biggest hurdles for public officials trying to save money and improve services, particularly for newly elected or appointed officials. Reasonably accurate information about costs is the key to making almost every other change initiative possible. ABC/M data are a great enabler. Yet most governments and government organizations simply do not have sufficiently good information about their costs—perhaps on their expenses, but not on their costs.

WHAT ABC/M IS NOT

It is a mistake for ABC/M project teams to refer to ABC/M as an improvement program or a new change initiative. When that occurs, managers and employees often label the project as a fad, fashion, or "flavor of the month." The ABC/M data are simply used as a means to ends. They make visible the economics of the organization and the consumption of resource expenses by its work activities/outputs. Money is continuously being spent on organizational resources whether ABC/M measuring is present or not.

ABC/M is analogous to a physician's stethoscope that allows listening to one's lungs and heartbeat. Your heart is beating and you are breathing regardless of the presence of the stethoscope. In a similar way, an organization is continuously burning up its resources through its processes and the work activities that belong to them, and it then traces the activity costs to who or what is consuming the resources. This is occurring whether ABC/M is monitoring these events or not.

I am deliberately dumbing down and understating ABC/M for an important reason. In the early 1990s, when ABC/M was beginning to get serious attention, the management consulting community began selling the system as consulting services. Unfortunately, in those days the consultants hyped and oversold ABC/M as a magic pill that could possibly solve all of an organization's problems. This raised management's expectations too high. If the consultants did not solve the problems that their client thought it had engaged them for in the first place, the blame fell on ABC/M for not working. But ABC/M worked just fine. It was just that some of the consultants did not accurately sell the system—nor at times adequately understand how to interpret and use the data. But that has changed now. The consultants have realized that their value-add is to help their clients solve their problems, and the ABC/M data is an important enabler to the solutions.

In many cases, organizations oversized the initial ABC/M model well beyond the size needed to see results and get quick hits. It is important that an organization realize early on that ABC/M provides fundamentally good data to be used for understanding, discovery, and decision making. Then ABC/M is better positioned for longer-term and wider acceptance.

So I am deliberately managing expectations about ABC/M by reducing one's perceptions that it provides all the answers. ABC/M restacks the costs but does not root them out. ABC/M's data can be a great enabler for providing answers; the key phrase is *it is an enabler*.

There are many acronyms related to organizational improvement—TQM and BPR, to name a couple. They all focus on continuing improvement of work and the pursuit of excellence in daily operations. Many of these programs emphasize the following:

- Management of processes rather than resources
- Elimination of waste

One common thread runs through all of these improvement techniques: a focus on work activities and their relationship to services or products provided to customers. ABC/M data can turbocharge all these performance improvement programs. When ABC/M is combined with operational information, such as performance measures, it becomes an even more powerful tool in making sensible and substantial changes.

In my opinion, it is inevitable that all organizations will eventually rely on some form of an ABC/M information system to assist in effectively managing their affairs. So there is no reason to hype or overstate the power of ABC/M. It will continue to claim widespread global acceptance simply based on its merits and based on the utility that the ABC/M information provides.

LET "HOW" AND "WHY" DRIVE THE EFFORT

In the end, 90% of ABC/M is organizational change management and behavior modification, and 10% of it is the math. Unfortunately, most organizations initially get those two functions reversed. They spend way too much time defining and constructing their ABC/M information system and very little time thinking about what they will do once they have the new ABC/M data. This is a huge problem.

Poor implementation has adversely affected the rate of adoption of ABC/ M. When ABC/M systems fall short of manager and employee teams' expectations, it is usually because the initial ABC/M system design was substantially over-engineered in size. The typical initial ABC/M system is usually excessively detailed and is well past diminishing returns on extra accuracy for each incremental effort of extra work. One manager reacted to seeing his first ABC/M report by saying, "I feel like a dog watching television. I don't know what I'm looking at!" With a fraction of the effort and in a much shorter timeframe, the implementation team could have started to produce reasonable and comprehensible results.

It is important to start getting results from ABC/M quickly because of the potential organizational shock that managers and employees may experience when they receive the new ABC/M data. That is, it is important to start realizing what kind of new (and possibly disturbing) information might come from ABC/M.

When people see the ABC/M data for the first time, they should see things they have never seen before—even though some of it will not be pretty. For example, there may be a manager who for years believed that his or her services were very efficient relative to those of other departments, functions, or agencies. But when ABC/M finishes more properly tracing the *true* consumption of expenses, the result may be an unpleasant surprise. The total costs of that manager's department services, as well as the calculated unit costs per each output of service, may be well above comparable benchmarked costs of similar services elsewhere! That manager will not be happy to see this information, nor whomever reported that information. Do not underestimate the level of resistance that can come from exposing managers and employees to the ABC/M data. You are dealing with human nature.

There is an important lesson here. Treat the ABC/M data responsibly. ABC/M is not an accounting police tool, but rather an organization-wide managerial information system to be used for self-improvement. Its data are not intended to embarrass anyone and should not be used to punish anyone. In many cases no one really knew what the true costs were. Many suspected that the existing expense and cost allocation was wrong, but they did not know what the correct calculations would reveal. ABC/M finally gives managers and employee teams the hope that they can see the truth. But seeing the data and using the data are not the same thing. There is much more thinking required when it comes to using the ABC/M data for managing and decision-making.

There is an old fable that says that all truth passes through three phases:

1. First, it is ridiculed.
2. Next, it is violently opposed.
3. Finally, it is accepted as being patently obvious.

Whether the perceived villain is the ABC/M methodology, or the output data computed by the ABC/M system, keep this in mind. There will be resistance to ABC/M. And the resistance is not so much due to people being afraid of change—although that is a factor—but due to people being afraid of uncertainty. The irony is that ABC/M brings truth, but until the ABC/M data are revealed, people are not sure what will be shown or how it might be used.

In short, even if an ABC model is in place, do not expect ABM to automatically follow. Using the data is the hurdle.

> **"Poor management accounting systems, by themselves, will not lead to organizational failure. Nor will excellent management accounting systems assure success. But they certainly can contribute to the decline or survival of organizations."**
> —H. Thomas Johnson and Robert S. Kaplan,
> *Relevance Lost: The Rise and Fall of Management Accounting*
> (Boston, MA: Harvard Business School Press, 1987), p. 261.

DIFFERENCES AND SIMILARITIES AMONG ABC/M USERS

ABC/M advocates generally find the doubting-Thomas syndrome more prevalent in the public sector than in the business world. In making their argument against the applicability of ABC/M to their activities, government employees most often cite two facts: (1) government does not operate with a profit motive in mind, and (2) government is normally a supplier of services rather than products. Both are true. In this section, we will look at these and other differences among ABC/M users as well as the growing similarities.

In the final analysis, I believe that ABC/M can offer real value to the public sector while taking into account its unique attributes.

Commercial Businesses vs. Government Entities

Activity-based cost management has a different flavor when applied to not-for-profit organizations and governments rather than commercial businesses. The general concepts of ABC/M remain foundational. But there are some different purposes and conditions that alter the focus and even the design of ABC/M for government organizations.

A significant difference in contrast to commercial businesses is a government agency's absence of a profit- and wealth-maximization motive. The system of reporting layers of profit contribution margins used by commercial organizations to focus on opportunities is meaningless. Some quasi-private public sector organizations, such as a military base commissary, pursue full cost recovery through pricing and fees, and do not have to maximize profit to enhance the owner's or investor's wealth. Just breaking even with sales covering costs may be the goal.

Many other public sector organizations have no fee or price structure and no revenues from buyers or consumers. The organization is funded with a spending budget issued by an authorized body, such as a municipal board of directors or the U.S. Congress, and delivers services to other agencies or citizens without any exchange of payments. A local police or fire department and a national aviation agency are examples. Citizens are not expected to purchase their safety in pieces or on an as-needed basis; it is an expected service.

Another difference between the private and public sectors involves the targeting of specific markets and customers. Not-for-profit and government organizations usually do not have the luxury of determining whom they wish to serve. Tax authorities deal with all taxpayers, and their work is defined by law. Public hospitals are required to attend to all patients, water municipalities cannot easily withhold their product from different groups in society, and so forth. Not-for-profits cannot simply abandon or ignore certain types of recipients of their products or services, even those making relatively high demands. Hence, they cannot easily adjust their cost structure by simply targeting certain groups to serve or to avoid in the way that commercial businesses can.

Despite these differences, the similarities between commercial and not-for-profit organizations are substantial and growing with time. Some public sector agencies are managed indistinguishably from for-profit businesses, are increasingly adopting private sector business practices, and in some cases are competing with commercial businesses. They can and do benefit from the same management tools and techniques used by the private sector. For example, when a government agency introduces a previously non-existent surcharge or converts to a fee-for-service arrangement, isn't this comparable to a commercial business charging higher prices to those willing to pay more in exchange?

The most important common element among private and public sector organizations is the concept of *value*. Defining value has ambiguities, but regardless of how value is defined and measured, it ultimately becomes a determinant for many types of decisions. ABC/M provides a basis for introducing the concept of value into the language of management and also assigning measures to it. This leads to a much better evaluation of options and tradeoffs to determine both what levels of service should be offered and what levels of manpower and resources should be supplied to deliver the services.

To reinforce the notion that commercial and public sectors are converging in their similarities and uses of modern managerial improvement methods, Figure 2-2 shows how in the United States the Congress, the President, and subordinate managers are similar to the management structure in a private sector corporation. Congress is like a corporation's Board of Directors and the President is like a CEO. In the private sector, members of the Board are elected by shareholders who as investors have a high interest in good outcomes; the parallel in government is the stakeholders (i.e., voting citizens) who elect their senior officials. Below the position of CEO, many corporations combine titles under a single individual; in government, the hierarchy of authority mirrors that of a corporation. Regardless of whether an organization is public or private, its managers increasingly need to know how to improve their performance, because doing so is increasingly expected from shareholders or stakeholders.

Service-based vs. Product-based Organizations

In an earlier reference to outputs such as "finished reports" that may be intangible but can still be defined, we were distinguishing between cost structures of product makers and of service providers. As pointed out, the ABC/M methodology and its principles are applicable to either case. This is because ABC/M is concentrating on how any output is consuming the work activities, including whatever costs support those work activities.

However, a few differences between a service provider and a product maker/distributor with a high reliance on equipment are important:

- In service organizations, the resources generally are more flexible and interchangeable than in capital-intensive organizations where equipment may be dedicated to making only certain products or only doing certain things. In service organizations, some people can multi-task or

FIGURE 2-2 Commercial versus Government "Business" Model

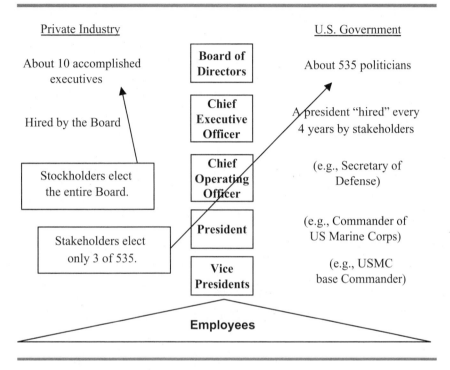

move among different tasks. In contrast, in capital-intensive companies that make and distribute products, the moment that their equipment is purchased, they have committed themselves to a certain level of available capacity (and cash outlay expenses) regardless of the level of subsequent use of that equipment. Service companies effectively have the luxury of "postponing" the addition of resources—mainly workers—until they are needed. In short, service companies can more quickly adjust the level of their capacity. With people as their most flexible resource, it is also the capabilities, not just the capacity, of their workers that allow more variety of outputs to be delivered. The more capabilities, the more flexibility. That is one reason that organizations are increasingly investing in training and education of their workforce, and even their suppliers' and contractors' workforces.

- When an organization is operating at near full capacity and needs to significantly alter its own cost structure, service organizations have an advantage over a hard goods provider. Presuming that the service organization in this case truly is as lean and agile as it can be, it can still alter its own cost structure by influencing the "future demand workload" side of the supply and demand equation. It may be able to offer a greater number of service level options (with varying prices or promotional features) to induce customer behavior more in harmony with its cost structure. Providing service-level options would be similar on a personal basis to choosing to ship a package with overnight delivery or with two-day, three-day, etc., rates. By inducing the customer or service-recipient to make the appropriate choices, an organization can shift the demand workload away from workers operating at full capacity and toward workers with some idle and unused capacity.

In the end, if one steps back and views service sectors versus producing sectors, the two forms appear to converge. There are more similarities than dissimilarities. ABC/M can be easily modeled for both forms using common ABC/M principles. If anything, service organizations arguably have some advantages in adapting to the guidance provided by use of an ABC/M model.

> "Judging by common sense is merely another phrase for judging by first appearance....The men who place implicit faith in their own common sense are, without any exception, the most wrong-headed and impracticable persons."
> —John Stuart Mill, English political economist, *The Spirit of Age* (1870).

> "The majority of people believe in incredible things which are absolutely false. The majority of people daily act in a manner prejudicial to their general well-being."
> —Ashley Montagu, American anthropologist, *In fact* (newsletter) (1940)

EXAMPLES OF ABC/M IN GOVERNMENT

The following are examples of ABC/M applications in government.

ORGANIZATION: U.S. General Services Administration (GSA), Public Buildings Service (PBS), Office of Property Disposal (PR)

MISSION: The role of the GSA's Office of Property Disposal is to promote responsible asset management throughout the federal government by satisfying its customers' utilization and disposal needs.

ISSUE/PROBLEM: The primary problem was to reduce the overall expense to fulfill its mission while concurrently improving its service levels.

SOLUTION: The solution was to develop an ABC/M system that enabled PR to identify the full costs of doing business and to assign these full costs more equitably to business activities and selected cost objects (e.g., customer project, type of disposal). PR was also asked by its executive management to provide cost data to allow management to analyze the business activities in terms of value added and non-value added work tasks.

ABC/M MODEL STRUCTURE: PR developed an ABC/M system called Activity Based Costing Operating System (ABCOS) that relied on its Time Tracking System (TTS). The commercial ABC/M software Oros, from ABC Technologies Inc., was used as the ABC/M calculation engine. These systems were integrated with what the PR calls its Disposal Module. ABCOS' cost object model provides information by state, agency, and type of disposal effort.

RESULTS: The data from the ABC/M system allow management to analyze the business activities in terms of value added and non-value added work tasks. ABCOS also identifies high-impact opportunities for process improvement, consolidation, and right-sizing. The ABC/M model provides cost information to support management decisions along with improving project management, forecasting the level and type of resources, and identifying GSA's true cost of disposal services for customer agencies.

LESSONS LEARNED: Start with a small pilot. Make sure activities are well defined. Stress constantly the iterative process and the fact that although the ABC/M workplan allows you to get your ABC/M model up rather quickly, it still requires time to realize results and benefits.

ORGANIZATION: Internal Revenue Service (IRS)

MISSION: The U.S. government's tax collection agency, with a $7.4 billion budget.

ISSUE/PROBLEM: In anticipation of electronic filing of income tax returns, the IRS wanted to understand the cost differences between annual paper filings (200 million) and expected electronic filings (15 million). Once the costs were known, they then wanted to estimate the impact of the shift in their workload and the cost of new resources.

They had three problems:
1. The existing financial system was designed to provide administrative funds control. It was not set up for managerial cost accounting.
2. While the local IRS service centers had reasonably effective labor time tracking systems, direct labor expenses were not linked to a specific type of tax return.
3. None of the non-labor and indirect support organizational expenses were associated with a specific type of tax return.

SOLUTION: The IRS applied ABC/M to calculate the total and unit costs for each type of tax return.

ABC/M MODEL STUCTURE: They defined approximately 50 types of tax returns (e.g., 1040, 1040A, 1040EZ).

RESULTS: They successfully computed the total and unit costs for each type of return. With ABC/M, they also discovered the unit costs of many previously unknown intermediate outputs of work, such as the cost per various types of phone calls.

They applied the ABC/M data to predict the expected shift in workload and new levels of required resources. They identified substantial cost savings. The ABC/M data introduced internal benchmarking cost data useful to identify and then share best practices.

LESSONS LEARNED: Opportunities opened up to apply user fees. Some support functions established service level agreements with their customers. The ABC/M system was then used as a user chargeback system between the support functions and their users.

ORGANIZATION: U.S. Army Garrison at Fort Detrick

MISSION: The Fort Detrick Garrison provides a broad set of services to military personnel.

ISSUE/PROBLEM: Their goal was to answer the question, "What resources are required to meet specified performance requirements for an Army installation support service?"

Ideally, answering this question allows an installation commander, functional manager, resource manager, or cost analyst to make more informed decisions about policy changes, resource allocations, and business process changes. Answering this question would also help ensure that managers can quantify the resources needed to meet service goals and to determine the impact on service levels if sufficient resources are not provided to meet the service-level goals.

SOLUTION: The goal for the ABC/M project was to segment expenses for the garrison's principal missions, processes, products, and business activities. An ABC/M system was implemented for the entire garrison.

ABC/M MODEL STUCTURE: The initial ABC/M pilot included 122 service-lines.

RESULTS: For many of the managers, cost accountability was now provided at their level to facilitate decision-making and to better control resources in reaction to changing budget constraints.

LESSONS LEARNED: Support from senior management proved to be an essential ingredient for success. Achieving that support took a while to cultivate. This was accomplished by explaining why there was a need for the more refined cost data and by demonstrating that the existing pre-ABC/M cost information was inaccurate or insufficient to aid in decision-making.

ORGANIZATION: Immigration & Naturalization Service (INS), Office of the Budget

MISSION: The INS manages the inflow of immigrants into the United States. The responsibility of the function that applied ABC/M, the Fee & Policy Rate Setting Branch, is to ensure that user fees recover the full costs of services provided.

ISSUE/PROBLEM: A public pledge was published in the *Federal Register*, January 20, 1994. The pledge proposed that the INS would improve the management of the finances of fee accounts and the development of fee schedules. Specifically, the proposal was that future fee adjustments would reflect improved classification and definitions of direct and indirect expenses and their allocation to service-recipients.

SOLUTION: An ABC/M system was implemented. Significant attention was placed on balancing the effort of data collection with the needed accuracy as well as required credibility to achieve buy-in from the user community. Substantial work in the ABC/M implementation went into developing data sampling methods that would obtain 95% reliable results.

ABC/M MODEL STUCTURE: Eleven categories of INS applications served as the final cost objects. Some categories had further segmentation.

RESULTS: With the ABC/M data, there was a much better understanding of how different volumes for different types of applications affected the cost structure. This information was used to better manage resource levels.

LESSONS LEARNED: A key need was for the ABC/M team to initially invest time with the resource managers who would eventually use the ABC/M data and to address their concerns before implementing the ABC/M system.

ORGANIZATION: U.S. Postal Service

MISSION: As with any nation's postal service, its mission is to deliver letters and packages to residential homes and to the workplace.

ISSUE/PROBLEM: The ABC/M project originated from the Postmaster General's mandate to develop a standard cost accounting system designed to compare performance amongst the various mail processing facilities.

The intent of the system was to provide comparable benchmarking data to identify best practices using unit cost data and then allow drill-down capability to assist in focusing on opportunities.

SOLUTION: An ABC/M system was developed, and it evolved into an effective resource allocation and financial budgeting tool.

ABC/M MODEL STRUCTURE: The ABC/M model was rich in transaction quantity and volume data from machine counts for activity drivers.

The initial model had 58 direct and support work activities. Intermediate equipment activities included trucks, planes, rail, and other carriers. There were 9 final cost objects for types of delivered products:

- Letters
- Flats
- Machinable parcels
- Large parcels
- Priority mail
- Express mail
- Registered mail
- Cross-dock containers
- Trays and sacks

RESULTS: In the initial pilot site, there was a 13% reduction in costs resulting from a shift from manual to automated equipment.

Equipment maintenance activity costs were reduced substantially due to a shift to more frequent preventive repairs.

Mail sorter equipment was relocated from airport facilities to non-airport operations where it could be utilized more cost effectively.

LESSONS LEARNED: Key lessons included:

- Use existing data
- Develop strong cross-functional teams
- Keep the model relatively simple
- Do not oversell ABC/M

ORGANIZATION: U.S. Mint

MISSION: The U.S. Mint manufactures circulating, numismatic, and commemorative coins. It is a $3 billion business with 2,500 employees.

ISSUE/PROBLEM: There was increasing pressure for managers to better understand the U.S. Mint's cost structure and its cost behavior, particularly its overhead. Senior management set a strategic goal to reduce the unit costs of coins by 15%.

SOLUTION: An ABC/M system was implemented. A guiding principle for the project was to focus on deliverables and keep the project moving rapidly. There was a strong belief that organizational buy-in would mainly come by producing tangible results.

ABC/M MODEL STUCTURE: The U.S. Mint has a very similar structure to any traditional manufacturer and is fairly capital-intensive. As a result, the ABC/M model design and architecture emphasized the machinery activities; people run equipment, and the equipment makes products. The various types of equipment also consume a fair amount of support, in widely varying proportions. The equipment also consumes substantial non-wage related expenses, such as energy and supplies.

RESULTS: A tremendous amount of previously unmeasured cost data was produced, including:

- The total and unit cost of each product, detailed by each manufacturing process
- The resource expenses of each manufacturing process
- Equipment utilization and capacity information

The managers were provided more robust modeling capability to predict the impact of various scenarios involving different volumes and mix of outputs.

LESSONS LEARNED: Reported critical success factors were:

- An accepted work activity and process library
- Quick demonstration of results
- A commitment to get trained in advance
- Anticipation of organizational resistance with methods to deal with it
- A cross-functional team.
- Improvement to processes that result in better, faster, and cheaper services to customers
- Empowerment of employees to create change

ORGANIZATION: U.S. National Institute of Health (NIH), the Office of Research Services (ORS)

MISSION: NIH is the U.S. leader in biomedical research. It funds and conducts biomedical research aimed at improving human health. The ORS is one of the primary support functions of NIH that provides for municipal services, building and space acquisition, property management, and research program support. The ORS also ensures regulatory compliance.

ISSUE/PROBLEM: The service-recipients within the NIH needed a better framework to transact business with the ORS. Due to increasing budget pressures, service-recipients needed to know what types of services the ORS provided, why, and how much they cost.

SOLUTION: An ABC/M system was implemented to provide service cost analysis and lead to an improved budget methodology.

ABC/M MODEL STUCTURE: The ABC/M model reflected eight ORS organizations and contained six program areas, 40 types of service groups, and 175 discrete service-lines comprised of their unique and shared work activities. These costs were traced to 60 customers relative to their consumption. The largest component of the resource expenses is those of outside contractors, which are 50% greater than the wage-related expenses of the ORS employees.

RESULTS: Reliable costs for all of the ORS services were derived. Service costs were benchmarked against market rates of commercial providers, and cost gaps were closed or narrowed, realizing substantial cost savings.

LESSONS LEARNED: A top-down support needs to be blended with bottom-up involvement and ownership of the ABC/M data. It was critical to replace fear and skepticism by ORS employees with confidence that the ABC/M data can be used for internal improvement.

ORGANIZATION: U.S. Army Forces Command (FORSCOM)

MISSION: FORSCOM is a major U.S. Army Command and acts as the Army component of the U.S. Atlantic Command. They train, mobilize, and deploy combat-ready ground forces of America's Total Army to meet operational requirements for the United States. They are stewards of the Army's resources and provide care for soldiers, civilians, retirees, and their families. In 1998 they maintained and served eleven Army installations and four sub-posts.

ISSUE/PROBLEM: Budget pressures created a need to understand much better their cost structure and behavior. In one public seminar the FORSCOM presenter said, "Until recently, we managed our installations much as we did in 1940!" The initial goal was to provide managerial information for use in applying activity-based management. A key was to provide comparable and reliable benchmarking data on the costs of outputs to aid in the search for best practices.

SOLUTION: By implementing ABC/M systems at each installation, FORSCOM was able to apply the data to reinvent operations and processes, reduce unnecessary spending, and ensure higher value-added in their products and services. One of the keys was to integrate the ABC/M data with ongoing reengineering efforts, particularly in high payoff areas. The ABC/M data were used at the "micro level" to manage processes; ABC/M data were fed into FORSCOM's Service Based Costing for managing at the "macro level."

ABC/M MODEL STUCTURE: The initial focus was on unit costing of output cost objects. However, as the true costs were reported, focus shifted to the work activities that belong to the processes that produce those outputs and services. After eight pilot ABC/M models were constructed in 1996, five ABC/M models were built for six installations and focused on logistics, public works, community activities, training/airfields, and information management.

RESULTS: A significant result was simply to create an awareness of costs—not only of the output products and services but also of the work activities that comprise them.

The ABC/M data were thought-provoking in that they caused serious questioning of accepted regulations, rules, and business practices. For example, they discovered that a negotiated formal contract award could cost three times more than a sealed bid formal contract award. In another example, they identified where the administrative costs to process a report regarding an asset or property exceeded the value of the asset or property. As a benchmarking example, they discovered that childcare costs were twice that of the commercial sector on a comparable basis. They applied the ABC/M data in A-76 studies.

Although fee-based full cost recovery is not a universal policy, they discovered that lunches, on average, cost roughly $7.50 to serve yet were priced at about $5.50.

Several of the installations reorganized from numerous silo-directorates into more process-oriented business centers.

LESSONS LEARNED: They learned that much of what ABC/M is about is learning and discovery. Once equipped with fact-based data, managers and employees could ask better questions about existing operations and consider opportunities for change.

They also learned that there can be considerable organizational resistance to change. Some managers and workers are threatened by having data revealed about their practices. Resistance was overcome by persuading these individuals that it is far better to manage using reliable information rather than intuition.

ABC/M is only data and not a silver bullet. Realizing true change with economic impact requires a willingness to take—not just plan—actions and to make tough decisions.

ORGANIZATION: U.S. Patent & Trademark Office (PTO), U.S. Department of Commerce

MISSION: By evaluating and approving high-quality patents and trademarks, the U.S. PTO stimulates innovation and economic growth for the U.S. economy. It also protects the investments made in research and development.

ISSUE/PROBLEM: Due to many forces sparked by accelerating innovation, the PTO was experiencing substantial increases in submitted applications. The PTO capacity to handle this increasing workload did not keep pace. Service slipped while customer expectations for speedier processing increased.

Since the PTO is not funded by taxpayers, but rather is a fully fee-funded organization, it needed to operate very much like a commercial business. It needed to better understand how to apply specific fees and increases to those fees to recover their costs.

In addition, the U.S. government was issuing new regulations for external financial reporting (e.g., GPRA), and the PTO's existing financial systems fell short.

SOLUTION: PTO implemented an ABC/M system.

ABC/M MODEL STUCTURE: Resource drivers continued to use program codes from their legacy system, but examiner surveys were added. The work activity dictionary was grouped into eight broad business processes. For the unit costing of outputs, these same activities were traced to cost objects using 29 activity drivers.

Cost objects included: utility patents, design patents, plant patents, reissues, re-examinations, printed patents and OG, appeals, and interferences.

RESULTS: Some of the calculated ABC/M results challenged the PTO's beliefs. For example, costs related to trademarks were higher than expected; now they knew why and the sources of those higher costs.

The output of ABC/M also provided performance measurement data for the PTO's balanced scorecard system and for its improved fiscal budgeting process.

LESSONS LEARNED: Much good came from the visibility revealed by the ABC/M data. The lesson, however, was to not underestimate the magnitude of organizational resistance to the ABC/M data. A considerable amount of extra time was spent dealing with skepticism about the calculated numbers and revalidating the inputs and cost assignment assumptions despite minimal change in the numbers.

ORGANIZATION: Animal and Plant Health Inspection Service (APHIS)

MISSION: To protect American agriculture from exotic pests and diseases, to minimize wildlife/agriculture conflicts, and to protect the welfare of animals used for research or sold whole-sale for pets.

ISSUE/PROBLEM: As a shared-services provider of administrative support to three USDA agencies, APHIS has long needed to identify an equitable way to charge for its services and to be accountable to customers for services provided. Portions of the agency are also funded by user fees, and there is a need to monitor how well they are recouping charges as well as establishing a basis for future fees. As with nearly all federal agencies, APHIS also needs to connect its GPRA goals and results with resources.

SOLUTION: APHIS has used ABC/M in several ways. The first use was to track costs to customers for administrative services through an ABM system that has now been in place for three years. ABC/M has also been applied to identify a basis for user fees in one program delivery organization and to monitor user fee costs in a laboratory support organization. ABC/M also has shown potential for connecting GPRA goals to cost in a more specific way than is currently done.

ABC/M MODEL STRUCTURE: For the administrative unit, each division has its own model with customers as cost objects. For the program organizations, each model contains the whole organization's structure, and cost objects are set up as budget line items or major service categories, depending on the needs of the organization.

RESULTS: For the administrative organization, an output-based system for charging customers is in place, and the results may soon be used in budget allocations. Program organizations are preparing to restructure fees based on results or develop new fee proposals.

LESSONS LEARNED: The ability to automate data gathering and to make maximum use of existing data is crucial to any large-scale application of ABC/M. Managers need early involvement and training to be able to make the best use of ABC/M results in cost management and to be willing to accept output-based budgeting. Traditional ways of tracking costs in user fee situations may underestimate indirect charges.

ORGANIZATION: U.S. National Security Agency (NSA), Directorate of Support (DS)

MISSION: The Directorate of Support Services contributes to the accomplishment of the Signals Intelligence and Information Security missions of the NSA by providing a comprehensive array of high-quality, cost-effective support services including hiring, retention, workforce development, security, information services, facilities, and logistics services. The Directorate of Support Services sets corporate standards in customer services and is leading the

NSA into the use of business practices through Activity-Based Costing/Management and the Balanced Scorecard.

ISSUE/PROBLEM: In order for the NSA to understand and determine the cost of its mission support services, it needed a comprehensive analysis of its cost drivers and resource consumption. The DS set out to identify and map all mission support processes in order to allocate cost to mission customers through notional billing and Fee For Service models. The requirement to trace expenses to the customer has been driven by congressional mandates to reduce overall Agency support cost and allocate dollars to missions and their customers.

SOLUTION: The NSA applied ABC/M to trace its costs.

ABC/M MODEL STRUCTURE: Using the Oros ABC/M software from ABC Technologies, each area of support was modeled to reflect the consumption of its expenses associated with facilities, human resources, training, logistics, security, information services, and management business support. With a total of over 150 cost objects, products, and services, about 600 work activities, and as many activity drivers, the DS ABC Models gave a comprehensive, detailed view of work performed, customer support in most areas, and the resources applied.

RESULTS: DS was the NSA's first key component to begin allocating its total manpower cost against its products, services, and work being done to indirectly support its corporate mission. It allowed DS to begin the research and analysis necessary to implement a Fee For Service Model that will eventually also include the chargeback of working capital to customers. The current DS models are being incorporated into a new Agency-wide Corporate Accounting System for allocation of all agency costs.

LESSONS LEARNED: Knowledge is power. With the Directorate of Support's ability to speak to cost and drivers of cost, defending and requesting budget dollars became validated. Without continued management understanding of the full capabilities of ABC/M and using the results to make decisions and improvements, ABC data will provide nothing. A robust and agency-wide ABM is where the entire NSA intends to go.

ORGANIZATION: U.S. Transportation Security Agency (TSA)

MISSION: The TSA provides protection to travelers.

ISSUE/PROBLEM: The TSA's goal was to answer the question, "What are the costs and resources required for screening airport passengers?"

The TSA was under pressure to explain its cost structure and demonstrate it was applying good practices at reasonable service levels. Answering this question also helps ensure that TSA managers can quantify the resources needed to meet service goals and to determine the impact on service levels if sufficient resources are not provided to meet the service-level goals.

SOLUTION: The goal for the ABC/M project was to determine the unit cost of screening passengers in terms of the work activities performed. An ABC/M system was implemented to review screening costs at both privatized and federalized airports in order to identify key cost drivers and potential best practices.

ABC/M MODEL STUCTURE: The initial ABC/M was kept relatively simple rather than defining hundreds of work activities at the task level.

RESULTS: The unit cost per passenger was found to differ greatly across airports. However, the size of the unit cost differences were reduced after the necessary costs of required but idle capacity for readiness were segmented. Airport commonality exists at the process level due to standard operating procedures (SOP), indicating a standard relationship between cost and capacity. Readiness was revealed as the largest cost component of the screening process; unnecessary waiting time by passengers can be reduced by increasing the maximum lane capacity per hour and using fewer lanes. The adjusted unit cost data aided in focusing on opportunities.

LESSONS LEARNED: Maximum capacity, screening process unit costs, and detection rate can be successfully benchmarked across TSA airports. The benchmarks facilitate discussions about best practices for operations improvement. Costs should not be examined in isolation of performance and service levels. Process efficiencies can be achieved by reducing the number of redundant screenings and unnecessary manual bag movements.

ORGANIZATION: "XYZ" Air Force Base *

MISSION: "XYZ" Air Force Base is an Air Force material command base located in the U.S. It is home to many operational and support missions. The base performs depot maintenance, repair, and remanufacture of various Air Force combat weapon systems, including fighter and cargo planes. The annual operating budget for the remanufacturing operations is over $200 million.

ISSUE/PROBLEM: Leadership was tasked to demonstrate that it can quantify improvement opportunities using ABC as a methodology. Not only did the activities have to be quantified, they needed to be classified as value-add or not. Leadership wanted to separate how much indirect support was going to each of the various weapon systems that were being worked on in the depot. Leadership also wanted to see the difference in the unit costs of each block of planes being repaired. The blocks represent age grouping of aircraft. One block might consist of planes made more than 25 years ago. Another block might be planes made 15–20 years ago, etc.

SOLUTION: Use process mapping that has already been performed to produce an activity/process based view of the organization. Review the initial model structure with supervisors to revise and include rework, indirect support, work interruptions, etc.

ABC/M MODEL STRUCTURE: This was a classic manufacturing job shop model, with direct processes modeled to the projects/weapon systems and indirect support modeled to the other areas. The different modifications being made were the first set of cost objects, the individual aircraft by tail numbers were the next set of cost objects, with the customers requesting the repair and maintenance work being the last set of cost objects. The resources and activities were placed in organizational hierarchy so that management could understand the model better. The departmental activities were grouped into overall organization-wide processes, which lead to the outputs by modification and by tail number. Funding sources of the various resources used were added to get visibility to funding output.

RESULTS: The model was completed in 10 weeks. Three people were on the core team. The resulting analysis showed several areas where improvements could be made. The first was in the area of work interruptions. The real cost of a plane's "tour of duty" when in service was over $1,000,000 in set up, clean up, put away, get back out, and get back to work type costs. This did not include the lost opportunity cost of production capability. Other costs of rework and redundant work were also made visible (over $600,000). These results were considered very confidential, because of the magnitude of the findings and the potential impact on future program funding. Plans were put into place to change and improve the operating environment, without disclosing the results of the ABC model.

LESSONS LEARNED: Many process maps show only the steps used to deliver "good" outputs. Quantifying the various other outputs ("bad" and "lost opportunities") yields great insight for improving operations. Some of the best ABC in the government and military is performed clandestinely because of the need to improve operations without other management misinterpreting the information.

*Contributor: Stu Schaefer, CEO, Spectrum Group Management Consulting, www.spectrum groupMC.com

ORGANIZATION: "XYZ" Army Depot *

MISSION: Performing a wide range of vehicle conversions and upgrades, maintaining tracked combat vehicles and their components, and maintaining towed and self-propelled artillery. The depot also performs maintenance on individual and crew-served weapons as well as land combat missiles and small arms.

ISSUE/PROBLEM: Net Operating Results (NOR) are very unpredictable. They swing positive and negative, seemingly regardless of workflow. Clearly the real costs are not quite right, compared to what they are forecasted/budgeted to be. The depot is paid a "price," based on its standard cost system, for each product delivered. The classic cost distortion of overhead spreading without regard to reality and the classic government issue of not having all the costs counted in one place were contributing to the obscurity of true cost. Leadership needs to understand the true costs and what is causing them, so that it can do a better job of forecasting results and planning workflow.

One of the first things to do was get a handle on a real picture of how big the organization is. Officially it has approximately 2,500 employees, yet it modeled 3,223 FTE. Officially it has a $250M operating budget, yet it modeled over $500M in cost. Officially it has a $120M payroll, yet it modeled a personnel cost of $190M, with an additional $75M in associated contractor support costs, which equals an additional estimated 900 FTE. The overall real workforce brought to bear is over 4,000 strong, 55% more than the official count. The overall cost is almost double what the official operating budget is said to be. With this sort of clarity, the depot began to model the processes and outcomes.

SOLUTION: Implement an ABC/M system that will include all the costs that are relevant to the outputs of the organization. The costs were substantially more than appear on just one department's budget when viewed in isolation from the other departments. Determine true, overall costs per project (PCN) and then by weapon system, including support costs. Compare those to the standard cost system figures to understand where the distortions are.

ABC/M MODEL STRUCTURE: This was a classic manufacturing model, with direct processes modeled to the projects, and indirect support modeled to the areas supported. The hundreds of individual PCNs were the first set of cost objects, with weapon systems being the second set of cost objects. Customers were the last set, so the amount of work done for other organizations besides the Army became visible.

RESULTS: The resulting comparison showed several items that were significantly deviating from the standard cost system, with a classic S-curve chart reported. When comparing single unit versus volumized deviations, it became clear that some high volume products with small single unit deviations were causing large overall differences. This realization enabled leadership to understand the effect the true cost was having, versus the reported standard costs.

These results were considered very confidential, because they gave insights that would enable the command to pick out the work that would be most beneficial to it. As a result, the command is able to plan its NOR much more accurately and petition for the work that will be most beneficial to it.

LESSONS LEARNED: Small unit cost variances on high volume products/services can have a greater overall effect than the low volume items that have extraordinary variance. Information of this caliber is so strategically important that management does not want others to know it possesses the information. The organization only agreed to let this be published on the basis of anonymity.

*Contributor: Stu Schaefer, CEO, Spectrum Group Management Consulting, www.spectrum groupMC.com

ORGANIZATION: Not-for-Profit Blood & Tissue Center

The blood and tissue center has mainly local/regional blood distribution and several tissue distribution centers throughout the nation. All production is local.

ISSUE/PROBLEM: The organization's board consists of several customer representatives. One of the board's financial objectives for blood services is to break even with cash outflows recovered via priced billing charges. Although yearly financials show that blood services breaks even, management thinks that tissue sales are subsidizing the blood side, because of the way overhead (especially support functions) is allocated between the two. However, there is no proof of this subsidy that would justify changing fees for blood products and services.

Unit cost for both tissue and blood products were desired in order to set appropriate rates and be able to cost new and developing products.

The local blood market basically operates as a monopoly without competition. In case a competitive situation ever exists in the local blood market, the organization wants to be ready and equipped with essential cost information to appropriately mount a strategic response.

SOLUTION: An ABC/M model to determine true product, customer, and process costs is needed. The most recent model is the fourth iteration of ABC/M at the organization. Although prior models were already useful for blood product/service/process decisions, this was the first model that attempted to quantify all the necessary elements of tissue operations.

ABC/M MODEL STRUCTURE: The G/L was reshaped from departments into more logical resource pools of common types of resources regardless of their departmental cost center. The work activities by department were defined in detail, but not overly so. The final cost objects used were the traditional ABC/M cost assignment network's products and customers with the customer-caused work activities traced directly to the customers as a cost-to-serve rather than improperly allocating them to product costs.

RESULTS: Management can now see the true product cost for blood and tissue products, with and without overhead/support costs. The model was able to show the cost-to-serve different customers and gave insights on how volume affects this cost. Management now has monthly profit and loss statements for each tissue branch based on ABC cost.

Management now sees support departments (HR, IT, facilities, etc.) assigned to operational departments based on actual consumption of support. One tangible benefit is that this allowed for higher Medicare reimbursement of reference laboratory cost since support overhead was directly assigned to it in a logical fashion that Medicare agrees to. Proper allocation of support cost showed that the blood side of the organization was using about

$1 million more in overhead support than the GAAP allocations (based on percent of sales) assumed. Based on this new information, the governing board allowed the organization to adjust its fees accordingly.

LESSONS LEARNED: It takes time. It takes experts from outside, and able and willing people on the inside to think about the operations and the model. Proper top management backing and communication to the organization is essential. Unutilized capacity in some areas can make certain unit costs appear very large. Constant awareness of where unutilized capacity might be hiding is necessary. Future explicit modeling of capacity is planned, which would then enable proper management and accountability of capacity.

*Contributor: Stu Schaefer, CEO, Spectrum Group Management Consulting, www.spectrum groupMC.com

---

ORGANIZATION: United States Navy Family Housing, Pacific Northwest*

MISSION: The role of Military Family Housing is to provide, support, and maintain housing for all active duty military families. Family Housing provides counseling, relocation assistance, real estate referral, and other services directly related to the unique requirements of military personnel and their families.

ISSUE/PROBLEM: Family Housing had no way to determine all labor, support, and maintenance costs, by geographic area, type of unit, age of unit, type of construction, etc., in order to identify funding requirements. Family Housing wanted reasonable, repeatable means to determine costs associated with existing facilities in order to make decisions on a master plan involving Public/Private Venture (PPV), renovation, demolition, and new construction and the budget requirements to support that master plan. Additionally, Family Housing wanted to determine the best application of staff labor to meet the needs of multiple geographically dispersed housing offices whose workload had changed as a result of Base Realignment and Closure Act (BRAC) tenant relocations.

SOLUTION: The solution was to develop an ABC model that identified all costs associated with each type of housing support and maintenance service provided, by unit type, within each housing complex. Management wanted to identify specific, detailed cost by housing type, housing complex, service provided (such as scheduled versus unscheduled maintenance, municipal versus military provided, utilities cost per unit/complex), average time to turn a unit around by complex and housing type, etc. Management also wanted an analysis of each complex and housing type to determine the best use of PPV/renovation/demolition and new construction funding. Further, management needed to determine cost of staff-related family support services and service level demand at each site to develop a staffing plan to meet the needs that were changing due to BRAC-related changes in base tenant composition.

ABC/M MODEL STRUCTURE: An ABC model was constructed using the commercial ABC/M software SAS ABM, from The SAS Institute, as the ABC/M calculation engine. The model was designed to allow its incorporation into the overall regional ABM system.

RESULTS: The model immediately identified specific areas for cost recovery that required little more than a reallocation of service provider responsibility. The data clearly showed the cost to support each housing type and complex, identified maintenance costs in excess of value, and identified opportunities for consolidation of utility costs. The data were used to further refine the regional family housing master plan. The data from the ABC model allowed management to analyze the staff business activities in terms of value added and non–value added services and to reallocate staff resources based on service level needs. The ABC model provided cost information to support management decisions, improve future year cost projections, and provide quantifiable data to support budget requests.

LESSONS LEARNED: Process map staff requirements prior to building the model to ensure the activities described are well-defined and the activities scope is agreed to. Ensure budget information provided is understood; where possible, ensure budget line item costs are applied specifically to what they support and not evenly applied across a general support area. Start with a small pilot. Stress constantly the iterative process and the fact that although the ABC/M work plan allows you to get your ABC/M model up rather quickly, time is required to realize results and benefits. It is important to ensure that a good communication plan is in place and that all staff understand the purpose and expected outcome of the study.

*Contributor: Joe Clark, Director, Vision Technologies, www.visntec.com

Chapter 3

If ABC Is the Answer,
What Is the Question?

"Nine times out of ten, in the arts as in life, there is actually nothing to be discovered; there is only error to be exposed."
—H.L. Mencken, American editor, *Prejudices* (1922, third series)

"The resources added by the President for fiscal years 2000–2005 in no way diminish the U.S. Department of Defense's resolve to shrink the portion of its budget consumed by infrastructure."
—William S. Cohen, Secretary of Defense, March 2, 1999

O NE CAN ONLY refer to "ABC/M" for so long before needing to visualize it and understand it as a cost-flow mechanism. That is what we do next. Chapters 3 and 4 will describe what an ABC/M system looks like, how it works, and how to design it. In this first segment, I address some of the questions that invariably loom large in the minds of organizational planners contemplating ABC/M application to their problem-solving. I also introduce some of the concepts and terms that are basic to understanding ABC/M as an accounting tool and—more important—as a management tool for encouraging behavioral change.

SO, WHAT'S THE BIG PROBLEM?

Why do some public sector managers shake their heads in disbelief when they think about their organization's cost accounting system? I once heard a public official complain, "You know what we think of our cost accounting system? It is a bunch of fictitious lies—but we all agree to them." Of course, he was referring to the misallocated costs based on broad averages that result in flawed and misleading information. What a sad state it is when the users of the accounting data simply resign themselves to a lack of hope. And unfortunately, many of the accountants are comfortable if the numbers all foot-and-tie in total; they care less if the parts making up the total are correct. The total is all that matters, and any arbitrary cost allocation can tie out to the total.

Imagine if you were a roving reporter and asked managers and employee teams throughout your organization, "How happy are you with the financial and accounting data that now support policy decisions aimed at improving effectiveness, efficiency, and performance?" Thumbs up or down? Many would give it thumbs down. When you have the *wrong* information coupled with the *wrong* measurements, it is not difficult to make *wrong* decisions.

How can traditional accounting that has been around for so many years all of a sudden become considered so bad? The answer is that the data are not necessarily bad so much as somewhat distorted, woefully incomplete, and partly unprocessed. Figure 3-1 provides the first hint of a problem. The left side shows the classic monthly report that responsibility-center managers receive under the general ledger system. Note that the example used is a back-office department of a license bureau, such as for driver or hunting licenses. It is a factory, too, only its outputs are not tangible products but documents. This is to demonstrate that, despite misconceptions, indirect white-collar workers produce outputs the same as factory workers do. You can substitute any department, government or commercial, for the license bureau department in the example, and the lessons will hold.

If you question managers who routinely receive this report, "How much of these expenses can you control or influence? How much insight do you get from this report into the content of your employees' work?" they will likely answer both questions with a "Not much!" This is because salaries and fringe benefits usually make up the most sizable portion of controllable costs, and all that the manager sees are those expenses reported as lump-sum amounts.

When you translate those "chart-of-account" expenses shown under the general ledger or fund accounting system into the actual work activities that consume these expenses, a manager's insights begin to increase. The right side of Figure 3-1 is the ABC/M view that is used for analysis and as the starting point for calculating the costs both for processes and for diverse outputs. In effect, the right-side ABC/M view begins to resolve the deficiencies of traditional financial accounting by focusing on work activities. ABC/M is very work-centric, whereas general ledger and fund accounting systems are transaction-centric.

Another key difference lies in the language used to depict cost allocations (i.e., absorption costing). ABC/M describes activities using an "action verb-adjective-noun" grammar convention, such as "process building permit" or "open new taxpayer accounts." This gives ABC/M its flexibility. Such word-

FIGURE 3-1 The Language of ABC/M

Stating activities with an "action verb-object noun" grammar convention creates an atmosphere for change by providing a new way of looking at something people are already familiar with, rather than something that is foreign.

From: General Ledger

Chart-of-Accounts View

License Processing Department

	Actual	Plan	Favorable/ (unfavorable)
Salaries	$621,400	$600,000	$(21,400)
Equipment	161,200	150,000	(11,200)
Travel expense	58,000	60,000	2,000
Supplies	43,900	40,000	(3,900)
Use and occupancy	30,000	30,000	—
Total	$914,500	$880,000	$(34,500)

To: ABC Database

Activity-Based View

License Processing Department

Key/scan licenses	$ 31,500
Analyze licenses	121,000
Suspend licenses	32,500
Receive provider inquiries	101,500
Resolve member problems	83,400
Process batches	45,000
Determine eligibility	119,000
Make copies	145,500
Write correspondence	77,100
Attend training	158,000
Total	$914,500

Reprinted with permission of the McGraw-Hill Companies, from Gary Cokins, *Activity-Based Cost Management: Making It Work.* © The McGraw-Hill Companies, Inc., 1996.

ing is powerful because managers and employee teams can better relate to these phrases, and the wording implies that the work activities can be favorably affected through change, improvement, or elimination. General ledger and fund accounting systems use a chart-of-accounts, whereas ABC/M uses a chart-of-activities as its language. In translating the data from a general ledger or fund accounting system into activities and processes, ABC/M preserves the total reported budget funding and costs but allows the individual elements to be viewed differently.

To be further critical of the left side chart-of-accounts view, notice how inadequate those data are in reporting the costs of processes that run cross-functionally and penetrate through the vertical boundaries of a government agency's organization chart. The general ledger and the fund accounting system are organized around separate departments or cost centers. This presents a real reporting problem. For example, with a city's department of public works, what is the true total cost for processing equipment repair requisitions that travel through so many hands? For a service organization, what is the true cost of opening a new account for a citizen or service-recipient?

Many organizations have flattened and de-layered such that employees from different departments or cost centers frequently perform similar activities and multi-task in two or more core workflow processes. Only by reassembling and aligning the work-activity costs across the workflow processes, like "process home buyer permits" or "open new taxpayer accounts," can the end-to-end process costs be seen, measured, and eventually managed.

The structure of the general ledger and fund accounting system is restricted by cost-center mapping to the hierarchical organization chart. As a consequence, this type of reported information drives *vertical* and hierarchical behavior, not the much more desirable *process* behavior. In effect, with traditional accounting systems, public sector managers are denied visibility of the costs that belong to their end-to-end workflow processes—and what is driving those costs.

In summary, the general-ledger and fund-accounting view describes "what was spent," whereas the activity-based view describes "what it was spent for and why."

HOW DO COST DRIVERS WORK?

Much additional information can be gleaned from the right-side view of Figure 3-1. Look at the second activity—"analyze license," at a total cost of $121,000—and ask yourself what would make that cost significantly increase or decrease. The overall answer is the number of licenses analyzed. That is that work's activity driver. Figure 3-2 illustrates that each activity on a stand-alone basis has its own activity driver. At this stage, the costing is no longer recognizing the organization chart and its artificial boundaries. All the employees' costs have been combined into the work performed. The focus is now on the cost of that work and on what influences and affects the level of that workload.

There is yet more that can be gained from this view. Let's assume that 1,000 licenses were analyzed during that period for the department shown. Then the unit cost per each analyzed license is $121 per license. If one specific group—senior citizens over the age of 60, for example—was responsible for half those claims, then we would know more about the sources of demand (i.e., workload). The senior citizens would have caused $60,500 of that work (500 claims multiplied by $121 per claim). If married couples with small children required another fraction, married couples with grown children a different fraction, and so on, then ABC/M will have traced all of the $121,000. If each of the other work activities were similarly traced, using the unique activity driver for each activity, ABC/M will have piled up the entire $914,500 into each group of beneficiary. This reassignment of the resource expenses will be much more accurate than any broad-brush cost allocation applied with traditional accounting systems that use broad averages.

This cost *assignment* network is one of the major reasons that ABC/M calculates costs of outputs more accurately. The assignment of the resource expenses also demonstrates that all costs actually originate with the ultimate end-user, service-recipient, or beneficiary of the work. That location/origin of costs could be a citizen, welfare recipient, new home-buyer seeking permits, or another government agency relying on those services. This is at the opposite end from where people who perform "cost *allocations*" think about costs.

Cost allocations are structured as a one-source-to-many-destinations redistribution of costs. They ignore that the destinations are actually the origin for the costs. The destinations, usually outputs or people, place demands on work, and the work draws on the resource capacity (i.e., the spending)—hence the costs measure the effect by reflecting backwards through the ABC/M cost assignment network. In sum, accountants have historically allocated "what we spend" from the general ledger, whereas ABC/M assigns "what it costs."

FIGURE 3-2 Each Activity Has Its Cost Driver

In addition to seeing the "content of work," the activity view gives insights to what drives each activity's cost magnitude to fluctuate.

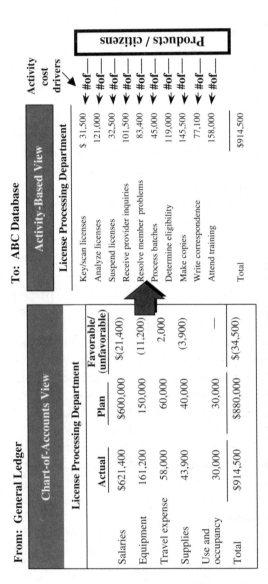

From: General Ledger

Chart-of-Accounts View

License Processing Department

	Actual	Plan	Favorable/ (unfavorable)
Salaries	$621,400	$600,000	$(21,400)
Equipment	161,200	150,000	(11,200)
Travel expense	58,000	60,000	2,000
Supplies	43,900	40,000	(3,900)
Use and occupancy	30,000	30,000	—
Total	$914,500	$880,000	$(34,500)

To: ABC Database

Activity-Based View

License Processing Department

Key/scan licenses	$ 31,500
Analyze licenses	121,000
Suspend licenses	32,500
Receive provider inquiries	101,500
Resolve member problems	83,400
Process batches	45,000
Determine eligibility	119,000
Make copies	145,500
Write correspondence	77,100
Attend training	158,000
Total	$914,500

Activity cost drivers

#of → (Products / citizens)
#of →
#of →
#of →
#of →
#of →
#of →
#of →
#of →
#of →

When managers get this kind of report, they are either happy or sad, but they are rarely any smarter!

> "No feature of cost accounting is more difficult than burden distribution...The impression is too widespread that burden is extremely elusive. Cost accountants can do a great deal to counteract this impression by taking advantage of every opportunity to explain the modern methods of distributing burden."
> —Gould L. Harris, "Calculation and Application of Departmental Burden Rates," *National Association of Cost Accountants (NACA) Bulletin,* vol. 1, no. 3, April 1920.

WHAT ARE COSTS?

Although the two cost views—the cost assignment and the process view—seem logical, people who design or use ABC/M systems often have difficulties deploying the power of these two views. In practice, they often confuse the two.

Part of the problem in defining and designing costing systems involves understanding just what exactly *costs* are. What are *costs,* anyway? Costs themselves are abstract and intangible. One cannot see costs or hold a couple of them in one's hands. Yet we all know they are there. Like an echo, we know they exist whether we measure them or not.

We know that costs increase or decrease as changes in the workload affect the activity costs via changes in the quantity or frequency of their cost drivers. Work activities are triggered by events, and the costs react as the effect. In one sense, since costs are not tangible, ABC/M operates as "an imaging system" similar to radar, sonar, or an electrocardiogram. Like a digital camera, ABC/M records the image.

As just stated, costs measure effects. And, costs measure effects more than they illuminate root causes. However, ABC/M systems can provide an enterprise-wide image of *all the collective effects* plus the *causal relationships* that result in an organization's costs. So costs give insights to root causes, but mainly through their inferences. This may sound ironic, but "cost management" can be considered an oxymoron (such as "jumbo shrimp" and "hospital food")—-a contradictory phrase. You do not really manage costs; you understand the *causes* (and drivers) of costs. Then you manage the causes.

So, in effect, an organization does not manage its costs—-it manages: (1) *what* causes those costs to occur (i.e., its cost drivers), and (2) the *effectiveness and efficiency* of the organization's people and equipment in responding to those causal triggers.

It is sort of amazing that, when one designs a cost measurement system, the resulting information is actually measuring something *intangible and invisible*! But in its own way, ABC/M "tangibilizes" data to represent things that most people believe are intangible.

To sum up, in one sense, the report on the left side of Figures 3-1 and 3-2 represents more of an "accounting police" or "budget police" command-and-control tool. This is the most primitive form of control. Have you overspent your budgeted target? If you have, who says that budgeted target amount was fair when it was initially imposed? As I've said before, when managers receive the left-side report, they are either happy or sad *but rarely any smarter*. That is unacceptable in today's world, which expects much more out of organizations than in the past. We will all witness the emergence of the "learning organizations," not ones that are straight-jacketed with spending restrictions. The right side of our graphics restates the same expenses as on the left side, but the costs are reported in a much more useful format and structure for decision support.

When expenses are expressed as activity costs, they are in a format to be traced into outputs. Expenses are transformed into calculated costs. As a result, employees can never say, "we could care less about what anything costs." People care more when they know what things cost and believe in the accuracy of those costs. Cost accounting is outside their comfort zones. ABC/M makes "cost" understandable and logical.

HOW DOES ABC/M INTERSECT WITH TRADITIONAL COST ACCOUNTING?

Figure 3-3 uses the analogy of an optical lens to show how ABC/M serves as a *translator* of general ledger and fund accounting system data to provide more focused data for improved decision support. The lens not only translates the ledger expenses into a more useful and flexible format but provides more sensory information. The data from the ABC/M lens can serve as an early warning detector that some resource level of spending may be out of alignment, perhaps with the goal or strategy of the organization or with the needs of its customers. For quality managers, ABC/M makes visible all the work related to the cost of quality (COQ)—for example, where quality-related costs are located and which outputs and products the COQ costs have gone into.

As shown in Figure 3-3, ABC/M is not a replacement for the traditional general ledger and fund accounting system. Rather, it is a *translator* or overlay that lies between the traditional expense account accumulators and the

FIGURE 3-3 ABC/M Doesn't Replace the Accounting System

An ABC/M system does not replace the accounting system. It restates the same data and adds operating relationships to support decision-making more effectively.

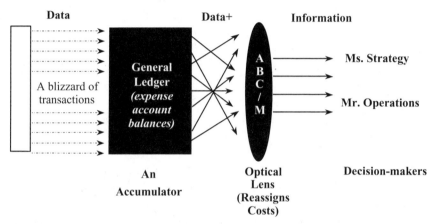

Reprinted with permission of the McGraw-Hill Companies, from Gary Cokins, *Activity-Based Cost Management: Making It Work.* © The McGraw-Hill Companies, Inc., 1996.

end-users. Examples of end-users include the government agency's own managers and employee teams who apply cost data in decision making, as well as governing authorities or oversight committees who may evaluate how to better re-deploy spending budgets.

ABC/M translates expenses into a language that people can understand. It translates expenses into elements of costs, namely the work activities, which can be more flexibly linked or assigned to processes or cost objects based on demand-driven consumption patterns. It is not a simplistic and arbitrary system of broad average cost allocations.

The reason ABC/M is becoming popular in government and public sector organizations is that general ledger and fund accounting systems are now recognized as being *structurally deficient*. The data from those systems are not in a format that will provide good managerial information for decision support. Traditional accounting is a sound mechanism for collecting and accumulating transaction-intensive expenses, but not for converting those into costs for useful decision-making support.

In the simplest terms, the general ledger or fund accounting system acts like a checkbook. One can read the amount of money spent but not really know the what-for's and why's of any individual "check." And, unfortunately, the spending ledger's largest "check" amounts are employee payroll-related, which gives managers virtually no visibility into the *content* of the employee work activities being performed. Further, the payroll-related costs do not reveal the interrelationships of that work with other work or with products and service-lines for service-recipients or beneficiaries. Moreover, there are no insights into what events cause or drive variations in work activity costs. Since an organization's work activities probably represent the costs most subject to management control, it is critical to know and to understand them.

In contrast to traditional accounting, ABC/M focuses on the work activities associated with operating and managing any institution, including those in the not-for-profit or government sector. As noted, ABC/M is work-centric, whereas the general ledger or fund accounting system is transaction-centric. Both have their place and purpose, but the data provided by traditional accounting are too raw to be considered business intelligence for decision support. ABC/M solves that problem and does much more. Just translating the ledger account expenses into their work activities is an incomplete view of ABC/M. The total picture includes ABC/M's linkage of these activities into networks to calculate the cost of outputs useful for performing analysis, for determining tradeoffs, and for making decisions.

The modern movement toward "managing with a process view" has created a growing need for better managerial and costing data. Managing processes and managing activities (i.e., costs) go together. By current definition, a *workflow process* comprises two or more logically related *work activities* intended to serve end-receivers and beneficiaries; thus, a means of integrating processes, outputs, and measured costs has become an even more important requirement for managers and employee teams. ABC/M data provide a logical way to visualize and report on these linkages.

In sum, ABC/M resolves the structural problems inherent in the general ledger and the fund accounting system by first converting account balances into activity costs. ABC/M then assigns the activity costs to cost objects or reassembles the activity costs across processes. These new and transformed cost data can be used to identify operating relationships that are key to making good decisions affecting products, service-lines, and customers.

WHY THE INCREASED INTEREST IN ABC/M?

In the early 1980s many organizations began to realize that their traditional accounting systems were generating inaccurate or incomplete costing information. The typical organization's cost structure had been changing substantially as overhead and indirect costs increased and displaced direct labor and material costs. As alluded to earlier, the three primary causes for this shift were: (1) increasing organizational complexity resulting from proliferation in the variety of product and service-line offerings, (2) a more diverse group of delivery channels and service-recipients, and (3) increased automation, new technologies, and new methodologies.

In the past, the system of calculating costs by using simplistic volume-based allocations may have been acceptable and may not have introduced excessive error. The rapid rise in indirect and overhead expenses changed all that. The traditional costing method became increasingly invalid because of its failure to tie actual consumption costs to the broadening array of products and service-lines. The unfavorable impact of these costing distortions was becoming much more intense than in the past.

Some managers understood intuitively that their outdated accounting system was distorting product and service-line costs, so they sometimes made informal adjustments to compensate. However, with so much complexity and diversity, it was nearly impossible for managers to predict the magnitude of adjustments needed to achieve reasonable accuracy. ABC/M was seen as the way to resolve the problem of poor indirect and overhead cost allocations and to provide additional information that would serve as a basis for positive actions, both strategic and operational.

The rise in ABC/M is also the result of external factors. The level of performance and service that is expected of most organizations has increased dramatically. In the past, many organizations were reasonably comfortable in their mistakes. There was adequate time or resources to mask the impact of any wrong or poor decisions. In many cases, there simply was no accountability with consequences. Errors and poor service were more easily tolerated.

Today the pressure has intensified, and the margin for error is slimmer. Governments and not-for-profit organizations cannot make as many mistakes or use excess capacity and expect that they will not be noticed. Cost estimates for new projects, capital investment decisions, technology choices, outsourcing, and make vs. buy decisions today all require a sharper pencil. More private sector organizations are behaving like predatory competitors. These companies are becoming strong rivals to government institutions by better understanding the cause-and-effect connections that drive costs and by fine-tuning their processes and competitive bid prices accordingly.

The resulting squeeze from the existence of more and possibly better options for service-recipients is making life for some government organizations much more difficult than in the past. Budget tightening has worsened the problem. Knowing what products, service-lines, and service-recipients truly cost is becoming key to survival. With ABC/M visibility, organizations can understand what drives their costs and identify where to remove waste, low-value adding costs, and unused capacity. They can also see the degree of alignment of their cost structure with their organization's mission and strategy.

Today an organization's road is no longer long and straight; it is winding, with bends and hills that do not give much visibility or certainty to plan for the future. Organizations need to be agile and continuously transform their cost structure and work activities. This is difficult to do if they do not understand their own cost structure and economics.

HOW DOES ABC/M YIELD MORE ACCURACY?

As described, ABC/M was developed as a practical solution for problems associated with traditional cost management systems. In traditional cost accounting, the indirect expenses are usually too aggregated to serve any purpose, thus ruining any likelihood of an accurate calculation of cost by type of output.

Moreover, these overhead cost allocations are generally determined by applying broad-brush average cost rates to a volume-based factor, such as employee labor hours or department expenses. Overall, this system may reflect inputs used or outputs produced but will not accurately measure the segments. This flawed basis for allocating costs rarely reflects the specific cause-and-effect relationship between the indirect overhead expense and the product, service-line, channel, or service-recipient (i.e., the cost object) that is actually consuming the cost. Many managers are tired of the "allocation foodfights."

Because allocating is a zero-sum error game, the result of inaccurate cost allocations is that some cost objects get over-costed while the remainder must be under-costed. In practice, the under-costing of some cost objects can be substantial. That is because these service-lines, service-recipients, or perhaps even other government agencies require far more technical attention or consume more employee time than the broad-brush averages applied. Some people refer to traditional cost allocations as *spreaders*. In effect, we have allowed the accounting profession to construct a costing scheme that distorts reality and violates rules of cause-and-effect as a manager understands them.

ABC/M corrects for these flaws by identifying the work activities that are responsible for costs. It builds a cost-flow assignment network, which allows the work activity costs to be continuously reassigned or passed on only if the products, service-lines, or service-recipients, or in some cases *other* work activities, actually use and consume the activity. Remember the restaurant example? Figure 3-4 shows a diagram popularly called the ABC/M Cross, which is critical to understanding this concept.

FIGURE 3-4 The Activity-Based Cost Management Framework

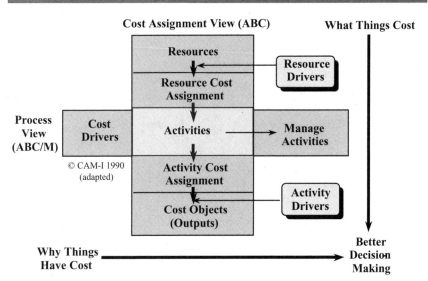

Reprinted with permission. The Consortium of Advanced Manufacturing—International (CAM-I).

Costs represent the belief system of the organization. Many employees accept the reported costs as true strictly because the accountants report them. Other employees are suspicious. An allocation-free cost system is like a smoke-free environment—no pollution. In short, don't allocate—prorate. ABC/M brings in the "myth grenades" that blow up the old flawed beliefs and replaces them with real facts.

The ABC/M cross reveals that work activities, which are located in the center intersection of the cross, are integral to calculating and reporting both the costs of workflow processes and the costs of cost objects. *Cost objects* are the persons or things that benefit from incurring activity costs; examples are products, service-lines, internal or external recipients (e.g., customers), stakeholders, and outputs of internal processes. Cost objects can be thought of as *for what and for whom work is done*.

Figure 3-5 takes us a step closer to understanding the importance of the cross by listing the questions that the vertical cost-assignment view answers. The vertical cost-assignment view explains *what specific things cost*,

FIGURE 3-5 The ABC/M Framework—What Questions Are Answered?

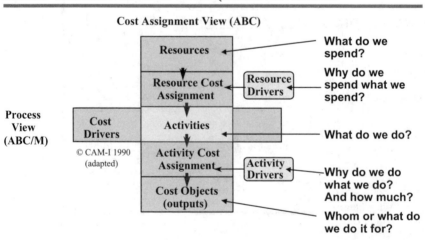

Reprinted with permission. The Consortium of Advanced Manufacturing—International (CAM-I).

whereas the horizontal process view explains *what causes costs* to exist and to fluctuate.

The vertical axis reflects costs and their sensitivity to demands from all forms of product and service-recipient diversity. The work activities consume the resources, and the products and services for the end-users, citizens, and beneficiaries consume the work activities. The vertical ABC/M cost-assignment view is a cost-consumption chain. After each cost is traced based on its unique quantity or proportion of its driver, all of the costs are eventually reaggregated into the final cost objects.

The horizontal view of the ABC/M cross is the workflow-process view. A workflow process is defined as two or more activities or a network of activities with a common purpose. Activity costs belong to the workflow processes. Across each process, the activity costs are sequential and additive. In this orientation, activity costs satisfy the requirements for popular flow-charting and process-modeling techniques and software. Process-based thinking, tipping the organization chart 90 degrees, is now dominating managerial thinking; ABC/M provides the cost elements for process costing that are not available from the general ledger and the fund accounting system.

Figure 3-6 illustrates the mechanism of the vertical axis of the ABC/M cross. It reveals that an activity cost has an output cost rate that is synonymous with the activity driver rate.

WHAT ARE DRIVERS?

Other than "activity," there probably is no term that has become more identified with activity-based cost management than the term "driver" and its several variations. The problem is that it has been applied in several ways with varying meanings. To be very clear, a *cost driver* is something that can be described in words but not necessarily in numbers. For example, a storm would be a *cost driver* that results in much clean-up work, which in turn has related costs. In contrast, the *activity drivers* in ABC/M's cost assignments must be quantitative, using measures that apportion expenses into costs. In the ABC/M vertical cost-assignment view, there are three types of drivers, and all are required to be quantitative:

- Resource drivers—trace expenditures (cash or fund outlays) to work activities
- Activity drivers—trace activity costs to cost objects
- Cost object drivers—trace cost object costs into *other* cost objects.

FIGURE 3-6 Activity Drivers

Activity drivers are factors that govern the assignment of activity costs down to the product or service for customers.

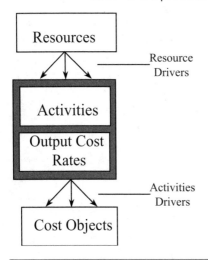

- All activity drivers (including "intermediates") reflect cause-and-effect relationships

- Activity drivers trace and reassign activity costs to their cost objects in direct proportion to the object's consumption of the activity

- The last set of activity drivers links the cumulative costs of upstream activities with the final product or customer

In the ABC/M cross's vertical cost-assignment view, activity drivers will have their own higher-order cost drivers. Events or other influences, which are formally called cost drivers, cause work activities. Think of a cost driver as a work order that triggers the work activity, which in turn uses resources to produce outputs or results. Activity costs are additive along the process and therefore can be accumulated along the business and value chain process.

Cost drivers and activity drivers thus serve different purposes. Activity drivers are output measures that reflect the usage of each work activity, and they must be quantitatively measurable. An activity driver, which relates a work activity to cost objects, "meters-out" the work activity based on the unique diversity and variation of the cost objects that are consuming the activity. It is often difficult to understand whether use of the term "activity driver" is related to a causal effect (input driver, such as "number of labor hours worked") or to the output produced by an activity (output driver, such as "number of licenses processed" or "number of meals prepared"). In many cases, this is not a critical issue so long as the activity driver traces the relative proportion of the activity cost to its cost objects.

Figure 3-7 illustrates how activity drivers are lower-order drivers of cost drivers. ABC/M relies on activity drivers for tracing costs. Collectively they are useful when combined with quality management (QM) problem-solving tools for identifying root causes.

Driver data, whether it is cost-driver or activity-driver information, sparks root cause analysis. Generally, the activity drivers used for ABC/M costing are output-based. Therefore, as the quantitative measures of the drivers rise or fall over time, ABC/M can report the historical trend in terms of *per-unit cost of work* rates for the activity outputs and ultimately for the products as a whole. Alternatively, it can also provide the *per-unit cost of each output* rates for use in predictive planning and what-if scenarios, which are popular uses of the ABC/M data.

Cost estimating with ABC/M is very natural because the activity costs react and behave linearly with changes in their activity drivers. Too often with traditional costing, the cost rates do not directly vary with changes in volume; this fault then results in mis-estimates and ultimately in errors, poor decisions, and lost profits.

As mentioned, in the vertical cost-assignment view, the term "driver" is prefix-appended in three areas. The first deals with the method of assigning resource costs to activities—called a *resource driver*. The second deals with the method of assigning activity costs to cost objects—called an *activity driver*. The third—a *cost object* driver—applies to cost objects after all activity costs have already been logically assigned. Note that cost objects can be consumed or used by *other* cost objects.

In this context, references to old 1990s language of "first" and "second" stage drivers are being abandoned as being obsolete. Their use today would give a misleading impression that ABC/M can be easily accomplished as a simplistic two-step allocation. ABC/M practitioners have come to recognize that ABC/M is a multi-stage cost assignment scheme (which will be discussed in Chapter 4). By limiting the use of the word "driver" to four clearly defined areas—cost driver plus the three just mentioned as appearing on the vertical axis—I hope to prevent misinterpretation or misuse of the term.

Figure 3-8 reveals the link between an activity driver and its work activity. In a simple fashion, it describes how each work activity can be judged based on its need by the service-recipient, its efficiency, or its value content. Some managers believe that the only real way to cut costs is to eliminate the

FIGURE 3-7 Drivers Have Drivers

Activity drivers have their own cost drivers. It is best to use "symptomatic" and physical output drivers in the ABC model to measure unit driver rates and segment the diversity of the cost objects . . .

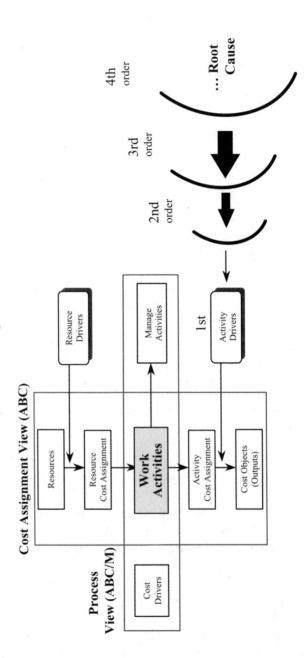

. . . and rely on employees to determine the "nth order" drivers using TQM problem-solving techniques outside of ABC's cost flowing.

FIGURE 3-8 Activity Analysis

Activity analysis judges work based on need, efficiency, and value.

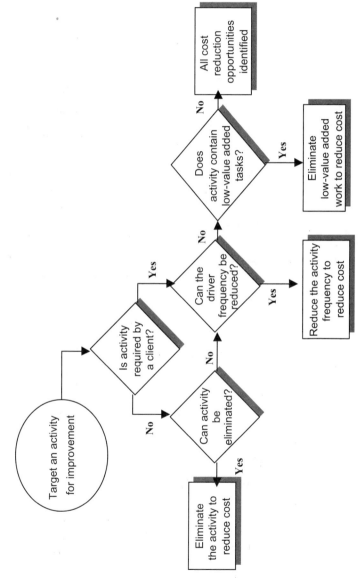

work activity altogether. Their reasoning is that trying to prune costs is rarely effective. There is little point, they say, in trying to do cheaply what should not be done at all; that is, a job not worth doing is not worth doing well.

Regardless of how management decides to achieve improvements, the main message here is that work is central to ABC/M. The effort will provide useful inputs to the decision-making process. ABC/M will answer these important questions: What do we do? How much do we do it? For whom do we do it? How important is it? Are we very good at doing it?

WHY IS MINIMIZING THE SIZE OF THE ABC/M SYSTEM IMPORTANT?

In practice, ABC/M systems will sometimes trace work activity costs to two or more other *intermediate* work activities that consume the work upstream from the ultimate products and services that initially trigger the demands on work. The reassignment network of cost-segmented consumption is key to ABC/M's superior costing accuracy. ABC/M can tolerate reasonable cost-driver estimates as proxies for actual-transaction detail drivers because the error does not compound—it dampens out on its way to the final cost objects. Although counterintuitive, with ABC/M, precision inputs are not synonymous with accurate outputs. This property significantly lightens the load for data collection. And this is why the mantra of ABC/M advocates is, "It is better to be approximately correct than precisely inaccurate!"

Figure 3-9 illustrates the impact of the error-dampening property. The figure shows several curves that all have the same destination—100% perfectly accurate cost results. The vertical axis represents the accuracy level, while the horizontal axis represents the "level of effort." For each *incremental* level of effort to collect more and better data, there is *proportionately* less improvement in accuracy. So the phrase, "Is the climb worth the view?" is truly applicable to ABC/M.

This graphic also draws attention to efficient and inefficient performance levels exhibited by ABC/M project teams in finding the *right combination* of accuracy and ABC/M administrative effort. There will always be a balanced tradeoff of *more* data for *higher* accuracy. But the appropriate questions being raised here are, "*Which* data? And *what* is the effort to collect those particular data?"

Unfortunately, most ABC/M project teams perform too far to the right on Figure 3-9 and usually on a much lower "frontier curve." That is, they have put in much *greater* effort than was needed, and they received *less* accuracy

FIGURE 3-9 Balancing Levels of Accuracy with Effort

Poorly designed ABC/M systems will yield less accuracy despite greater effort! Even the best-designed systems will yield less increase in accuracy per unit of effort expended as the size of the collection effort increases.

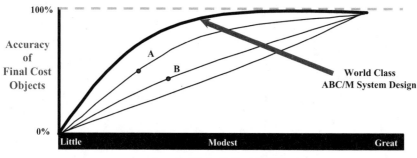

With better design, ABC/M Project Team A is achieving higher accuracy with much less collection effort relative to ABC/M Project Team B.

in costing than they could have achieved if they had been more clever in two areas of developing their ABC/M model. First, they need to select beforehand what data are most important to collect. Second—and more important—they need to design a good cost assignment structure. The challenge for today's ABC/M teams is to determine how to *right-size* their ABC/M model—-and to right-size it appropriately. Few organizations can afford excesses. In the end, the level of accuracy and detail needed depends on what decisions are going to be based on the data. And usually the accuracy requirements are not unreasonably harsh.

ABC/M's property of error-dampening means that an ABC/M model does not need to be very granular and, consequently, very large in size. Unfortunately, because this is counterintuitive, many ABC/M systems are over-engineered in size. They go well beyond diminishing returns in extra accuracy for extra levels of effort of work. I refer to this as "ABC/M's leveling problem."

What level of detail and precision do you need? The rapid prototyping design methods described in Chapter 9 create maximum value with minimum effort.

No one knows in advance how detailed to build the first ABC/M model. The project team, often led by accountants, errs on the side of excess detail. As a result, some ABC/M projects are exposed to high risk because they collapse under their own weight as the system becomes unnecessarily difficult to maintain long before the users comprehend how they can apply the ABC/M data usefully. ABC/M is a solution, but a solution to a problem should not become the next problem. ABC/M rapid prototyping accelerates the learning of the properties of ABC/M model design and architecture.

Some of the lessons learned about ABC/M and profitability analysis are:

- Information, even though not precise, can provide an organization with substantially improved support for decision making and can greatly improve its understanding of profitability.
- An organization does not need "excellent" ABC/M analysis to make great improvements.
- No system providing ABC/M information and its analysis is perfect. Good judgment and additional qualitative information are necessary before final decisions are made.
- Excess ABC/M model structure—such as number of activities and drivers—saps the strength of ABC/M in the initial stages.

A simple rule that will be repeated in this book is to constantly ask, "Is the climb worth the view?" That is, by building a more detailed and slightly more accurate ABC/M model, will your question be better answered? Avoid the creeping elegance syndrome. Larger models introduce maintenance issues.

WHAT IS THE EXPERIENCE OF MATURE USERS?

Some governments and government organizations have been routinely updating their ABC/M data for many years. They are advanced and mature ABC/M users who are interested in two goals: (1) to institutionalize ABC/M organization-wide into a permanent, repeatable, and reliable production reporting system, and (2) to establish the ABC/M output data to serve as an enabler to their ongoing improvement programs, such as quality management, cycle-time compression, workflow process reengineering, and service-line and service-recipient rationalization.

Recently, new issues have been emerging for these advanced and mature ABC/M users. These issues include:

- Integrating the ABC/M output data with their decision-support systems, such as their cost estimating, predictive planning, activity-based planning and budgeting systems, and balanced scorecard performance measurement systems
- Learning the skills and rules for resizing, reshaping, releveling, and otherwise readjusting their ABC/M system's structure to solve new problems with the ABC/M data
- Collecting and automatically importing data into the ABC/M system
- Automatically exporting the calculated data out of their ABC/M system into other systems

With experienced ABC/M users, it is evident that ABC/M eventually becomes part of their core information technologies.

More specifically, the output data of an ABC/M system are frequently the input to another system, such as an order-quotation system that is used prior to accepting a commitment to fulfill a request to a service-recipient. ABC/M data also complement other productivity- or logistics-management tools, such as simulation software, process modelers, workflow-process flow charters, executive information systems (EIS), and on-line analytical programs (OLAP).

In the next several years, there will be a convergence of tools, as these now somewhat separate software applications become part of the manager's and analyst's tool suite. This portfolio of tools is now being popularly referred to as *performance management*. Chapter 6 describes performance management and how ABC/M data links to an essential pair of components: strategy maps and the balanced scorecard.

WHY ARE ATTRIBUTES KEY?

Advanced mature users are also masters with employing ABC/M "attributes," which are scored and graded against the activities. Revisit Figure 3-8 to note that attributes address the third question related to activity analysis. ABC/M attributes allow managers to differentiate activities from one another. A popular attribute involves scoring activities along their "high vs. low value-adding" scale so that an organization can focus on the work that is more important. Multiple activities can be simultaneously tagged with these attri-bute grades, and of course the amount of spending money trails along as part of the activity data. Another option is to score or grade each activity by how well the organization performs its work.

Two or more attributes can be combined to gain further insights. A popular combination is the level of importance and the level of performance. With these two independently judged scores for each activity, organizations can see, for example, if they are very, very good at things they have judged to be very unimportant—and yet they are spending a lot of money doing it! Although some attributes are subjectively scored or graded by managers and employees, the process introduces emotionally compelling issues. I have often said that, "ABC/M adds the air-conditioning to the ABC/M data." We will further discuss the power of using attributes in Chapter 5.

WHY FOCUS ON BEHAVIORAL CHANGE?

Public sector organizations are discovering some realities. They must improve performance levels if their organizations are to be adequately funded. The needed improvement exceeds what is possible from conven-tional, highly vertical, functional organization forms. The traditional orga-nizational model is becoming less valid as required workflow processes transcend the old departmental boundaries.

Future cost avoidance and performance improvements can be achieved only through reconfiguring work activities into fewer, more integrated jobs. Optimizing a stovepiped functional department can be non-optimal for the total organization. On occasion, there are competing performance measures where, "As I do good, you are adversely affected." With this new way of thinking, traditional managerial accounting comes up short. It fails to provide appropriate data for decision support and cannot produce the kind of metrics needed as inputs into balanced scorecard and performance measurement systems.

How will managers and teams learn how to operationalize and actualize their process-based thinking? How will they measure their processes or ever know whether cost-saving benefits are truly being realized? How will work-flow processes and their outputs be managed, measured, and validated to ensure that they are indeed creating value relative to their effort and cost?

One important way to answer these questions is to provide managers and employee teams with fact-based data in place of assertions and intuitive guesses. In addition, public sector managers can benefit from visual aids that are supported by real and tangible metrics. Organizations will increasingly leverage diagrams and pictures, not just racked-and-stacked cost tables, in order for managers and employees to truly visualize, discover, internalize, and learn. And the *rate of organizational learning* is considered by many as today's primary differentiator between gaining and losing organizations. A slow learning rate is increasingly viewed as a major impediment to an organization's growth and sustaining power.

ABC/M project managers have been slow on the uptake in recognizing the behavioral-change management aspects of ABC/M systems. ABC/M is a socio-technical tool, and the emphasis should be on the social side. Many managers and ABC/M project teams see ABC/M as simply a better measuring scheme or cost allocator. However, its real value is in introducing undebatable fact-based data that an organization can use to build business cases, to quickly recognize problems or opportunities, and to test hypotheses.

ABC/M has many of the characteristics of an organizational methodology. Because many managers are frustrated by the difficulties in bringing about change within their organizations, behavioral-change management is receiving wider attention. ABC/M data are playing an important role, and I encourage you to be part of this change. A description of old age is that it starts as soon as your attachment to the past exceeds your excitement for the future. Since you will live the rest of your life in the future, think young and be progressive.

WHAT IS MAKING ABC/M CHEAPER AND MORE USEFUL?

For years, activity-based cost management was considered an expensive project that only large organizations with extensive resources could undertake. But today, with the proliferation of high-tech computers, the cost of data collection and measurement has fallen as information processing has improved. Not too long ago, it was cost-prohibitive to accumulate, process, and analyze the data necessary to run an ABC system. Cost accounting was restricted to a big-box mainframe computer and data stored as flat-files.

Today, such activity measurement systems are not only affordable, but much of the data already exist in some form within the organization. For example, quality management systems of ISO 9000-registered organizations have an abundance of data—usually disconnected from the accounting system. Also, a few knowledgeable employees can usually estimate a large portion of any remaining data that may not be available. Estimates such as these will have a minimal adverse impact on accuracy. Better yet, information technology has dramatically improved the deployment of ABC/M data for viewing, planning, and decision-making. Powerful database-management systems and computer engines mean that data processing is no longer the impediment to understanding costs.

Business intelligence is one of the fastest growing areas of information. Its leaders, such as the analytical and data-mining software company SAS, integrate ABC/M with other methodologies that comprise the portfolio of performance management systems.

What makes ABC/M even more realizable are the lessons learned that most data for decision-making need not be accurate to several decimal places. Also, a technique for implementing ABC/M based on rapid-prototyping scale models, discussed in Chapter 9, is ensuring implementation success. In contrast to the multi-month, one-chance, single-design approach, the ABC/M rapid-prototyping technique follows the quick build of an initial model, built roughly in two days, by iterative remodeling of increasingly larger-scale ABC/M models. Eventually the larger-scale ABC/M model becomes the organization's repeatable and reliable production system.

The primary use of ABC/M shifts from that of an accounting tool to that of a management decision-support system for operational streamlining and strategic thinking. ABC/M is managerial intelligence. Information technology gathers and manages this ABC/M information, combining not just cost but non-financial information and performance measures. As more managers have become aware of the information that is available, additional applications for ABC/M have emerged, including unused-capacity management. ABC/M provides the lens that focuses an organization's efforts.

HOW ABOUT THE FUTURE?

It is an understatement to say that business, government, and commerce are swiftly changing. Why are incumbents losing ground to reinventors, i.e., those who can transform themselves? Today you cannot move at the pace of evolution; this is revolution. You cannot just continue to follow the existing way of doing things but a little better. It must be much, much better.

Unfortunately, an overarching issue with ABC/M involves its perception as just another way to spin financial data rather than its use as mission-critical managerial information. The information age we find ourselves in can be mind-boggling. As technology advances, so will the demand to access massive amounts of relevant information. The companies that survive will be those that can answer these questions:

- "How do we access all these data?"
- "What do we do with the information?"
- "How do we shape the data and put them in a form with which we can work?"
- "What will happen when we apply technologies developed *during* the information age *for* the information age?"

Clearly, as information technology evolves, governments will increase their levels of service and their effectiveness. Further, as the needs of citizens and service-recipients change, governments will run into global competitors, perhaps even other governments, that increasingly look to information and information technology for competitive advantage. ABC/M is involved in this broad arena of "outsmartmanship."

ABC/M puts the "management" back in management reporting. For those people who are involved with ABC/M projects, the key is to create and orchestrate change rather than merely react to it and attempt to make the best of a poor situation. It will be fun watching government move from the learning stages into mastery of building and using ABC/M systems.

"To grammar even kings bow."
  —Moliere, French dramatist, *Les Femmes Savantes* (1672) Act II, sc. vi

"I shall not mingle conjectures with certainties."
—Sir Isaac Newton, English mathematician, *The Correspondence of Isaac Newton*
    (edited by H.W. Turnbull and J.F. Scott, 1959-74)

"Type the field name Name in the Field Name field."
  —an instruction in a software manual awarded the worst-of-the-month (April 1996) winner by Corecomm, a Houston, Texas-based technical writing company.

Chapter 4

Fundamentals:
What Is ABC/M?

"Finally we shall place the sun itself at the center of the Universe. All this is suggested by the systematic procession of events and the harmony of the whole Universe, if only we face the facts, as they say, 'with both eyes open.'"
—Nicholas Copernicus, founder of modern astronomy,
De revolutionibus orbium coelestium (1530)

"Money ranks with love as man's greatest joy. And it ranks with death as his greatest source of anxiety."
—John Kenneth Galbraith, Canadian-born American economist,
The Age of Uncertainty (1977)

N THIS CHAPTER, we will get into a lot more of the nitty-gritty involved in designing an ABC/M system. We will explain how to collect, validate, report, and analyze managerial accounting data and describe how to apply ABC/M in choosing among alternative management decisions. After describing the five stages of evolution of cost management systems and a chronological history of ABC/M, we will cover:

- An overarching framework of accounting as a taxonomy
- The expanded ABC/M cross, from a two-stage to a multi-stage cost assignment network
- Six advances of ABC/M systems since 1990
- The role of ABC/M applied to shared service centers, including the information technology (IT) department, and chargebacks
- Project accounting, earned value management (EVM), and ABC/M: a choice or blend?
- Local operational ABC/M for department cost management versus enterprise strategic ABC/M for performance management
- ABC/M's support of supply chain management and e-commerce

Let's get down to fundamentals. . . .

STAGES OF EVOLUTION OF COST MANAGEMENT SYSTEMS

In the early 1990s, Professor Robert Kaplan of the Harvard Business School described four stages of cost management systems. Figure 4-1 extends his stages of evolution with a fifth stage that may be

FIGURE 4-1 Stages of Evolution of Cost Management Systems

System Aspects	Stage 1 Broken	Stage 2 Financial Reporting Driven	Stage 3 Customized / Stand-alone	Stage 4 Integrated	Stage 5* Decision Support
Data Quality	• Many errors • Large variances	• No surprise • Meets audit standards	• Shared databases • Stand-alone systems • Informal linkages	• Fully linked databases and systems	• Fully linked databases and systems
External Financial Reporting	• Inadequate	• Tailored to financial reporting need	• Stage II System for financial transactions and periodic reporting	• Financial reporting systems	• Financial reporting systems
Product/ Customer Costs	• Inadequate	• Inaccurate • Hidden costs and profits	• PC-based ABC models • Product-focused	• Integrated ABC/M systems • full absorption	• Integrated ABC/M systems • Predictive costing
Operational/ Strategic Control	• Inadequate	• Financial feedback only • Delayed/ aggregated	• Kaizan costing; pseudo profit centers, timely non-financial	• Operational and strategic performance measurement systems	• Operational and strategic predictive scenario • Links to scorecards • Reflects economics

*Column 5 added by Gary Cokins

Source: Reproduced with permission from *Management Accounting,* published by the Institute of Management Accountants, Montvale, NJ. www.imanet.org.

more relevant to the public sector than the private sector. The fifth stage that I propose focuses exclusively on decision support, going beyond the fourth stage, which Kaplan referred to as *integrated* cost management systems. Let's briefly review the standard four stages before going on to my proposed fifth stage.

The Standard Four Stages of Cost Management Systems

Stage 1: Broken—Stage 1 cost management systems are primitive and fairly useless for managing an enterprise. At an extremely primitive level, an example would be a cigar box for cash and coins at a child's lemonade stand. The box serves the two purposes of providing change for customers and determining at the close of business whether any money was made. If there is more money in the box than there was when the day began, after allowing for the purchase price of the ingredients, the child knows he made a profit.

Small retailers whose pricing is simply a cost-plus markup of their purchases to cover operating expenses are only a step above the lemonade stand in terms of cost management system sophistication. An additional step above that are small manufacturers or distributors who may not be able to justify the extra expense to maintain a formal record-keeping system, and so the quality of their data is inadequate for making decisions.

In the public sector, this poor level of control might have existed in 19th century town government, but most governments are at least at a Stage 2 system.

Stage 2: Financial Reporting Driven—Stage 2 cost management systems are used by bankers or firm owners to comply with external reporting requirements, such as those for tax reporting. In the public sector, cost management systems are designed to apportion spending that was approved and budgeted by a sanctioning body. These are called fund accounting systems. Some are more complex and involve the need to monitor spending requests prior to spending approval to validate that the budget money is available. Extra steps of this sort, prior to the actual spending, are called encumbrances or commitments. In short, the emphasis of government Stage 2 systems is controlling spending.

The financial data may minimally meet reporting requirements, but may distort the true costs of the specific products or service-lines that the organization delivers because of poor cost-allocation methods and assumptions. This financial information may be reported weeks or months after the period in which business was conducted. It may be too aggregated to draw any insights about where to focus or what to control better.

Manufacturers and distributors tend to focus on the direct material and labor expenses that can be logically associated with product- and service-lines. The remaining support, distribution, sales, and administrative expenses are either ignored or loosely linked to the costs of outputs. Simplistic overhead expense allocations introduce distortions that can be large relative to the true costs.

Stage 3: Customized and Stand-Alone—Stage 3 cost management systems are designed to provide reasonable accuracy and visibility for decision-making. This is the stage where activity-based costing began to emerge. The variety and diversity of the product- and service-lines for these organizations will have expanded so much that indirect and support overhead expenses are a significant portion of the cost structure. Simplistic cost allocations, usually volume based, are no longer sufficient to reflect how the individual outputs or service-recipients consume those expenses.

In governments, Stage 3 systems include work order systems and project accounting systems. Some of these systems apply work breakdown structure (WBS) planning and reporting. These types of systems (discussed later in this chapter) place a greater emphasis on direct expenses.

Whether the expenses are direct or indirect, the cost assignments are computed in a parallel or off-line model, not necessarily in a repeatable system. The operational data, such as the basis for tracing the non-direct expenses into costs, are usually inserted as a separate step. For manufacturers, the assignment of overhead for inventory costing may be based on simplistic assumptions, whereas the ABC will be more reflective of use. The two methods produce different results for different purposes. The inventory costing is used for external reporting and the ABC for strategic decision-making or pricing.

Stage 4: Integrated—Stage 4 cost management systems are what many organizations aspire to. The databases are linked to the calculation logic that traces the expenses to processes and into outputs. The resulting information can be reported for monitoring performance or simply to more accurately report spending for control or profit margin purposes. The administrative effort to refresh the input data and update the results is much less than in Stage 3 systems. The reporting is highly automated and is supported by powerful query and analysis tools. The distribution of the calculated results is more widely accessible to various users throughout the organization.

The Fifth-Stage Cost Management System

Stage 5: Decision Support—Stage 5 is my addition to Kaplan's framework. Stage 5 represents more of a value management system. It goes well beyond simply calculating and distributing accurate and relevant cost information. It provides decision-makers information and the flexibility to configure assumptions.

In Stage 5, managerial accounting evolves into managerial economics. There is a shift from cost control to cost planning and shaping, due in part to recognition that most resources cannot be quickly adjusted in the short-term. Determining what level and type of resources are required to match future demands and plans receives more attention. In Stage 5, the emphasis shifts to forecasting and predictive analytics.

All decisions affect the future, not the past. The past reflects prior decisions, for good or for bad. Stage 3 and Stage 4 cost management systems originate with historical revenue and expense data. They are descriptive rather than prescriptive. I often refer to them as cost autopsies—because it is too late to do anything about what already happened. What ABC/M accomplishes, however, is the logical and defensible tracing of expenses so that managers and employee teams can gain insights and make inferences that are useful in determining where to focus and what to change.

The formal step of actually taking actions based on inferences from past information leads us into the broad realm of predictive costing and rebudgeting (during and after cost overruns). This will be the focus of Stage 5 systems. Today this activity resides in pockets of an organization where cost estimating and budgeting take place. Cost estimating is usually performed as ad hoc analysis aimed at a single decision, such as a capital investment justification or a make-or-buy outsourcing decision. It also is used in evaluating proposals to privatize public sector services.

Another application of cost estimating may be to determine a suitable price quotation for securing a customer order. In price quoting, there are implicit assumptions about cost rates and about whether expenses are fixed or variable. In some cases, these assumptions may not be totally valid. A more powerful predictive-costing calculation engine and system will allow for more formal and flexible configuring of assumptions regarding the consequences of decisions, including their impact on the specific inputs and outputs involved. These more sophisticated assumptions will also take into account the impact on capacity as well as increases or decreases in specific expenses deriving from the decision.

As the Internet continues to shift power to buyers, a defense for suppliers will be to influence customers' demands by offering a variety of options. These options will be various combinations of products, promotions, and alternative service levels offered at appropriate pricing scales. Much of this will be web-based and automated. Stage 5 systems will recognize the existing capabilities and capacity of an organization and take them into account in carrying out predictive costing. The new requirements shaped by 21st century e-commerce clearly make Stage 5 ABC/M systems all the more imperative.

Although government agencies don't have profit margins, the concept of a buyer-seller relationship is valid. Indeed, it is possible that power will be shifting from government to citizens as a result of the Internet's explosion of offerings. Government itself could use web-based automation to manipulate citizens' behavior and demands for limited resources. For example, it might charge premiums for express and expedited services, as it already does when issuing short-turnaround passports.

In any event, it is increasingly likely that organizations will have to rely on more powerful methodologies and technologies to predict accurately the cost impact of different decisions under various scenarios.

THE CHRONOLOGICAL HISTORY OF ABC/M

ABC/M has gone through a metamorphosis. Figure 4-2 illustrates various eras through which it has passed. In the next century, historians of cost management may look back and briefly describe each era like this:

- **Pre-1950s**—Since 1492, when the Italian monk Lucas Pacioli documented double-entry bookkeeping, accountants have put a lot of energy into developing methods to better assign costs. Many assignment methods, such as project accounting and standard costing, appeared adequate. Some organizations used industrial engineering techniques focusing on cross-functional work activity analysis.
- **Early ABC/M experimenters**—The financial controllers in a few organizations were clever and used cost assignment methods based on "event drivers." They were basically performing primitive forms of ABC.
- **Educators**—A few university faculty members began to realize that traditional cost allocations were not adequately causal based. Often the methods used were political or simply convenient. Professor Robert S.

FIGURE 4-2 The Chronological History of ABC/M

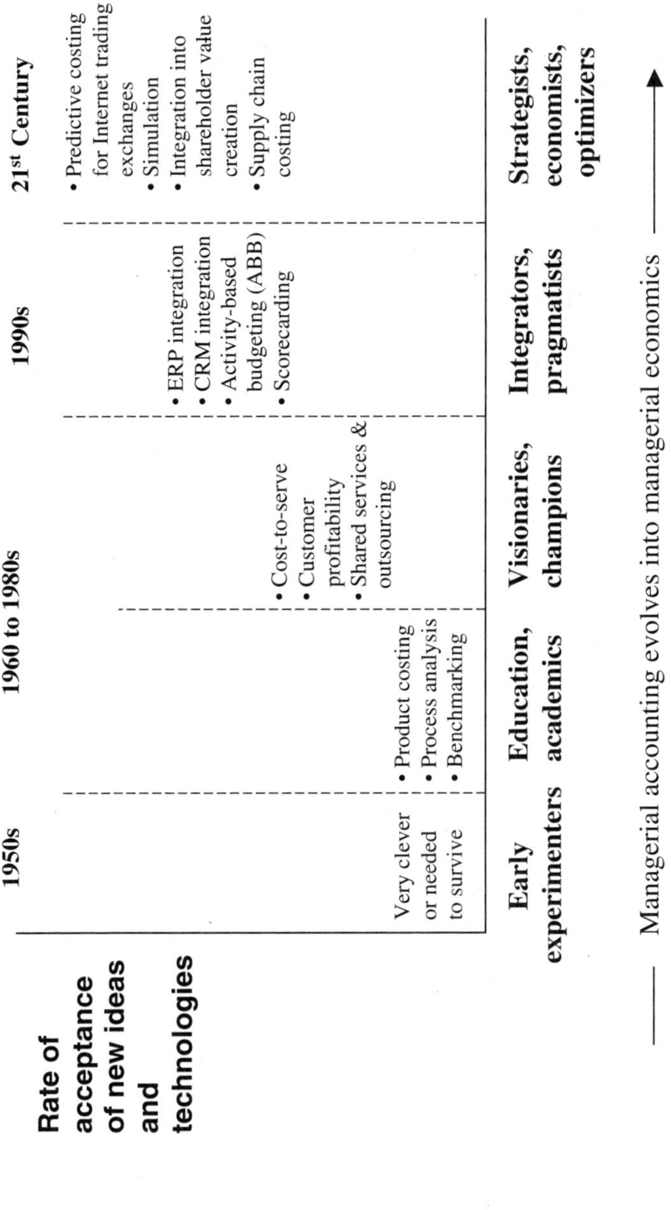

Rate of acceptance of new ideas and technologies

1950s	1960 to 1980s		1990s	21st Century
Very clever or needed to survive	• Product costing • Process analysis • Benchmarking	• Cost-to-serve • Customer profitability • Shared services & outsourcing	• ERP integration • CRM integration • Activity-based budgeting (ABB) • Scorecarding	• Predictive costing for Internet trading exchanges • Simulation • Integration into shareholder value creation • Supply chain costing
Early experimenters	**Education, academics**	**Visionaries, champions**	**Integrators, pragmatists**	**Strategists, economists, optimizers**

—— Managerial accounting evolves into managerial economics ——→

Kaplan of the Harvard Business School received the most attention. (He was also my personal trainer on ABC/M when, in 1988, he contracted with KPMG Peat Marwick to implement ABC/M systems.) It is useful to realize that Professor Kaplan did not invent ABC/M; he researched it and was a loud voice advocating that organizations apply it.

- **Visionaries**—Initially, companies applied ABC for more accurate product costing. This also allowed a much more credible reporting of profit margins. However, many of the users saw that the same data could address other problems. The ABC/M data were next applied for process analysis, business process reengineering, and benchmarking. It didn't take long for people to realize that the ABC/M method could be applied beyond products to other outputs, such as channels and customers. In commercial industry, this led to applying ABC/M for customer profitability analysis.

  In government and the public sector, visionaries were simply being pragmatic. They recognized that the level of resources needed to satisfy citizens or sanctioning bodies originated with the demand. Cost allocations were really a form of tracing backward to the workload. The pragmatic accountants realized that the basis for the allocation needed to be logical, and thus used a form of ABC.

- **Integrators**—In 1998, Germany-based SAP, the world leader in ERP software, purchased a minority equity investment in ABC Technologies, Inc., the world leader in ABC/M software. (ABC Technologies, Inc., was subsequently acquired from SAP in 2003 by SAS, the world leader in business intelligence and predictive analytics software.) This signaled to the world that the large ERP production and planning systems acknowledged ABC/M as credible and important. Soon other ERP vendors began to announce the availability of limited forms of ABC/M functionality. ABC/M began to be integrated with other business performance management (BPM) software tools as well.

  Concurrently, public sector accountants realized they could use the same type of ABC software to accurately compute the costs of outputs.

- **Strategists, economists, and optimizers**—As described in the section earlier in the chapter about Stage 5 of cost management systems, the thought leaders in cost management have begun to integrate ABC/M data into decision-making support. This involves predictive costing, not simply segmenting and tracing historical costs. In the commercial sector, linkages of trade-offs between customer profitability and increases or decreases in shareholder value have begun to receive intense study. In the public sector, linkages of results with resources for future capacity and headcount planning are being computed via activity-based budgeting (ABB), which is described in Chapter 7.

In the next few sections, we will discuss how ABC/M systems are constructed and highlight some of the major advances since 1990 in ABC/M thinking.

> **"It is a common criticism of cost accountants that they spend too much time in working out elaborate distributions of expenses which are unimportant in themselves and which do not permit of an accurate distribution. Undoubtedly some of that criticism is deserved, but it should also be remembered that once the basis for distribution has been worked out, it can generally continue in use for some time."**
>
> —H. G. Crockett, "Some Problems in the Actual Installation of Cost Systems," *National Association of Cost Accountants (NACA) Bulletin*, vol. 1, no. 8, February 1921.

AN OVERARCHING FRAMEWORK OF MANAGERIAL ACCOUNTING

During the good times for governments and their various branches and agencies, funding is plentiful and the fun is in apportioning it via budgets. Leaner times bring more citizen watchdog groups and a greater sense of responsibility to taxpayers. In recent years, there has been a growing interest on the part of governments in understanding their costs and the behavior of what drives their costs.

The past several years have also brought: (1) confusion about how to understand costs; (2) competing cost-measurement methodologies (e.g., project accounting, activity-based costing, standard costing, throughput accounting, target costing); and (3) various professional consortia publishing their own custom brands of accounting research.

The resulting problem is that managers and employees are confused by mixed messages. They are confronted with too many solutions for costing problems. We may discover that there is no single correct approach; the best option might be a *blend*. Various costing methods do not necessarily compete; they can be reconciled and combined. They are all cut from the same cloth—they measure the consumption of economic resources.

Who speaks for the manager in a government agency or military branch that so many consultants and university faculty are presumably serving?

Managers do not want confusion. They simply want solid support and fact-based data to enable better decisions. For certain types of decisions, they also want to know what assumptions should be made about the inclusion or exclusion of specific costs and if certain costs should be presumed to behave as variable or fixed relative to changes in other factors.

An overarching framework to measure costs is needed. Creating an understandable framework is not rocket science. One can be constructed and articulated. A candidate framework is presented here. Is it perfect? Probably not. But it is an overarching view that has helped non-financial managers feel more comfortable with their understanding of accounting.

After this framework is in place, we can proceed to explore ABC/M in more depth.

MEASURING AND USING COST DATA IN MANAGERIAL ACCOUNTING

The sole focus of this section is on *managerial* accounting, not *financial* accounting. Financial accounting addresses external compliance reporting for banks, owners, publicly owned companies, and government agencies. These data are compulsory. Financial accounting is governed by laws and rules established by regulatory agencies.

From an international perspective, for most nations, financial accounting follows generally accepted accounting principles, known by the acronym GAAP. Some people jokingly refer to the GAAP-trap, because focus on these numbers may distract the organization from more relevant numbers or prevent it from adopting more appropriate ways to calculate costs and, if applicable, profit margins.

In contrast, managerial accounting is used *internally* by managers and employee teams for decision-making. If you violate financial accounting laws, you may go to jail. Although you don't risk going to jail if you have poor managerial accounting, you do run the risk of making bad decisions. And, as frequently noted here, the margin for error is getting slimmer as the pressure grows for better organizational performance.

At the highest level of managerial accounting, there are two broad elements: measuring the costs and using the cost data. These two broad elements can be broken down into five smaller elements. Figure 4-3 uses a tree, branch, and leaf structure to display an overarching framework for managerial accounting.

FIGURE 4-3 Management Accounting Framework

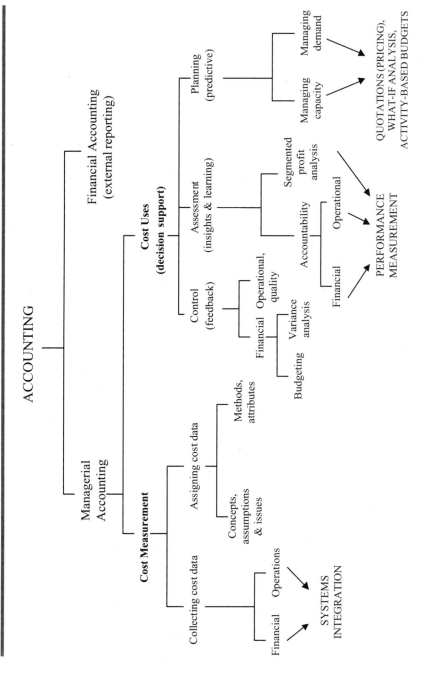

- **Cost measurement**—Cost measurement is made up of: (1) collecting data and (2) assigning the source expenses in a way that is meaningful for the organization.
- **Cost uses**—Chapter One of managerial accounting textbooks will usually state that there are three broad purposes for using cost data: (1) operational control, (2) assessment and evaluation, and (3) predictive planning.

By further separating these five elements of cost measurement and use into their individual parts, we can understand the landscape of managerial accounting. We can explore some of the terminology and highlight key issues.

Using this overarching view, we can discuss how managerial accounting involves information *systems integration* with an ultimate application for *assessing performance* (organizational execution) and for *forecasting costs* (strategic and operational planning that supports resource management).

The five elements in Figure 4-3 can be bordered, as shown in Figure 4-4, for clarification. The sections that follow go into these five elements in more detail.

Cost Measurement

As shown in Figures 4-3 and 4-4, there are two basic activities involved in measuring cost: collection and assignment.

Collecting Cost Data

This is where measuring and managing costs begins. As shown in Figure 4-4, the source for data can be financial (i.e., strategic) or operational (i.e., shorter-term tactical costs).

Financial data collection is a mature exercise dating back centuries to the days of trading and counting with rocks and gold coins, and even perhaps recording transactions on papyrus. These expenses were initially cash equivalents directly tied to cash payments for employee wages or to suppliers and contractors. General ledger bookkeeping handles these mechanics. This is all old stuff, with origins dating back to 1492 and our Italian monk, Lucas Pacioli, and his double-entry bookkeeping.

Operational data are non-financial. This information is measurable in the form of units such as minutes, pounds, gallons, or number of events. These are units of inputs or outputs that are consumed in making and delivering

FIGURE 4-4 Management Accounting Framework—with Borders

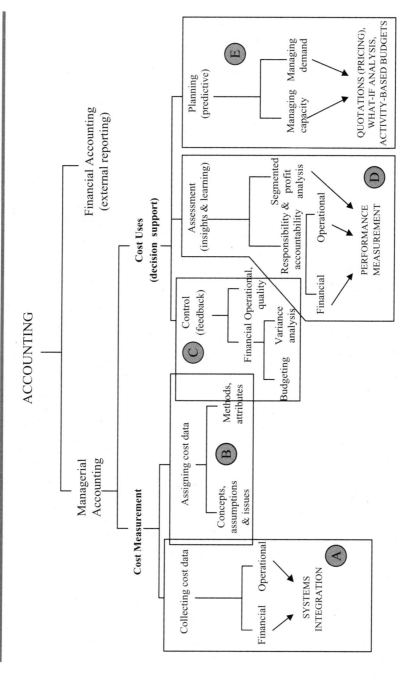

a product or service. Operational data are combined with financial data to produce cost data.

In our 21st century information era, systems integration and technology are used to convert these data for interpretation, use, and decision-making.

Assigning Costs

The assignment of expenses into costs depends on the managerial use of the data. And the managerial use of the data usually depends on pressing management problems. The assumptions and factors related to the assignment of cost data have a high level of complexity. As shown in box B of Figure 4-4, assigning costs involves both deciding on methods and deciding on assumptions. An example of the assumptions that must be determined is whether resource expenses behave in a manner that is fixed, semi-variable, or variable in relation to changes in the volume and mix of outputs.

Cost Assignment Methods: *Non-period costing* means that the time period for which the costs are accumulated is unique to a *specific* product, service-line, item of equipment, channel, customer, or cost object. An example is product life-cycle costing. The start and stop points (i.e., birth and retirement) for *each* product are as unique as a person's DNA or fingerprints. The cost object, not the processes and their capacities, is the focus and matters the most. The accounting and economics professions have not developed mainstream and accepted methods for calculating these life-cycle costs, although some engineering professional societies have defined various methods (e.g., parametric cost modeling).

Period costing means that the time period for which the costs are accumulated consists of fixed time intervals that are linked to a calendar cycle such as a week, a month, or a year. All the product, service-line, and customer costs are reported regardless of whether they had intra-period starts or stops. With period costing, the timeframe matters the most, and the focus is on the spending for process, not the products and customers using the spending. Life-cycle costs of a cost object are not usually important, except for job-order costing.

There are many methods for assigning costs, whether using period costing or non-period costing. These can include:

- Project accounting
- Earned value management (EVM)
- Job order and work order costing

- Process accounting
- Throughput accounting
- Kaizan accounting
- Standard costing
- Activity-based costing (ABC)
- Activity-based management (ABM)
- Supply chain costing
- Constraint-based costing
- Feature-based costing
- Parametric cost modeling

What the assignment methods generally all have in common is that they start with the source expenses captured from the transaction-based systems, such as payroll and purchasing systems. These expenses are initially recorded into general ledger or fund accounting systems.

Organizations are increasingly confused about what the best choice is for their cost assignment method. What is true is that every organization is consciously or unconsciously using a cost assignment method and system. But is it the best method for the organization? How is the organization to know?

Each of these cost assignment methods traces the consumption of source expenses (i.e., cash outlay expenditures) into a destination (i.e., cost object) that is of management interest. Where each assignment method differs is with the selected cost object or with assumptions involving how to assign the expenditure costs. Ideally, all expenditures are directly associated with their cost object, but in practice some costs are arbitrarily allocated or absorbed, which may produce misleading results. Most of these cost assignment methods further reassign the costs to group them, again to satisfy a management interest. Assumptions also apply for these cost reassignments.

Ultimately, all expenses can be accounted for as costs. The accountants and cost engineers know that the financial books must balance. But have the accountants properly assigned their expenses as costs given the conditions and according to the business problem, need, or interest for management?

Concepts, Assumptions, and Issues: Various categories and factors are involved in assigning expenses as costs. These factors are both uniquely configured for the cost assignment method and governed by management's need or interest. The list of cost assignment methods reveals that costing and economics are intertwined. The items in this list are the heart and soul of cost accounting. They are key to how accounting data support managerial decision-making. In sum, the specific assumptions for each of these depend on the decision being made with the cost data.

Cost Uses

There are three broad uses for cost data: (1) control; (2) assessment and evaluation; and (3) predictive planning.

Control

Controlling expenses has historically been a key use of cost data, particularly for mature organizations. Frequent reporting of expenses and costs provides a form of near-term feedback for managers to react to. Managers' reactions to the data depend on their expectations, their gut-feel intuition, or the formal budget and planned targets.

There is a growing belief that the emphasis in collecting and assigning cost data should shift away from *control* and toward the other two uses of cost data, *assessment (learning)* and *predictive planning*. The reasoning for this proposed shift is that it is usually too late and after-the-fact to control a process efficiently with historic expense and cost data.

There is also recognition and concern that repeated planning and replanning, with the resulting variance analysis, creates a full-time job for cost accountants performing as the accounting police. It is as if each quarterly plan update has as its goal to make unfavorable variances disappear. The focus caused by all of this financial estimating is almost on managing the plan and *not* the performance.

Knowing a lot about the past, in many cases, is less important than having a reasonable estimate about the future. The more successful organizations are those that understand their true, not planned, spending and costs and that determine and deploy future levels of resources (i.e., capacity costs) in anticipation of their demand level.

The logic for control is based on a "management by exception" approach intended to aid in focusing. A shortcoming surfaces if the planned targets or standards, from which the variances are measured, are themselves faulty. If they are, then people are misfocused. Figure 4-4 separates cost control into its financial and operational branches.

Assessment and Evaluation

The second purpose for using cost data is to assess what is happening and evaluate why. The emphasis here is on gaining insights and learning to better achieve the organization's goals. There is less emphasis on restricting or modifying behavior or on applying accounting police tactics to punish spending violators and those with reported unfavorable cost variances.

As we can see in Figure 4-4, box D, assessment divides into two branches. One branch reports data to assist those who are responsible and ultimately held accountable for performance, while the second branch illuminates the impact of complexity and diversity of output and delivery. Collectively, all these data are used for performance measurement; they are combined with non-financial data to provide weighted and balanced scorecard (dashboard) reporting.

Responsibility and Accountability: This branch further forks into financial and operational assessment branches. The *financial accountability* uses of cost data are the traditional enterprise-wide measures related to performance, particularly as viewed by the governing board.

The *operational accountability* uses of cost data are for learning, i.e., to better understand the driving influences that cause costs to occur. The key aims are to identify where there is waste or misalignment of work effort with the organization's strategy and to identify how well processes and practices are performing relative to benchmarks. One example of benchmarking costs involves measuring levels of quality. In cost-of-quality (COQ) analysis, as practiced by the quality management discipline, activity costs are classified across an accepted continuum (i.e., error free, prevention related, appraisal related, internal failure related, external failure related). The goal is to reduce non–error-free costs.

Segmented Output Costs: This branch is the traditional area of cost-volume-mix analysis. The new spin, however, is to further analyze process output costs by additionally recognizing the impact of diversity and variation, beyond products and service-lines, caused by customer or service-recipient choices (e.g., order type, channel, and customers' cost-to-serve). Recent advances in software technology, such as online analytical processing (OLAP), allow for multidimensional combinations (e.g., by geographic region, by person) to better understand the source of a complex mix of costs.

As previously noted, reporting these financial metrics along with non-financial measures such as customer satisfaction helps management communicate existing (and changing) strategy for better alignment and execution. Some of the measures also provide leading indicators (e.g., customer service levels) that will subsequently and predictably result in the lagging indicators (e.g., operating profit and strategy attainment). The branch of assessment and evaluation is directed toward the managers' navigational dashboard—weighted scoreboard performance measures.

Predictive Planning

Predictive planning is increasingly becoming a key purpose for using cost data. This branch involves what-if analysis, trade-off analysis, outsourcing evaluations, investment decisions, and the like. This fifth and last branch of the managerial accounting framework is best described as *cost forecasting*. Some might even argue that this does not qualify as cost accounting.

The two uses of cost accounting described earlier (cost control and cost assessment) are cost autopsies. There can be no debate that the spending occurred. It did. But predictive planning—the third use—is about estimating future resource expenses, not just past activity costs. Predictive planning, using historical cost data as its foundation, is becoming a mission-critical capability required by all managers, not simply by the accountants and financial analysts.

The prevailing thinking is that an organization should first manage the demand from its service-recipients and then plan for its level of supply of resources to match that demand. In other words, an organization should aim to *maximize* its strategic goal attainment while *minimizing* the unused capacity of its resources. Figure 4-4 displays branches for managing the supply of available capacity and managing demand. (Budgeting is, of course, a logical third branch but was implicit in the discussion of box A above.) The leaves of these branches cover both traditional cost-volume-mix analysis and cost-benefit analysis. With advances in information processing technology, managers and employee teams will be equipped with more powerful tools and data that are better structured to meet decision-making requirements.

Managing Demand: Demand can be affected by (1) rationalizing product or service-line offerings; and (2) influencing demand via pricing and non–price-related mechanisms. Rationalizing and repositioning products, service-lines, channels, customers, and service-recipients is pure strategy. What to promote? What to abandon? What new kinds of offerings? Increasing the satisfaction of service-recipients by influencing demand involves knowing consumer preferences and the impact of flexing and mixing service levels.

Managing Capacity: Managing budgets and planned spending is about the future, not the past. In the short-term, many costs behave as fixed; the existing capacity cannot be easily adjusted. Further, a portion of the resources behaves as step-fixed since resources cannot be added or removed in continuous amounts; they come in lumps or quantums (e.g., another machine, another worker). Therefore, having the proper level of future available capacity, including skills and capabilities, will be central to achieving strategies. Minimizing unneeded, unused capacity will become imperative. Knowing how costs behave prospectively will be essential to flex the supply of an organization's resources in sync with expected demand.

THE TAXONOMY OF ACCOUNTING

A taxonomy defines the components that make up a body of knowledge. There is rarely a single way to document knowledge, and alternatives always exist. The framework presented in the preceding pages is one attempt to put together the jigsaw puzzle that is confusing many managers. In the end, when it comes to selecting the best costing system, the right answer is not necessarily a single choice but a blend.

This book proposes that activity-based cost management (ABC/M) provides foundational financial information because it reflects work—a central factor in any organization. ABC/M data add information for decision support that is often missing or distorted. Below are two lists—the first describing information that traditionally has been available and the other detailing information needed as a supplement to the traditional data to provide decision support. ABC/M produces the data for the second list.

1) Data Required for Organizations
   - Fiscal Requirements
     Profit/loss
     Spending/investments
     Earnings per share
   - Regulatory Reporting Requirements
     Compliance and exception reporting
     Mandates
     Progress against commitments
   - Executive Information Requirements
     Budget performance
     Project completion reporting
2) Other Data Useful or Needed to Manage
   - Business Results
     Goal achievement
     Profitability
     Growth
     Risk

Sustainability
- Process Results
    Effectiveness
    Cost/efficiency
    Quality/variances
    Customer satisfaction
- Asset Results
    Performance
    Profitability
    Value
- Program Effectiveness
    Status/problems
    Outcomes produced
    Lessons learned

THE EXPANDED ABC/M CROSS

Chapter 3 briefly covered some of the basic concepts underlying the ABC/M model and introduced the ABC/M cross in its simplified form. For ease of reference, we repeat Figure 3-4 here as Figure 4-5. In this section, we will enlarge upon the basic view in Chapter 3 to show the fuller richness and complexity of the ABC/M model as it actually works.

Fundamentals of the ABC/M Cross

Figure 4-5 displays both the simple two-step allocation view and the process view of the ABC/M model. It captures a summary of the transactions that occur during a period of time. It does not display the volatile peaks and valleys when transactions, activities, or events occur within that time period. For example, it will not reveal that much of the expenses might have been booked in the last two weeks of the month.

The ABC/M basic model should be thought of as a template that can be adapted for various purposes. The model should not be thought of as a flow chart of an activity-based costing implementation plan or a flow chart of a business process. Figure 4-5 is meant to be a very basic diagram that allows the reader to gain an understanding of fundamental ABC concepts and relationships. The model views cost transformation from an activity's perspective. It somewhat oversimplifies ABC/M by having a single box for activities in the center. This represents just one node-in-a-network's view,

FIGURE 4-5 The Activity-Based Cost Management Framework (ABC/M Cross)

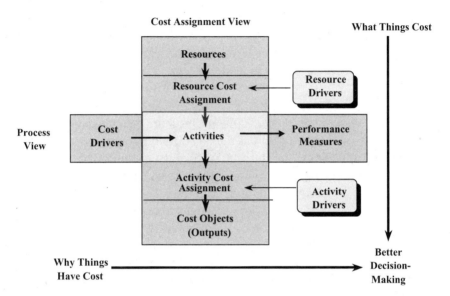

Reprinted with permission. The Consortium of Advanced Manufacturing—International (CAM-I).

where the "node" is a work activity. All work activities in an ABC/M system, and of course there are many, share this same view but with varying driver relationships.

The ABC/M model includes three modules—resources, activities, and cost objects—and two broadly labeled cost assignment methods—resources to activities and activities to cost objects. In this simplified presentation of the ABC/M model, it may appear as if there is only a single and direct cost assignment between each of the three modules. In practice, there are (1) multiple cost assignments unique to each driver, and (2) intra-module cost assignments prior to the cost assignment exiting a module and entering the next one.

The Vertical Assignment View

The vertical cost assignment view represents the calculation of the cost of cost objects (e.g., outputs, product-lines, service-lines, service-recipients).

It is basically a snapshot view of the business conducted during a specific time period. In this sense, the cost assignment view can be seen as the structure and rules by which cost assignment takes place for some specific time period. The time period may capture costs through the end of a month, a quarter, or any other period that may (or may not) coincide with an accounting reporting period. The cost assignment view reveals how resources and activities relate to cost objects.

Resources, at the top of the ABC/M model, are the capacity to perform work. They represent all the available means that work activities can draw on. Resources can be thought of as the organization's checkbook, since this is where all the expenditures from a time period are summarized. Examples of resources are salaries, operating supplies, or electrical power. These are the period's cash outlays and amortized cash outlays, such as for depreciation, from a prior period. Resources are traced to work activities. It is during this step that the applicable resource drivers are developed as the mechanism to convey resource costs into the activity costs.

We must now distinguish between *expenses* and *cost*. All costs are calculated costs. It is important to recognize that assumptions are always involved in the conversion and translation of expenses into costs. The assumptions stipulate the basis for the calculation. Expenses occur at the point of acquisition with third parties, including employee wages. At that special moment, "value" does not fluctuate; it is permanently recorded as part of a legal exchange. From the expenses, then, all costs are calculated representations of how those expenses flow through work activities and into outputs of work.

A popular basis for tracing or assigning resource expenses is the time (e.g., number of minutes) that people or equipment spend performing activities. Note that the terms *tracing* or *assigning* are preferable to the term *allocation*. This is because many people think of *allocation* as a redistribution of costs that has little or no correlation with the actual relationship between sources and destinations. Hence, in some organizations, overhead cost allocations are felt to be arbitrary and are viewed cynically. For work order and project accounting systems, more effort is required because the resource expenses (e.g., time spent) are also simultaneously linked to the work step, work order, or project. In contrast, ABC/M involves much less administrative effort.

The activities module is where work is performed within processes. It is where resources are converted to some type of output. The activity cost assignment step contains the structure to assign activity costs to cost objects (or to other activities), using activity drivers as the mechanism to accomplish this assignment.

Cost objects, at the bottom of the ABC model, represent the broad variety of outputs and services where costs accumulate. They are the persons or things that benefit from incurring work activities. Examples of cost objects are products, service-lines, distribution channels, customers, or outputs of internal processes. Cost objects can be thought of as what and for whom work is done.

Once established, the vertical cost assignment view is useful in determining how the diversity and variation of things, such as different products, service-lines, or various types of service-recipients, can be detected and translated into how they uniquely consume activity costs.

The Horizontal Process View

The horizontal axis is a process view. A process is defined as two or more work activities or a sequence of activities. Activities also belong to processes. But, in contrast to the cost assignment view, the horizontal process view displays (in cost terms) the flow chart–like sequence of activities aligned with the business processes through time. As noted earlier, events or other influences that cause work activities to be performed or to fluctuate are formally called cost drivers. A cost driver, such as a sales or work order, is the trigger that causes the work activity to utilize resources to produce output. Activity costs are additive along the process and therefore can be accumulated into a total cost of performing the process.

In summary, the vertical cost assignment view explains *what specific things cost*, whereas the horizontal process view demonstrates *why things have a cost*, which provides insights into *what causes costs* and *how much processes cost*.

The ABC basic model displays in a simple fashion that the work activities at the intersection of the vertical and horizontal axes are integral to determining the cost of an organization's processes as well as the cost of its cost objects. The activity at the intersection schematically represents an individual activity—a very local view. But, from a global perspective, the vertical (cost assignment) and horizontal (process) views may consist of many activities that are networked together based on their relationships to resources, cost objects, and other activities.

Expanding the Two-Stage ABC/M Cross Model

The ABC/M cross depicts the key relationship between ABC/M and the management analysis tools that are needed to bring full realization of benefits to the organization. ABC/M is a methodology that can yield significant information about cost drivers, activities, resources, cost objects, and performance measures. This information gives an organization the opportunity to improve the value of its products and services. The ABC/M data reflect how the organization is consuming its resources, and this image in turn serves as an enabler for inferences and decision support.

The fundamental structure of the ABC/M cross model appears to have withstood the test of time. But now it is showing some signs of age.

The initial focus of early ABC/M applications was the determination of product and service-line costs through better segmentation of resource consumption. Subsequent applications in larger and more complex organizations revealed that ABC/M data are useful in solving broader problems. For these solutions, the ABC cost calculation usually required more than a simple, so-called "two-stage" cost reassignment as indicated by the cost assignment view of the ABC/M basic cross model. Figure 4-6 illustrates the expansion of the cost assignment network from two stages to a multi-stage network.

The expanded ABC/M model includes *intermediate* stages of activities (i.e., activity outputs that are inputs to successive work activities). This expansion recognizes that overhead is complex and escalating in expense. Support departments do work for other support departments that in turn do work for other support departments ultimately doing work for the front-line primary work activities that produce products or deliver services for end-users, service-recipients, and customers. Specific usage, not time-based sequence, is the dominant factor for determining this cost assignment structure. These intermediate input/outputs cannot easily be traced directly to final cost objects (i.e., products, service-lines, or types of service-recipients) since there is no causal relationship. As a result, intermediate activities are two or more stages of cost assignment removed from a final cost object. These support-related activity costs raise the question, "How much of this activity is consumed by specific products or service-lines?"

It is virtually impossible to answer this question because the work is simply too indirect and remote from the products or service-recipients to detect or sense the relationship. However, these support activities can be traced in

FIGURE 4-6 Simple versus Expanded Multiple-Level Cost Flowing

Activity-Based Costing is a little more complex than what we have described up to this point. To segment resource consumption to reflect variety and diversity, the ABC axis expands somewhat.

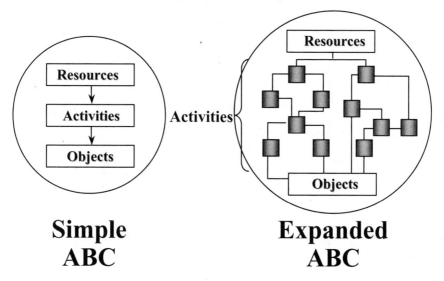

Simple ABC

Expanded ABC

Reprinted with permission of the McGraw-Hill Companies, from Gary Cokins, *Activity-Based Cost Management: Making It Work.* © The McGraw-Hill Companies, Inc., 1996.

proper proportions to other activities that require their input. Such support-related activity costs are eventually burdened into the primary activity costs. These intermediary activities support the work activities that do detect and react to, with workload, the variation and diversity of the products or service-lines.

The ABC/M model uses multiple stages to trace all the costs through a network of cost assignments into the final cost objects.

Figure 4-7 diagrams a generic cost assignment network in an expanded ABC/M model. The main difference between this diagram and the basic ABC/M model in Figure 4-5 is the presence of: (1) *intermediate* stages of activity-to-activity cost assignments, and (2) cost object–to–cost object assignments.

FIGURE 4-7 The Expanded ABC/M Cost Assignment Network

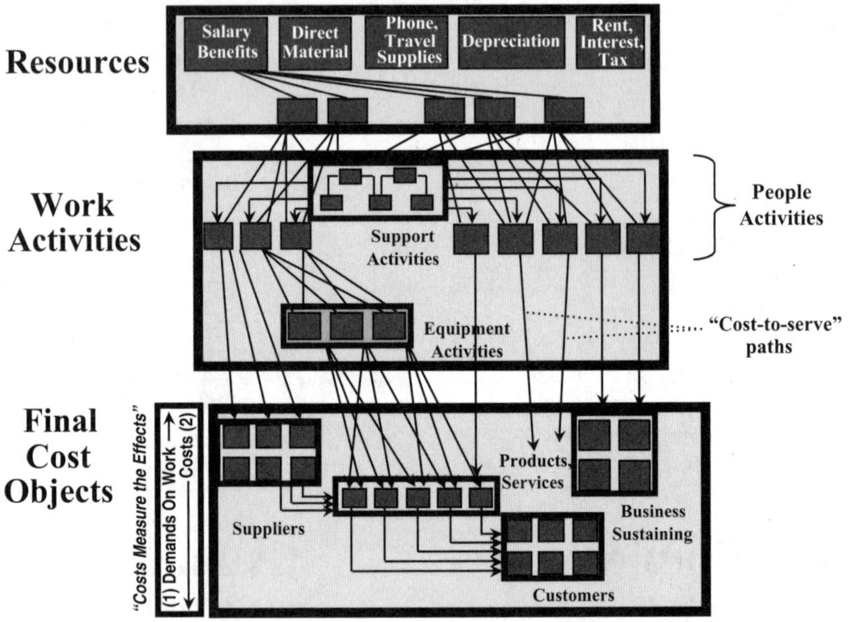

It is helpful to visualize the cost assignment paths of the generic expanded ABC/M model of Figure 4-7 as thin straws and wide pipes, where the diameter reflects the amount of cost flowing. The power of the expanded ABC/M model is that the cost assignment paths and destinations provide *traceability* from beginning to end, i.e., from resource expenditures to each type of (or each specific) product or service-recipient—the origin for all costs. It may be useful to mentally and visually reverse all the arrowheads in this diagram so that costs flow in the opposite direction. That is what is actually happening in an organization every minute, hour, day, week, month, and year. The customers, products, service-lines, and supplier-related costs are placing demands on work that in turn draws on the resource spending. The calculated costs then measure the effect in the opposite direction. Costs measure effects. This polar switch reveals that all costs originate with a demand-pull from customers and service-recipients and that the costs simply measure the effect on resources.

RECIPROCAL COSTING ISSUES

The increased flexibility from having intermediate activity-to-activity cost assignments has met pockets of resistance. Some people simply do not wish to take the extra effort and presume (if they are aware of it) that the error they are introducing will be immaterial. But there are others who believe that some sort of reciprocal costing technique is essential.

In effect, the advocates of reciprocal costing are saying, "If my department is serving you, while at the same time your department is serving me, then we need simultaneous costing. Admittedly, this produces an infinite circular loop, but we can use linear programming techniques and computer horsepower to make the numbers come out right."

Commercial ABC/M software products allow for the modeling of shared service costs. In addition, when these shared service costs are truly reciprocal in nature (i.e., "I do something for you, and you do something for me"), these software tools allow for that relationship to be modeled. The "reciprocal" nature of cost allocation involves three factors:

- "I do things for you and you do things for me." This means that both departments give and receive costs from each other. But the cost giving may not necessarily be exclusive, so other departments may be receiving the same type of cost from the sender. In many cases, *reciprocity* may be a less appropriate term than *shared service costing*.
- Cost modelers need to have traceability. Just because an organization wants to allocate costs to account for shared services does not mean that it should lose the ability to know where the costs came from.
- Just like with a traditional profit and loss statement, there should be a way to differentiate between direct and allocated expenses. Therefore, good commercial cost-accounting software offers a modeling environment where the allocated activity costs from another department can be separated from the direct resource expenses that have been consumed by an activity/department. Again, this allows for traceability.

"ABC/M purists" debate the advocates of reciprocal costing about how to perform what, on the surface, appears to be a simultaneous cost assignment calculation. The ABC/M advocates support solutions that rely on activity-based thinking and principles. Their solution is to disaggregate the "giving or doing" activity and the "receiving" activity into two or more granular activities. This allows the cost assignment network to trace costs at an activity-to-activity level where reciprocity no longer exists. In effect, the consumption properties are driven by diversity and variation of the cost objects, and the costs continue to flow unidirectionally. Those who take the simultaneous equation approach to cost allocations prefer a mathematical multiple and iterative reallocations approach. With computer horsepower, these types of accountants can, if they choose, calculate circular reallocations for hundreds of loops until the residual unallocated cost becomes nominally small. But although this accomplishes assigning the costs, it demolishes any sense of understanding causal relationships. For some government organizations, the computerized simultaneous equation may be preferable to an ABC/M solution because the sources of the fund grants or accounts must legally be audited. The ABC/M solution introduces extreme flexibility to model the answer, and it does have a familiar debit-and-credit appearance the accountants are comfortable with. Commercial ABC software supports either solution.

Figure 4-7 also demonstrates that assets and equipment perform activities, too, and they are another example of an intermediate activity. As examples, people operate machines and machines make products, or people drive buses and buses deliver passengers. These are activity-to-activity cost assignments. In capital equipment–intensive organizations, the equipment essentially performs the mainstream work that fulfills the needs of service-recipients. Equipment-related activities often require support activities to operate effectively. The equipment activity costs are usually assigned to cost objects using activity drivers that are based on:

- Units of time (e.g., per minute), or
- Equivalent inputs or outputs (e.g., number of units produced), by which measure the relative processing time per unit of output is roughly equal among products or service-lines

Some people are initially intimidated by Figure 4-7. It makes logical sense the more you work with ABC/M. The ABC/M cost assignment network is related to an observation that has become known as Metcalf's Law:

The value of a network increases as the number of nodes increases.

My experience with ABC/M has convinced me that the key to a good ABC/M system is the design and architecture of its cost assignment network. The "nodes" are the sources and destinations through which all the expenses are reassigned into costs. Their configuration helps ensure the utility and value of the data for decision-makers. And, although this is counterintuitive, the number one determinant of the accuracy of the final cost objects is the network design itself. By detecting how the diversity and variation of outputs relates to the work, the cost assignment network's paths influence cost object accuracy more than the quantities in the cost drivers.

Identification and Treatment of Organizational Sustaining Costs

The final cost object to the far right in Figure 4-7 is the *organizational sustaining costs*. Many activities in an organization do not directly contribute to value, responsiveness, and quality. That does not mean that those activities can be eliminated, or even reduced, without doing harm to the organization. For example, preparing required regulatory reports for other government agencies certainly does not add to the value of any cost object or to the satisfaction of the customer or service-recipient. However, this activity does have value to the organization: it permits the organization to function in a legal manner. These types of activity costs are usually traced to a sustaining

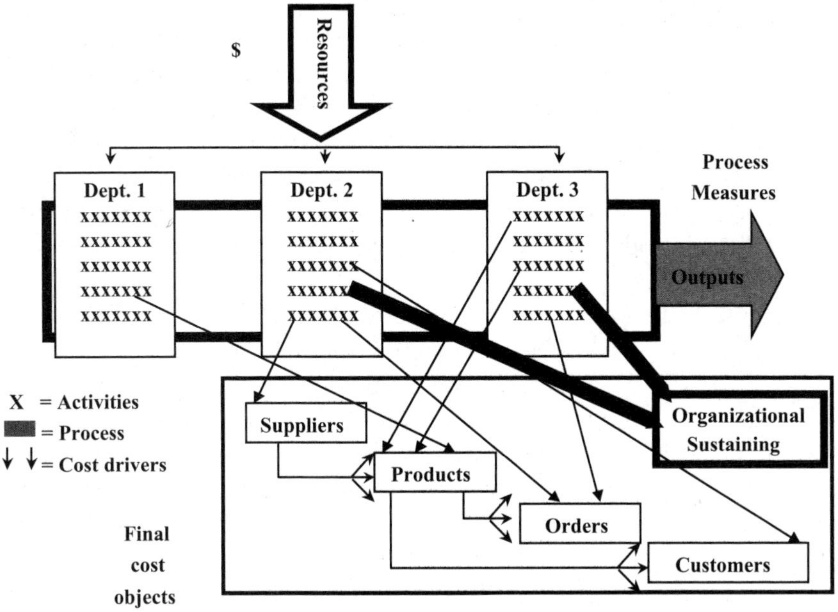

FIGURE 4-8 Identification and Treatment of Organizational Business Sustaining Costs

cost object group. This prevents these organizational sustaining costs from being charged to the activity costs for making or delivering a product or serving a customer or service-recipient.

Organizational or infrastructure sustaining costs are those costs not caused by products or customer-service needs. The consumption of these costs cannot be logically traced to products, services, customers, or service-recipients. One example is the cost associated with the accounting department closing the books each month. How can one measure which service-line or service-recipient caused more or less of that work? Another example is the cost of lawn maintenance.

Organizational sustaining costs cannot be directly charged to a service-line in any possible fair and equitable way; there is simply no use-based causality originating from the service-line or service-recipient. (Yet, overhead costs are routinely and unfairly "allocated" this way despite the result being misleading costs.) Recovering these costs via pricing or funding may eventually be required, but that is not the issue here; the issue is fairly charging cost objects when no causal relationship exists.

In early ABC/M cost assignment structures, ABC teams conveniently allocated all support and general administrative expenses to activities or directly to final cost objects (e.g., products, service-lines) despite no cause-and-effect relationships. This also overstates the true costs of costs objects.

The structure of expanded ABC/M systems leverages the use of sustaining activities traced to sustaining cost objects to segregate activity costs related to products and service-recipients from activities that have little to do with delivering services. "Sustaining costs" can be included or excluded in the final cost of cost objects depending on the nature of the decision to be made; that is, the assumption of applying full versus marginal cost absorption is decision-dependent.

Organizational sustaining costs for government and not-for-profit organizations can eventually be fully absorbed into products or service-lines, but such a cost allocation is blatantly arbitrary. There simply is no cause-and-effect relationship between an organizational sustaining cost object and the other final cost objects. If and when these costs are assigned into final cost objects, organizations that do so often refer to them as a "management tax" representing a cost of doing business apart from the products and service-lines.

Final cost objects that constitute business sustaining cost objects may include senior management (at individual levels, such as headquarters, division, and local) or other government regulatory agencies (such as environmental, occupational safety, or tax authorities). In effect, these organizations—via their policies and compliance requirements or via their informal desires, such as briefings or forecasts—place demands on work activities not caused by or generally attributable to specific service-lines or service-recipients.

Other categories of expenses that may be included as organizational sustaining costs could include idle but available capacity costs or research and development (R&D). Remember that ABC is managerial accounting, not regulated financial reporting, so strict rules of generally accepted accounting principles (GAAP) do not need to be followed, but they can be borrowed.

Tips on Identifying and Classifying Activity Drivers

Basically, the ABC/M cost assignment network is the next-generation absorption costing system. It is much more flexible than traditional step-down cost allocation schemes, yet it still accomplishes the goal of absorption costing—to calculate the costs of outputs.

Identifying and collecting data for activity drivers is an early challenge for ABC/M project teams. It is equally important, regardless of what activity driver is selected, to determine to which cost objects the activity's cost should be traced. Figure 4-9 lists a series of if-then questions that address both the "what activity driver" and "to where."

The second question in this figure arises when there is no final cost object that can directly receive the activity costs. When this condition exists, the activity cost must then go into *another* activity (or possibly be traced to a business-sustaining final cost object). In the figure, the answers to the early questions have a greater impact on accurate costing, but unfortunately some ABC/M project teams devote much of their energy to only the last question—the actual driver quantity measures.

One of the insights gained from ABC/M is an understanding of how final cost objects (such as suppliers, products, channels, customers, and service-recipients) vary with the work-related activities that they consume. Some activities, such as renewing a customer's annual license or placing a product into a box, vary directly with each specific supplier, customer, or product (i.e., cost object) processed or serviced. We classify these as *unit-level* costs. Workloads vary directly with each activity driver quantity, and they can be recognized as specific to an individual supplier, product, service-line, customer, or service-recipient.

FIGURE 4-9 Assignment Rules for Activity Drivers

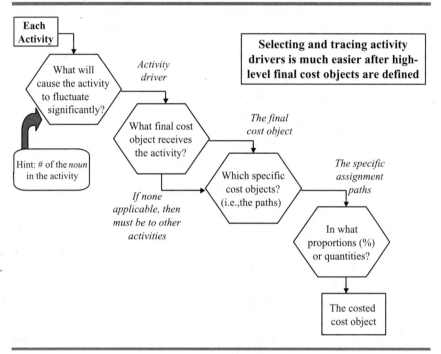

There are other work activities, such as teaching a course, for which the time or work effort varies independently of the batch size (i.e., the number of students in the classroom). In this case, work activities vary directly in accordance with the number of times a class is taught. Another example, customer-related, is where the length of time processing a license renewal is independent of the license fee. These are referred to as *batch-level costs*. The activity drivers for both unit-level and batch-level activities can be quantified by the number of occurrences.

Both unit-level and batch-level costs can be attributed to specific suppliers, products, or service-recipients without debate since they are the final cost objects causing and consuming the work. There is another higher-level activity referred to as cost object sustaining costs. Sustaining drivers reflect policy or strategy, or response to the importance of the object. Infrastructure or business-sustaining costs generally are applied to the organization as a whole—although some can also be applied to service-recipients, customers, products, or suppliers.

Figure 4-10 illustrates how different activity costs will trace to cost objects with unit, batch, or a sustaining driver.

In short, activity costs—including those that are related to support or overhead work activities—can be attributed to suppliers, products, service-lines, channels, or customers. In fact, those final cost object categories will even have their own "sustaining" cost objects. These are separate sustaining cost objects from the "business sustaining costs" that have little to do with making a product or delivering a service.

ABC/M logic begins with demands-on-work triggering the need for and magnitude of activities. With ABC/M, the demands-on-work are communicated via activity drivers and their driver cost rates. Activity driver cost rates can be thought of as "very local burden rates" or VLBRs. They reassign expenses into costs similar to traditional ways but at a more local, granular level and with arterial flow streams (not rigid step-down cost pools-to-pools). Cost behavior is initially determined at the level of work activities, and then linked up to the resource level.

Some implementers are intimidated by what appears to be excessive complexity in constructing and maintaining an ABC/M information system. They soon realize that one "hits the wall" trying to calculate ABC/M in spreadsheet software. This is because the racked and grid-like columns-to-rows math of a spreadsheet cannot be configured into a cost assignment network. Fortunately, the good news is that commercial ABC/M software, like SAS' SAS ABM product, can take the conceptual paper-based model, as in Figure 4-7, and import all the input data to calculate the costs. The calculations from ABC/M software are robust, and they never double-count costs. They continuously foot-and-tie and maintain an audit trail, like an optical fiber network, that connects each output back to all its resource expenses.

One way to think of the ABC vertical assignment is as a network of internal supply-value chains that are *locally* direct costing process outputs and then *globally* accumulated into the end-products and services exchanged with third-party suppliers and customers. In general terms, the costs of the work activities in the expanded ABC/M model's *cost assignment view* are sensitive to the diversity relating to the mixes of widely varying outputs and cost objects. In contrast, activity costs in the ABC/M model's horizontal *process view* focus on how the activities chronologically relate to each other as ele-

FIGURE 4-10 Assigning Activity Costs to Different Levels

Some activity drivers vary with unit and batch volume. Others trace costs based on different time or effort spent. All cost objects eventually go to service-recipients.

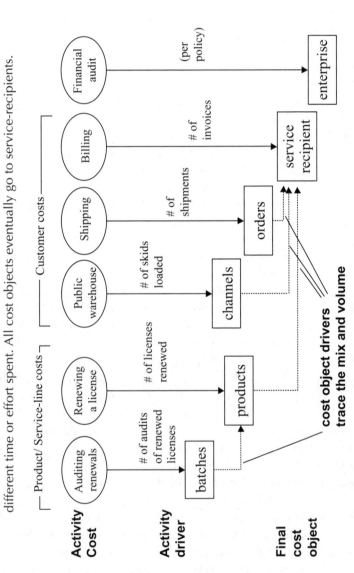

ments in a sequence and as an activity-network traversing across organizational boundaries.

> **"No facts that are in themselves complex can be represented in fewer elements than they naturally possess. While it is not denied that many exceedingly complex methods are in use that yield no good results, it must still be recognized that there is a minimum of possible simplicity that cannot be reduced without destroying the value of the whole fabric. The snare of the "simple system" is responsible for more inefficiency ... than is generally recognized ..."**
> —Alexander H. Church, "Organization by Production Factors,"
> *Engineering Magazine*, April 1910, p. 80.

THE SIX ADVANCES IN ABC/M MODEL DESIGN AND THINKING

As government agencies flatten their organizational structures and strengthen their commitment to the interests of their customers, effective business processes become critical to improved performance—if not to survival. An organization's processes are the integrating theme for its work and are the vehicles that ultimately achieve value for customers. Managing business processes, and their outputs, requires understanding what the business processes and their outputs cost, as well as knowing what their value is perceived to be by taxpayers, service-recipients, and governing bodies. That brings us to the reason that a more effective measurement of costs is becoming so important.

The focus of this book is on why and how well government organizations are applying ABC/M. Chapter 10 provides sufficient examples for you to draw your own conclusions. But before going into the specifics of ABC/M in government, let's explore the six key ABC/M advances in thinking that I believe are essential to appreciating why ABC/M is effective.

(1) Evolution of the Cost Assignment View

As described earlier, ABC cost assignment structures are now recognized to have multi-stage, not just two-step, reassignments. There are activity-to-activity assignments for overhead and support costs, which cannot directly reflect variation with final cost objects, and there are also cost object–to–cost object assignments.

Figure 4-11 is analogous to Charles Darwin's model for the evolution of species. The left graphic represents single-celled paramecium. The middle graphic represents reptiles, amphibians, and snakes. The right graphic represents man beginning to walk upright.

FIGURE 4-11 Darwin's Evolution of Cost Assignment Methods

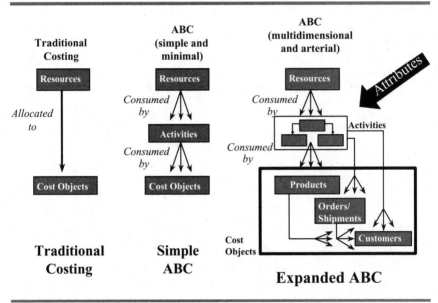

The evolution of the vertical ABC cost reassignment network starts with the simplistic allocations of the traditional accounting system and ends with a multi-stage network of costs flowing through ABC's three cost modules. This multi-stage arterial costing network is capable of detecting greater diversity and variation not only in product costs, but also in all final cost objects, including different types of service-recipients.

In Figure 4-11, the view on the left is primitive. It represents traditional accounting's "cost allocation" method, which simply redistributes the source costs into destinations, such as product costs, without regard to logical causality. The results are inaccurate costs. Sadly, the financial controllers who continue to allocate costs this way are misleading their end-users with flawed data. It is irresponsible on their part.

The middle view represents the basic ABC/M cross model, where the expenditures for resources are assigned at the work activity level, not at a department level (i.e., using verb-adjective-noun grammar to define activities). At the work activity level, the amount of activity costs varies linearly with changes in the quantity of their activity driver. In this ABC/M cross model, the use of multiple resource and activity drivers reflects the unique consumption relationship among resources, activities, and cost objects. As a result, the calculated costs of the cost objects are more accurate. This is the minimum entry into ABC, but it is too simplistic to be adequate.

The right-hand side of the graphic shows the ABC vertical cost assignment as a *multi-stage* cost assignment network with an expanded structure that allows for: (1) intermediate activities and activity drivers, and (2) cost objects being traced into other cost objects. This version is labeled an expanded ABC model to distinguish it from the obsolete two-stage ABC cross model. Thus, the three modules of the ABC/M cross model have now matured to become a multi-stage network of activities and objects. This cost assignment network has the flexibility to link resources to their cost objects, and the tracing relies on cause-and-effect relationships. Hence, the complete cost assignment network leads to much greater accuracy of cost object costs.

(2) General Ledger and Fund Accounting Data Require Transformation

ABC/M is now considered to be an analytical application by information technologists. By definition, analytical applications transform or draw on summary data from transaction-intensive operational systems. Analytical applications, such as ABC/M, are separate and apart from the transactional systems, such as ERP systems.

ABC/M's popularity is partly due to problems with using the general ledger and fund accounting data for decision-making. These chart-of-account schemes are now recognized as being structurally deficient for cost analysis (other than for historical spending control against budget or fund account) because the account balances do not reflect the traceability of costs with activities. ABC/M's chart of activities (a listing of work activities worded in verb-adjective-noun grammar) resolves that deficiency.

(3) The Two Views of Cost: Cost Object and Process Views

It is important for ABC/M design teams to correctly design their cost assignment networks and process views at the outset—not later, when the ABC/M system is large and making changes is difficult.

The expanded ABC/M approach calls for two separate cost assignment structures:

1. The horizontal process cost scheme is governed by the time sequence of activities that belong to the various processes.

2. The vertical cost reassignment scheme is governed by the variation and diversity of the cost objects.

In effect, think of the ABC/M cost assignment view as *time-blind*. The ABC/M process costing view, at the activity stage, is output *mix-blind*. The cost assignment and business process costing schemes are two *different* views of the same resource and activity costs. The work activity costs at the intersection of the ABC cross are *shared and common* to both views. These activity costs at the intersection are the starting point of their two alternative route networks for flowing costs—one diversity-based and the other time sequence–based. The activity costs are the *initial* translation of the general ledger or fund accounting expenditures that represent their resource consumption. After the work activities are costed from the resources via resource drivers, the activity costs may then either:

1. Be added across time for the process view, or
2. Be reassigned with their eventual accumulation into the products,

FIGURE 4-12 The Two Views of Cost—The Cost Object View

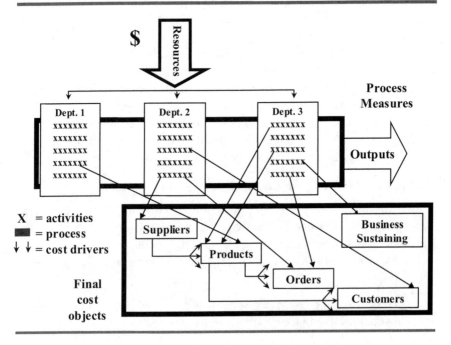

FIGURE 4-13 The Two Views of Cost—The Process View

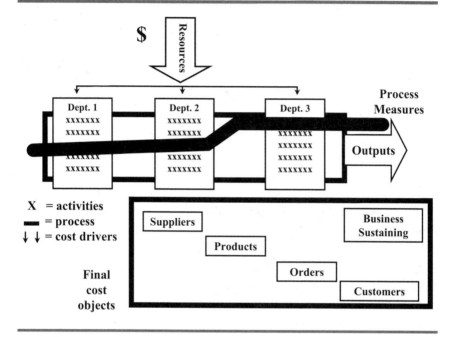

service-lines, channels, or service-recipients for the view of the mix of final cost objects.

Figures 4-12 and 4-13 show these two views of activity costs. After the resource costs are assigned to and translated into activity costs, one may prefer to think of the activity costs at the ABC cross's intersection as being on a pivot. In Figure 4-12, each activity cost is pivoted in the direction of diversity and variation; the activity costs are aimed at the cost object that is the originating source of that diversity. One way to think of the ABC/M vertical cost assignment view is that end-customers place demands on work in one direction, thus consuming the resources. Then the costs flow as a result ("costs measure the effect") in the opposite direction. These relationships preserve the basic tenets of a *full absorption costing* system.

In Figure 4-13 the activity costs are pivoted in the direction of time, the ABC/M horizontal process view. Managers and employees generally find the

ABC/M process view easier to understand since it aligns with the *sequence* of their actual activities. Managers are comfortable with a flow-chart view of their processes.

In summary, in the ABC cross, the *total* cost of the same activities going horizontally (i.e., total business process costs) and the *total* costs being assigned and causally traced vertically (i.e., total product, customer, receiver, or business infrastructure-sustaining costs) *must equal each other*.

Although the ABC cross is intended to communicate this phenomenon, the ABC cross's simplicity often eludes this subtlety. Tracing and measuring costs to their cost objects involves a *different combination* of activities than chain-linking those same activities and their costs in time along business processes.

(4) Leveling or Disaggregation Brings about a Three-Dimensional ABC Cross

One of the questions that organizations implementing ABC most frequently ask is, "How *many* activities should we include in our ABC system?" There is no one correct answer. The number of activities is dependent on the answer to several other questions, such as, "What problem are you trying to solve with the ABC data?" In other words, the size, depth, granularity, and accuracy of an ABC system are *dependent* variables; they are determined by other factors. The level of detail and accuracy of an ABC system depends on what decisions the ABC data will be used for.

Indeed, one of the challenges for ABC/M implementation teams is determining the level of detail to build into the system—specifically, how many activities to use. More refinement usually leads to more activities and greater disaggregation of activities (i.e., levels, or depth), which in turn results in increasingly larger ABC/M systems—despite accounting for the same amount of expenditures. Greater size implies greater administrative effort, but not necessarily more usefulness from the additional data. Greater size can lead to death by details.

Thus, the ABC/M cross can be displayed as layers that lie immediately below the single "box" for each of the three modules of the expanded ABC/M model. The three-dimensional view in Figure 4-14 reveals what the cross looks like with depth and layers of detail. Not only are there always two or more specific resources, activities, and final cost objects, but any one of these can be decomposed (or disaggregated, as in an indented "bill of cost").

FIGURE 4-14 Leveling or Disaggregation Brings about a Three-Dimensional ABC Cross

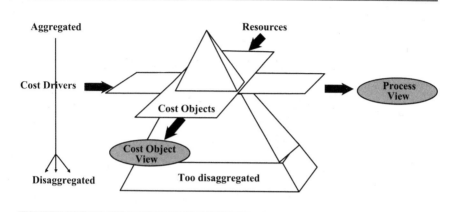

It is now known that the degree of ABC/M data detail—and its accuracy—should depend on its uses (i.e., the types of decisions to be made using the data). High accuracy in the cost of cost objects is not automatically achieved with additional disaggregation (i.e., depth). Moreover, if pursued too far, disaggregation may in fact hamper the effort to sustain an ABC/M system. Controlling the levels (i.e., depth) and size of an ABC system is an important ABC/M system design decision that affects how easily an ABC system can be maintained for updated reporting.

(5) Increasing Emphasis on Predictive Costing and Budgeting

Traditional costing, including ABC/M, takes a historical view of time and experience. As noted, it is akin to a *cost autopsy*. The management accountant basically strives to segment how past resource expenditures either directly trace or are fairly allocated to final cost objects. But all decisions, by definition, affect the future. The advanced and mature users of ABC/M data have moved on to applying their ABC/M data for predictive planning purposes, budgeting, and evaluating what-if scenarios.

Predictive ABC/M techniques are now in place to handle how resource expenses react in a fixed, semi-variable, or variable way with changes in the volume and mix of activity drivers. These predictive techniques will make activity-based budgeting (ABB) the reality that it was once expected to be, when it was at the embryonic, zero-based budgeting (ZBB) stage of talk. Chapter 7 discusses fresh thinking about ABB and predictive costing.

(6) Shortened Time Interval between ABC/M Recalculations

In the early days of ABC/M, many organizations recalculated their ABC/M models only on an annual basis. As the administrative costs needed to refresh and update their ABC/M models systems declined, and as end-users requested more frequent reporting of recent results, the frequency of calculating and reporting ABC/M data increased substantially.

Increasingly often, ABC/M systems are being recalculated monthly, in sync with the financial period-end accounting close. Not all the driver quantities are necessarily updated; those metrics from the prior period's recalculation are simply reused if it is felt that no substantial shift had occurred in the driver distribution. (ABC driver assignments normalize to 100%, so it takes a substantial shift to adversely affect cost accuracy.)

Given the foundation for how ABC/M works, some of the more popular applications of ABC/M, to be discussed in the next sections, are for competitive outsourcing studies, shared-service providers, or as an easier way to accommodate project and work order accounting systems.

THE ROLE OF ABC/M IN COMPETITIVE OUTSOURCING STUDIES AND SHARED SERVICE PROVIDERS

One of the forces driving federal agencies to improve operations is competitive sourcing, the practice of having commercial activities within federal agencies compete with the private sector for providing internal services. This requirement has been part of every presidency since Dwight D. Eisenhower's, and has been treated more or less seriously over the last half century. George W. Bush made it an important part of his President's Management Agenda, so competitive sourcing has become more frequent since 2000. ABC is an essential tool during these competitions.

Federal entities are required by the Federal Activities Inventory Reform Act (FAIR) to develop an inventory of their commercial-type services. The rules for engaging in competitions for the services are set forth in OMB Circular A-76, *Performance of Commercial Activities*. As part of the A-76 competition process, an agency first establishes a Performance Work Statement (PWS) of the commercial services up for competition. The PWS includes a description of the function's scope, workload volume, and performance requirements.

The government organization currently performing this work responds to the PWS by creating a *most efficient organization* (MEO) in its proposal.

An MEO is not necessarily how the government organization does its work before the competition, but rather how it *will* do the work should it win. Typically, the government organization will improve its operations and cut costs in order to be competitive with contractors from industry who also submit proposals to meet the PWS requirements.

Indeed, most of the time the government organization wins A-76 competitions. No matter who wins, taxpayers usually come out ahead because of reduced cost. Promised savings from these competitions are considerable. For example, OMB reported that government-wide data showed that the A-76 competitions completed in FY 2004 resulted in an annualized projected savings of approximately $22,000 per position involved, regardless of whether the winning service provider was internal (part of the government) or was external (a contractor).

Internal Shared Service Providers

For departments where competitive sourcing may not apply, the traditional "overhead functions," once widely despised by internal customers, are becoming "shared services organizations." The initial consolidation of multiple support functions into a single service provider may have begun simply as an effort to remove redundancies and to save costs. However, a pleasant consequence can be substantially improved levels of customer service.

ABC/M data can serve as the cornerstone for shared service providers. Fact-based information is required to transform overhead functions, the information technology (IT) function in particular, beyond simply performing as cost-effective internal suppliers. With ABC/M, shared service providers can perform like their counterparts in the external market.

Shared services have traditionally been called overhead functions. It is not an attractive label. Some users of the overhead services view them as a monopoly.

But a sea change is in progress. Today shared services are being defined as "the sharing and leveraging of resources, people, and information to more effectively meet the business needs of an organization" (Bill Langdon, The Society of Management Accountants of Canada, 1999). Figure 4-15 displays how an organization's internal services can be placed on a continuum that leads toward a competitive marketplace model.

FIGURE 4-15 A Continuum of Models for Shared Services

BASIC MODEL   MARKETPLACE MODEL

• Economies of scale • Reduced operating costs • Shared resources • Leverage of expertise • Chargebacks for services • Customer and business orientation	• Economies of scale • Reduced operating costs • Shared resources • Leverage of expertise • Chargebacks for services • Customer and business orientation

+ Customer choice of supplier
+ Market-based pricing
+ Separation of governance
   (policy/audit) role from services

Reprinted with permission. The Society of Management Accountants of Canada, "Adopting and Implementing Shared Services," Management Accounting Guideline, 1999.

The objective is for the internal services function to behave according to the dynamics and economics found in the external marketplace. This includes good customer service at a reasonable price. Ultimately, an internally shared service provider is like any business: customers and service-recipients determine its fate.

One extreme indicator of the growth of this movement is the choice some organizations have made to *outsource* services, such as for the employee cafeteria, uniform cleaning, purchasing, or information data processing. As Figure 4-15 shows, organizations may begin with a basic model of a shared service provider and progress from there. The marketplace model at the end of the continuum indeed becomes the marketplace! At this point in maturity, the shared service provider either remains internal or converts to an outsourcing partner.

Services are usually thought of as administrative or infrastructure support, such as accounting or janitorial services. Increasingly, the types of shared services being created are professional, technical, or advisory. These may include functions that were previously labeled as engineering, maintenance, or internal consulting.

Public sector, academic, and government organizations at all levels have recognized through experience that they are being asked to do more with less. The concept of shared services is one of the alternatives being examined and implemented to meet this request.

Why Establish a Shared Service Provider?

As noted, many organizations initially pursue a shared service framework as a means of reducing overall costs. Their reasoning, right or wrong, is that there is likely to be waste in the separate, internal functions. In some cases, a confrontational atmosphere exists between the service departments and their customers in the core business processes. Frequently, both parties are experiencing frustrations. The only thing that the internal customers seem to want are lower chargeback fees from their internal service provider. Often there is suspicion of duplication and redundancy of services across the organization. A single shared service provider consolidates multiple service providers under a single banner and minimizes overlapping work.

In time, organizations realize that a successful shared service provider improves the service levels for their internal customers. Further, as internal customer needs continuously change, the shared service provider is agile enough to match those changing requirements with cost-competitive services.

Ultimately, an effective cadre of shared services allows all the customers to focus on their own respective core products and service-lines, without nagging interruptions from poor support. After all, it is the performance of the core competencies that matters the most to the shareholders in a public or privately owned company or to the service-recipients of a government agency.

Chargeback Billing Systems

The premise behind the basic model in Figure 4-15 is that the support service function will attempt to maintain its cost structure in line with its volume of services and transactions. Simple economic theory acknowledges that all organizations have a barrier-to-entry fee of fixed costs. As volume grows, new resources and costs are consumed or added at either a variable or step-fixed rate (one can't purchase one-third of a machine or hire one-fourth of a person).

In a fair and equitable system, customers of the internal support services would be charged directly in proportion to their usage. Too often, however, these cost-recovery chargebacks are based on oversimplified cost allocation schemes. That is, the service organization's costs are too aggregated and too averaged to accurately reflect the relative use by each individual customer. As a result, some customers are always subsidizing others. Activity-based cost management resolves these inequities.

Because growth of sales volume for the internal service function spreads fixed costs across an increasingly broad set of services and customers, the economies of scale should increase in value in line with volume. The relative cost efficiencies may or may not be passed on to internal customers as lower prices or as reduced chargeback allocations. Regardless of the internal transfer pricing, these cost efficiencies should make the internal service function more cost-competitive with external market competitors.

The Power of Consolidations

When routine, transaction-based work is consolidated into fewer locations or individuals, the fixed and step-fixed component of the service provider's cost structure is reduced. In effect, functions previously decentralized or distributed throughout an organization become more focused and can deliver true cash savings through economies of scale.

The spirit of shared services is to create a situation where new and innovative thinking by the service provider is constantly inspired. This occurs in a competitive market environment. The service provider behaves as an entrepreneur and internal users and service-recipients are treated with a customer-for-life attitude.

One conflict exists. Although pricing ideally would be competitive with the external marketplace, special circumstances may put the shared service provider at a cost disadvantage relative to an unbridled competitor. An internal service provider's work involves two elements:

- **Policy and governance**—Compliance with government or senior management regulations, policies, and rules will add costs. For example, an audit is not free. This work (and its related costs) relates to risk management and financial control. There usually is no choice; the work is mandated.

- **Business unit services**—Customer order fulfillment is, of course, basic to the service provider's existence. This work is skill-based, scale-oriented, and customer-serving.

An example of this duality is the accounting and finance function, which must comply with specified procedures and a host of governing regulations while also delivering transaction-based processes such as payroll.

In the end, the chief goal of moving toward a basic shared service system and eventually to a marketplace model is to do more with less through improved efficiencies, reduced costs, and future cost avoidance.

Ground Rules for Shared Services

Proponents of shared services maintain that considerable customer service improvements, as well as lower costs, can derive from establishing such a system. These advocates strongly suggest, however, that the shared service provider be allowed to compete under the following rules:

- **Operate as a single entity**—The function should be a separate unit with its own profit and loss accountability. This encourages a pro-customer spirit.
- **Full-absorption cost recovery chargebacks**—By fully costing, not only does the shared service provider recover its costs via prices that are market-pegged, but the internal customers learn that they may be placing extra and unnecessarily costly demands on the service provider's work. Here is where ABC/M is imperative, because it can trace the service provider's costs based on the variation and diversity of its products, base service-lines, and high-to-low maintenance customers.
- **No permitted duplication of services**—This preserves fairness by preventing a boutique department from selling its services well below cost simply to remain busy.

A move toward shared services is not a rebirth of centralization. In today's virtual world, geographic location has become less relevant. What a shared service provider is allowed to do is increase its responsiveness and timeliness to its colleagues in the parent organization's core business processes. A common practice is for the buyer to formally sign a service-level agreement document specifying rates, contract length, and expected volumes. A typical agreement will cover the following:

- Description of the service(s) to be provided
- Service standards (e.g., deadlines, response times, other performance indicators)
- Pricing
- Operating principles (e.g., handling of excess demand)
- Improvement initiatives

One final note: Both service providers and customers may suffer organizational shock upon their initial exposure to fully loaded costs, i.e., the *true* costs for the organization to deliver support services to its internal customers. Some of these costs, however, are not directly caused by fulfillment of customer demand for services and products. These extraneous types of costs (such as completing reports for management or other authorities) are referred to as *business or organizational sustaining costs*, and ABC/M is capable of isolating them.

Migrating from the Basic to the Marketplace Model

Many organizations begin their shared service transformation with the "basic model." Sometimes the effort is launched as a result of a benchmarking exercise that brings bad news. An organization may discover, for example, that its accounts-receivable invoicing function is very poor compared with other organizations either in the public or private sector. The organization now has some new facts and a lot more focus. By moving to the basic model form of shared services, it predictably achieves substantial improvement in productivity per service-output (e.g., cost per invoice).

(Incidentally, the use of ABC/M data is becoming more popular as a metric for benchmarking. Often in benchmarking studies, there can be a bad case of apples-to-cookies. That is, lack of comparability among the participating organizations may go unrecognized, and lack of consistency in what work activities or outputs are to be included or excluded in the study may also skew the results. An ABC/M methodology introduces rigor and is sufficiently codified and leveled for relevancy to remove these shortcomings.)

The major change in going from the shared services "basic model" to the "marketplace model" is that the buyers (i.e., customers) are given free choice of suppliers, including external suppliers. Even if imposed constraints preclude a 100% free choice of suppliers, this approach almost certainly will bring radical change from the traditional relationship between an overhead department and its internal customers. The goal of this shift is to move from simply a cost-recovery model to a market-based pricing model.

A premature conversion of a shared service provider from the "basic" to the "marketplace" model can obviously create problems. From the outset, it is predictable that the shared service provider's cost rates will be non-competitive relative to the outside market (despite the outside market's added inclusion of a profit mark-up). One approach to introducing the internal service provider to the anticipated, fierce realities of the marketplace is a gradual and phased moratorium. During this grace period, the shared service provider may be protected by a policy that restricts its customers in choosing external providers. The internal service provider temporarily enjoys an *exclusive* supplier status, thus temporarily protecting its level of volume. Some minimal level is required simply to recover the entry-fee costs to provide the services.

During this transitional moratorium period, the shared service provider can learn, discover, rationalize, and generally get its house in order by attempting to:

- Understand its current costs of processes
- Understand its current costs of products, base-line services, and special services
- Perform benchmarking
- Rationalize which products, services, and customers to retain or abandon (strategic)
- Reengineer, streamline, and improve performance (operational)
- Develop performance measurements and scoreboards, including measures for customer satisfaction
- Separate and isolate its costs-of-governance from its pure costs-to-serve-customers
- Develop service-level agreements with its internal customers
- Develop a price-quotation process to deal with routine customer orders as well as with large-volume or special deals

ABC/M systems and data are essential for all of the above. While under temporary protection, the shared service provider can get its cost structure in order while altering its culture and attitude. It can also learn how to manage its unused but available idle capacity.

In practice, advocates of shared services strongly suggest that the governance and policy-related costs not only be separated from the cost-recovery chargeback prices to internal customers, but that they also be charged to and paid for by (or at least reported to) the executive management. ABC/M is very effective at segmenting these organizational sustaining costs.

To be clear, longer-term protectionism of an internal service provider is not necessarily in the best interests of the internal customers or of the organization as a whole. Although it may be a tough pill for the organization to swallow, outsourcing services deserves serious consideration if it provides more overall value to the internal customers. ABC/M is a powerful tool for analyzing outsourcing and for doing other trade-off or what-if analysis. A key question that should always be asked is, "If I stop (or add) this or that function, what costs remain, go away, or are added?" ABC/M answers this question because it is so work-centric.

Information Technology: A Prominent Shared Service

The recent explosion of information technology (IT) and network communications has taken many executives by surprise—and so has the astronomical price tag that comes with these technologies. Back in the 1990s, when IT was often simply called data processing and was not well-understood, senior management found its rising costs to be a nuisance. Today the sheer size of the IT budget has become astounding. Because IT is both a strategically critical support function and very expensive, it has become imperative to manage it cost-effectively.

In the earlier days of data processing, before personal computers became common and when mainframe computers were standard, the cost-recovery chargeback method was straightforward. All the IT department's costs were allocated to the user departments based on a central processing unit (CPU), which is a composite measure of time and load placed on the computer's central processor. As the complexity and diversity of the IT resources, services, and user needs have grown, so has the need for an improved cost measurement system. This, typically, has called for application of ABC/M.

As a partial solution, the cost of some IT functions can be directly traced using project accounting methods. However, this method is administrative-intensive and invasive, in that each employee may need to fill out a timesheet. To complete this solution, the costs of the remaining IT functions, such as communications or personal computer support, could be assigned to base services or users by using ABC/M activity drivers such as the number of user requests. In short, multiple activity drivers are now required, not a single volume measure such as CPUs, to equitably chargeback IT services to its users. And finally, these base-service costs are further traced to the organization's various products and customers based on individual consumption levels of those base services.

Unfortunately, most organizations have pursued IT costing methods that are rooted in conventional standard costing techniques. In these cases, allocated charges to the user departments continue to be based on easily measured resource usage (e.g., disk usage) plus a broadly averaged overhead cost-recovery calculation rather than on a more reflective cost basis. The accuracy of the cost calculations degrades as the IT environment diversifies and its support costs rise. Ultimately, chargeback costs for IT services stray far from reality. Then, all sorts of irrational behavior by managers in the user departments may ensue; for example, they may attempt to lower the number of phone calls or database inquiries and take other actions that adversely affect overall business performance.

ABC/M can play several roles in the IT arena.

Cost Assignment
Figure 4-16 describes the design of a high-level ABC/M cost-flow assignment network for an IT environment. The ABC/M system takes in all the IT costs, and it can even include support costs that IT incurs in other parts of the organization (e.g., senior management, human resources).

All the direct and indirect expenses for IT are restated using the ABC/M system. ABC/M first calculates the costs of IT services provided to the internal user community and ultimately flows them into the organization's business cost objects, i.e., its products, service-lines, and internal or external customers.

In Figure 4-16, the general ledger's resource expenditures can be classified as wage-related (i.e., employees and contractors) and non–wage-related (i.e., all the other expenses). The IT function's cash-outlay expenditures are traced into the types of work activities that it performs. Some of its work serves current operations while other activities serve the future.

The operational and support activity costs are assigned to IT service cost objects, such as financial software applications or help desks. The research and development and software development activity costs can be assigned to new systems, which in subsequent time periods become the costs of the current system.

FIGURE 4-16 IT ABC/M Cost Assignment Network

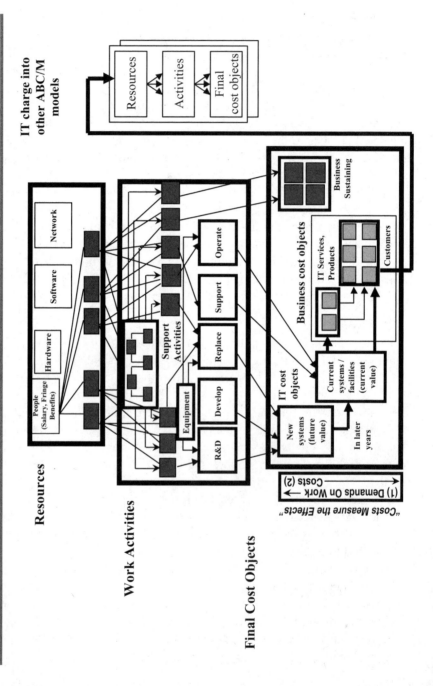

Ultimately, the full-cost-recovery chargeback costs are traced to the business cost objects, which are the entire organization's products, base service-lines, channels, and internal and external customers. These cost charges are derived from the volume consumption of the IT service cost objects. To ABC/M, IT is a business within a business. The assignment of the costs of IT services to the organization's products and customers assists in improving the accuracy and visibility of the IT resources consumed by each user department, which is important information for budgeting and, if applicable, the profit contribution margins. For government agencies requiring full cost recovery via pricing or fees, profit margin management is becomingly increasingly important as a means for them to relate their resources to the concept of value.

Cost Visibility

Equitably charging internal customers for their use of IT services is not the only application of ABC/M data. The same ABC/M data also provide IT managers and employees with the costs of their work activities and associated drivers. In typical ABC/M fashion, these data can be used either to (1) identify IT services and business services that are costly and lower value added, or (2) to benchmark cost rates against other IT organizations to search for indications of best practices. As pointed out previously, a recurring problem with benchmarking is the achievement of valid comparisons; there are always maddening differences that cloud results and analysis. ABC/M corrects for these inconsistencies, and it helps managers examine the levers that can increase the value provided by the IT function to its internal users.

The Role of ABC/M with Shared Services

ABC/M has been mentioned in several sections of this chapter. Figure 4-17 summarizes the multiple uses of this system as it relates to shared services overall.

The output of ABC/M is always the input to something else. Shared services are a very appropriate beneficiary of ABC/M data.

A case in point is the whole question of transfer pricing. As organizations move product or deliver services among multiple *internal* divisions and departments, they create internal commerce. The internal selling price is commonly referred to as a "transfer price." This is the monetary amount that reflects the exchange between the division or department that ships a product or delivers a service and the receiving division.

FIGURE 4-17 Uses of ABC/M Data for Shared Services

- Full absorption cost chargebacks—costs of products, base-line services, and special services
- Benchmarking—to ensure comparability and consistency
- Measuring the costs of business processes
- Reengineering and process improvement
- Performance measurement (balanced scorecard)
- Segmenting "governance" from "service" costs
- Assessing alignment of the cost structure with the service provider's strategy
- Developing a basis for price quotations
- Locating and measuring costs of unused capacity
- Evaluating outsourcing business case (tradeoff decision)
- Reporting customer profit and loss statements

The blunt fact of life is that a true price is established for a good or service only when the external market establishes a market price. It is not until independent third parties repeatedly exchange their money for something that one can assess its going market value. Whenever internal divisions within a larger organizational structure "sell" their product or service to another division, there are three risks:

- A cost-plus markup to add an internal profit is a mirage. The only situation where an item's proper price—not its cost—can be gauged is if an identical item is also being sold in the marketplace. For example, in petroleum processing or agricultural production, some intermediate grades or products are also sold as commodities. In those cases, prices are established that are independent of cost—which is the way they should be established. But when a manufacturing division transfers a component for assembly or finishing elsewhere, there is no market or market price. Transfer should occur at the true cost so that the accumulated cost buildup in the final division's cost appears as if it came from one business. In other words, contribution profit margins should only be measured when an exchange is made with an external party.

- Full cost-based transfer prices provide little incentive to the selling division to improve if all cost overruns can be passed on to the buying division.
- Regardless if the transfer is calculated as cost only or at cost-plus, if the allocated portion of the cost is flawed (and we have already described how commonly that occurs), then misleading information is distributed to the other divisions.

ABC/M provides the basis for a reliable transfer cost system. Some advocate using a marginal cost–based (not full) transfer price, but marginal cost is difficult to measure. And you still run into problems when the selling division operates below capacity—who then pays for the unused capacity? Fortunately, ABC/M resolves these difficulties with a computing platform.

(As a preview, the same ABC/M principles described here for internal purposes will be applied later in this chapter for supply chain management. That application will be for measuring interorganizational profit and cost measurement across multiple trading partners in the extended value chain.)

PROJECT ACCOUNTING OR EARNED VALUE MANAGEMENT (EVM) OR ABC/M: CHOICE OR BLEND?

Strong forces are pressing organizations toward doing more project-oriented work. Concurrently, there is an increasing appetite to measure results and their costs. In rising numbers, organizations are questioning the *adequacy* of their cost measurement systems. They are questioning not just data integrity and cost accuracy, but the entire approach and effort involved in cost assignment and accumulation.

Some public sector organizations have been using program accounting, project accounting, and work order management accounting systems for years. Direct costing of highly direct labor and material costs is not a foreign concept to them. But what has been surprising is the increasing shift of focus from direct to indirect costs. Indirect and support overhead costs are much trickier to trace and assign than direct costs.

Some organizations put great effort into their project accounting and work order systems and wonder if the heavy administrative cost exceeds the benefits. Others who have adopted ABC/M may conclude that a portion of their reporting requirements can be better satisfied with a program or project accounting (e.g., job and work order costing) system. Must organizations choose one over the other? Or can ABC/M and project/job order costing be combined? All these cost assignment methods involve a form of direct costing that applies calculated costs from expenditures into outputs. How can multiple cost assignment approaches be blended?

The broader question is under what conditions does an organization elect to measure its costs using project accounting or standard costing or actual costing? How does an organization know? And once the choice is made, how well does the system serve managers and employee teams? These questions will be increasingly asked as employees devote a greater portion of their workday to *projects* or to specific work orders, like maintaining or repairing a specific building.

There will increasingly be interest in knowing and reporting the *total* costs of each project or for all projects or all work orders totaled for a specific building, asset, or service-recipient. (Work orders are also referred to as *work packages*.)

ABC/M and Earned Value Management (EVM)

When the airline industry demonstrates that it can fine-tune "yield management" to squeeze remaining profits from available capacity, then commerce and government, as well as the rest of industry, take notice. Increasing productivity, improving project management, and the removal of excess and idle capacity are increasingly becoming an imperative.

Many organizations are exploring and adopting financial measures like value-based management (VBM). VBM is intended to influence managers to better use the assets that the organization has already purchased (or the assets of its trading partners). VBM measures are indicators. As the financial measures of VBM become better understood, there will be a need to manage the underlying influences resident in operations. A New York City Wall Street consulting firm, Stern Stewart & Company, has trademarked its VBM measure name as Economic Value Added (EVA). Asset utilization requires understanding capacity, and ABC/M can assist in quantifying capacity measures in terms of money-equivalents.

In regulated environments, such as for a contractor to a government agency, the law defines the cost recovery methods. Earned value management system (EVM) bookkeeping is sometimes required. EVM can be viewed as project accounting but with a greater emphasis on the dimensions of time and schedule. By integrating costs, schedules, and technical performance, EVM provides early, detailed, and ongoing tracking and understanding of a project as it progresses, with an emphasis on risk mitigation to manage deviations from the original plan's cost and schedule. EVM adds the monetary terms to project management.

Financial analysts recognize that a key influence on the actual return on investment of a project is not keeping the costs low, but rather having an early completion date, so that the substantial investment in assets and added installation expenses can be "turned on" to start yielding results. Hence, measures of program performance in terms of cost and adherence to the planned schedule both matter.

The U.S. Department of Defense (DoD) has practiced EVM for many years. Now, civilian agencies of the U.S. government are practicing it, too. The U.S. Office of Management and Budget (OMB) has legislated federal agencies to apply EVM. Section 300 of the OMB Circular A-11 states, "Agency will use, or uses an Earned Value Management system that meets ANSI/EIA Standard 748 and investment is earning the value as planned for costs, schedule, and performance goals," In addition, the Civilian Agency Acquisition Council and Defense Acquisition Regulations Council have created a set of guidelines for EVM to be applied with project management.

However, there can still be wiggle room as to how costs are charged to projects and eventually charged back to the customers. Substantial energy can be consumed by both the seller and buyer, or by the provider and user, scrutinizing how project-related costs were allocated.

Today's managers and employee teams are no longer tolerating unfair cost allocations or undeserved expense charges when they feel that some other department, workgroup, product, or service-line caused the original expense to occur. Likewise, contracting companies and government agencies are investigating how and what the contractor charged for. They no longer care to subsidize others at their own expense. How then does one design a cost measurement and assignment system that is fair and equitable?

Varying Cost Assignment Approaches

Figure 4-18 describes some alternative ways in which costs can reflect the diversity, variation, and complexity of the cost objects (e.g., products, services, outputs, projects, work orders, service-recipients, customers) that consume costs. Here is a short primer on how to charge-out costs. As earlier described with the ABC/M cross, any resource expense can be directly asso-

FIGURE 4-18 Improved Accuracy via Greater Direct Costing

Ideally, all costs should be <u>directly</u> charged, but as variety, complexity, and technology increase, more costs are <u>indirect</u>.

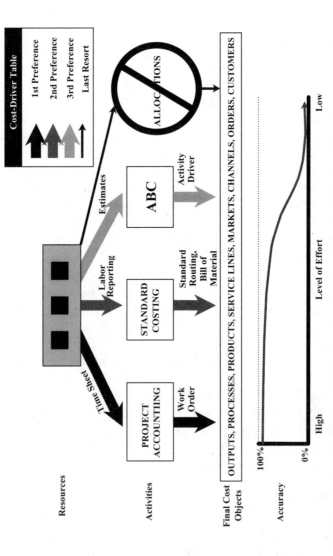

Reprinted with permission of the McGraw-Hill Companies, from Gary Cokins, *Activity-Based Cost Management: Making It Work.* © The McGraw-Hill Companies, Inc., 1996.

ciated or indirectly reassigned, and three elements will always be involved: the origin (i.e., resources), the transfer mechanism (i.e., the work activities), and the destination (i.e., cost objects). In costing lingo, the resources "supply" costs to work activities, whereas the products, service-lines, projects, or customers/beneficiaries "consume" the work activity costs.

These various cost assignment approaches include a less discriminating "allocation" approach, an ABC/M assignment based on causality, and the two popular direct costing methods—project (job order or work order) accounting and standard costing.

The applicability of the direct costing method ranks, left to right, from the most to the least preferred method. Note that *cost allocations* located at the far right are discouraged. There is no great mystery here. If the work activity was not consumed by or has no consuming relationship with a cost destination, then no meaningful assignment path can exist. There is no cause-and-effect. In practice, the bases or factors for many cost allocations are often at best directional (e.g., allocated by headcount or square foot) and at worst arbitrary (possessing no correlation). That is why cost allocations in Figure 4-18 are termed "last resort."

Cost assignment approaches are conditional and situational. The same expenses can be assigned two different ways to support two different questions. The most appropriate assignment approach depends on the end-users' needs. We next address how each of the direct costing approaches are similar yet different.

Project Accounting and Work Orders

Project accounting or its equivalent twin, *job order costing*, is the highest form of direct costing with regard to accuracy. This assignment method simultaneously captures the intersection of the resource's time-usage duration with the project plan's work step or with its recipient, such as the job/service work order or the product. That is, both the work activity and its recipient are coupled at the cost intersection. This form of costing is more applicable in law, consulting, or auditing firms as well as in contractor environments. In manufacturing, work order costing is popular in job shops where, at the extreme, the organization is building a one-of-a-kind. Project accounting is also prevalent in work environments that are regulated in compliance with laws stipulated by government agencies, such as the Department of Defense or the Department of Energy.

With this form of direct costing, the life of the cost object (e.g., a project) has a beginning and an end—a complete life-cycle to itself. Expenses are continuously charged while the work is in progress, and costing concludes by "closing out" when the project or job is complete. A drawback to project and work order accounting is the high administrative effort to collect, validate, and report the project or job costs.

When looking at a project hierarchy, the receiving legal entity is located at the top level, the next level is the stand-alone projects (say, constructing a dam), and so on until you reach a point that is deemed the lowest-level to attach costs to for purposes of project management. The lowest-level project is usually called a work order. Work is usually only captured at the lowest level (the "leaf of a tree" concept). There may be phases within each work order, such as electrical, plumbing, etc. At an even lower level within the work orders (below phases) are *tasks*. Tasks are elements of work that employees perform and that are traditionally recorded on timecards. Sometimes you will have a tie-in to your fleet/equipment rental system, so equipment-related activities can also be entered, via employee timecards or via equipment usage record cards if the usage is not tied to an employee. Remember that people and equipment perform work activities.

With project and work order accounting, usually what is lacking are the work activities provided by vendors because the financial accounts payable systems typically don't record the work activity information from the vendor. (For example, if you contract out engineering services and are billed for 1,000 hours, why shouldn't the system record the activity? You would if it were performed by employee labor!) Ideally you could aggregate the activity across the work orders to generate an activity cost-consumption report. You could then drill-through and drill-down to account for, compare, benchmark, and understand project costs and performance. Revenues and billings can be matched to projects to determine profits (a priori) or measure profits/losses after the fact.

Beyond the mechanics of recording transactions, you have to look at the purposes of a project or work order accounting system. Work orders are typically used to capture:

1. Construction costs for additions to fixed assets ("continuing property records" in utility nomenclature)
2. Maintenance work orders for capturing costs for performance analysis

and historical expense comparison (e.g., how much did watermain repairs cost this year versus last?)

3. Costs for billing purposes (e.g., to determine cost/cost-plus-overhead charges to external customers or to make benchmark fee-for-service comparisons with other providers)
4. Costs of providing shared services to numerous other service departments and operating departments

Regardless of its purpose, work order costing requires a lot of effort.

Standard Cost Accounting

Standard costing is the next highest form of direct costing. Here the actual time-effort of the work is still measured, but the reassignments of the work activity cost to its cost object are based on predetermined rates. The predetermined rates are often called *standards*—hence the name of this cost assignment approach.

Standard costing is more regularly applied when the products, services, or outputs are routinely and repetitively made or delivered. Regardless of whether the rates are determined based on historical averages or desired targets, the regularity and repeatability of the output is what matters. The actual input effort is still measured, and the cost accounting generates a whole host of variance-to-standard cost measures (e.g., efficiency, volume, price) used to reconcile the actual against planned costs. Even with standard costing, the standard cost plus cost variances must always equal the actual cost.

Standard costing addresses the key drawback of job costing in that it lessens the administrative effort. Standard costing assumes *standard* input or output rates, rather than each time measuring *actual* rates, for the work and the work's outputs. Standard costing does not require measuring at the cost intersection where actual work matches to the same and actual output. For that level of specificity, choose job order costing.

It should be apparent that ranking of preference for the cost assignment method to be selected takes into consideration the administrative effort as well as the desired accuracy of the costed cost object.

ABC/M: The New Kid on the Block

The third cost assignment method, activity-based costing, achieves substantial accuracy at a fraction of the effort. ABC/M has become popular because it is an economical direct costing method.

We have already described what ABC/M is and explained what has created interest in it. In short, ABC/M is a result of increasing variation, the resulting complexity to manage it, and the rise in overhead expense caused by both of these developments.

Relative to project accounting, ABC/M does not tolerate incurring the significant administrative effort to directly code every source-to-destination relationship for every transaction event at the cost intersection. Instead ABC/M allows the costs for common activities to be reasonably estimated, regardless of who performs them. Then a distribution of all the events, referred to as activity drivers, is used as the basis to assign the source work activity costs (traditionally called "cost pools" by accountants) to the final cost objects.

However, with ABC/M, the cost assignments are restricted to only the products or service-lines (or projects or work orders) actually consuming the activities; the driver quantities are the totals for the period regardless of whether they occurred earlier or later in the time period. In this way, ABC/M spares an organization from the tremendously greater effort to cost-link all the work activities at the *individual transaction level*. With ABC/M, the assignment path itself serves to ensure that there will be no charge to an undeserving (i.e., non-consuming) cost object. Hence, reasonable accuracy with minimal effort is attained.

The Impact of the Repeatability of Work
Some accounting practices begin by classifying people and equipment as being either *direct* or *indirect* (i.e., overhead). But as organizations flatten and de-layer, individuals tend to behave both ways. The distinctions between direct versus indirect costs cannot be made based on the person or machine, but rather by the type of work the person or machine is performing.

Although an objective of the cost assignment approach is to achieve reasonably high accuracy of the cost objects, the selection of the most appropriate cost assignment approach is strongly governed by the repeatability of the work being performed. For example, a cashier at a government licensing bureau tends to perform similar activities each work day, but a computer programmer in the same license bureau may be strictly project-oriented. Should the cashier fill out a project time sheet daily? Should the programmer not fill out a project time sheet? Figure 4-19 indicates when more administrative-intensive and costly data collection may or may not be applicable.

When work activities are non-recurring, such as with a law firm's client-billing or when constructing a skyscraper or earth-orbiting satellite, then a

FIGURE 4-19 ABC versus Project and Workorder Costing

In highly non-repeatable project work, project accounting is appropriate, but may only apply to a subset of workers. ABC increases in utility as an organization's continued outputs change slowly.

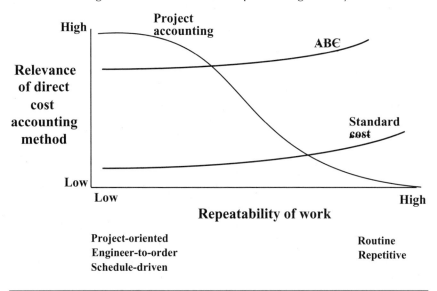

more exacting form of direct costing may be needed for higher accuracy. This is where project accounting, work order costing, or job costing is more appropriate. This approach to costing requires that all activity charges be made simultaneously and directly to the ultimate customer account or to a work-step in a project plan.

In Figure 4-19, the horizontal axis represents the repeatability of work, ranging left to right from non-recurring to recurring. The curve for project accounting, job costing, and work order costing descends in applicability as the type of work becomes less non-recurring—that is, more repeatable. With projects, the time schedule, including unplanned delays and their consequences, can severely govern the total costs. Project accounting serves well when the conditions of non-recurring work and lots of interdependencies are present. However, where work activities are recurring and repetitive, such as with the cashier in the license bureau, project accounting is less applicable.

Since there is broad diversity and variation in services and outputs, even for a cashier, organizations are keenly interested in the unit costs of the output of work ("what is the cost per license renewal of an individual versus a commercial customer?"). This is where ABC/M provides an economical solution. In Figure 4-19, the curve for ABC/M ascends in applicability as work activities become more recurring, though varying in time duration, even though the work produces or serves a broad variety of diverse products, services, customers, service-recipients, and taxpayers.

What If Recurring and Non-Recurring Work Co-Exist?

When a project-oriented organization has employees (or equivalently a substantial amount of work activities) that are not directly consumed by the projects, how should the costs of those employees be traced to the projects? To simply satisfy management's need for full cost recovery, or for legal compliance purposes, these costs will likely be absorbed based on some form of cost allocation. A popular way to accomplish this is to absorb these overhead-like support costs based on the project's direct labor hours (or dollars) or based on each project's expenses. But are there situations in which this method may unfairly overcharge a particular project or not represent a true cause-and-effect relationship? Of course there are. What if one project requires a significant amount of technical overhead support while another one does not?

One solution is to require the support staff personnel to have their timesheets completed (by that worker or by a department representative) and reported similar to how the project-assigned people report their time. But there will still be cases where it is not clear which projects or jobs to assign some of these costs to.

A good solution is to combine or blend ABC/M with the project accounting or job and work order costing system.

Figure 4-20 places project accounting and ABC/M under one roof. It depicts how the indirect or recurring costs, captured in the ABC/M system, can be streamed into the project accounting system or directly into the customers (i.e., service-recipients). Figure 4-20 also shows the four broad cost assignment "avenues" from the ABC/M cost assignment network:

- Work activity to project/job work activity (#1)
- Work activity to project (#2)

FIGURE 4-20 Combined ABC and Project Accounting

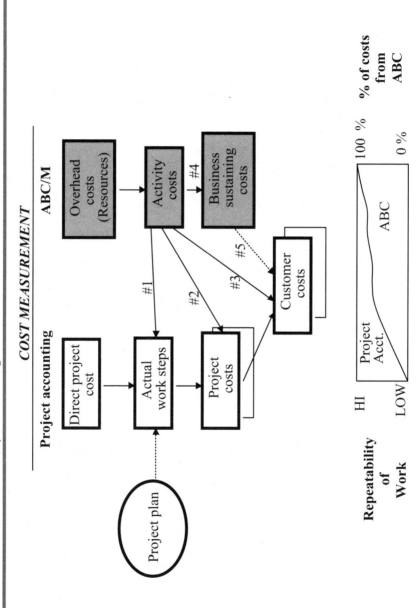

- Work activity to customer (#3)
- Work activity to organizational sustaining (#4)

With ABC/M, the administrative effort is very low. In all four of these assignment cases, the resource costs can still be estimated prior to their being reassigned from the work activities. From each of the work activities, the activity costs can either be:

1. Directly traced to worksteps (#1) in the project or jobs using an activity driver (e.g., the number of purchase orders for a procurement department's work) as a "local burden rate," or
2. Directly traced to the outputs of the project, job, or work order or directly traced to a separate cost object, such as the project (#2), a customer (#3), or an organizational-sustaining (#4) cost object. By tracing those activity costs directly caused by customers in assignment path #3, ABC/M segments how the costs-to-serve among varying customers reflect the substantial differences in how individual customers create unique work apart from the projects, jobs, or work orders themselves. Customers can be angels or devils independent of what they have ordered.

An appealing capability of ABC/M is that even after certain activities are traced into organizational-sustaining cost objects, one still has the option of stopping there with costs that are not fully absorbed into projects or service-recipients—or to further reassign those costs (assignment #5) to service-recipients or to projects. ABC/M is in effect a reassignment network that can always be extended further into additional cost objects.

ABC/M Does Not Always Tell the Whole Story, But . . .

ABC/M is in actuality a poor man's project accounting or work order system. ABC/M does not show the degree of completion of individual projects. It does not make visible cost overruns, as does a project accounting system. In a sense, since ABC/M is computing more as an "actual" costing system, it is not highlighting performance variances measured from a predetermined plan. ABC/M may trace costs into defined worksteps for a project plan, but project accounting systems are designed to also include and compare planned costs against actual costs to determine both schedule and spending cost variances.

One could conclude that project accounting has a larger breadth of purpose than ABC/M. It does a good job of answering the question, "What happened?" A component of project accounting is "earned value" book-keeping. Earned value is a management technique that relates resource planning schedules to technical cost and schedule requirements. Project work is typically planned, budgeted, and scheduled in time-phased "planned value" increments constituting a cost and schedule measurement baseline. The two major objectives of an earned value system are:

- To encourage contractors to use effective internal cost and schedule management control systems
- To permit the customer to be able to rely on timely data produced by those systems for determining the contract status. Some contract billing amounts are based on percentage-of-completion, and the earned value provides the numerator for that ratio

In contrast to the emphasis that earned value and project accounting have on historical bookkeeping, ABC/M seems to shine in the performance analysis piece, such as attaching attributes to resources and activities, breaking out associated idle capacity and costs, and answering "why" types of questions.

Moreover, although project accounting may have the larger breadth of purpose, it may not be complete in scope—accounting for all the organization's costs. One could make the case that work order costing and project accounting typically include only the labor, materials, and equipment costs that touch the work that ends up in the products and service-lines being delivered and sold. They omit all non-product and non-service-line costs that could and should be traced to customers, channels, and organizational sustaining cost objects. Therefore, a project accounting or work order system includes only a subset of the cost objects that would be found in an ABC/M system.

In the end, the desired level of detail and accuracy for measuring and reporting costs will depend on how the data are used for decisions and control. As multi-skilled employees in organizations spend increasingly more time multi-tasking in various business processes, projects, and work orders, the traditional general ledger and fund accounting system will be recognized as structurally unable to produce the information that managers and teams need. Fortunately, organizations have options and can design their cost measurement approach to balance the level of administrative effort to collect and report the data with the level of accuracy of the output information and with the needs of the end-users of that information. The final solution may well lie in a project accounting and ABC/M hybrid system.

In program and project management, funds are often appropriated for future spending. The sum of the appropriations for multiple programs and projects becomes the organization's total budget. There are entire procedures for handling budget adjustments for changes in customer specifications and for cost overruns, but that is a different topic for a different book.

Figure 4-21 illustrates the similarities and differences between a program and project accounting system and an ABC/M system geared for commercial organizations. There are multiple equivalent translations of the same amount of planned resource expenditures.

Both approaches have their strengths and weaknesses. Fortunately, in practice, both approaches can be blended, similar to how steel alloys produce desirable properties by forging separate elements, carbon and iron. The direct costs are usually traced through the program projects and work packages. The indirect costs can be traced via ABC/M. There are then lots

FIGURE 4-21 Program/Project Accounting versus ABC/M

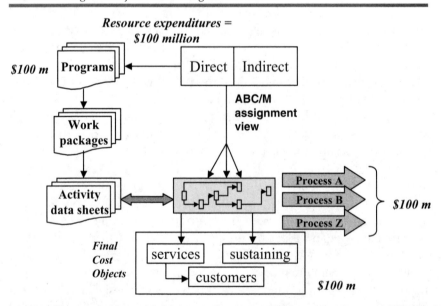

of options. The ABC/M costs can be further traced into the project costs, the processes, the service-lines, and customers. The key point is the multiple equivalent views of the same expenses.

LOCAL OPERATIONAL VS. ENTERPRISE-WIDE STRATEGIC ABC/M

A common misconception is that the scope of an ABC/M system must be enterprise-wide. That is, the expenses included in the system must account for *all* the employees in the organization and 100% of a time period's expenditures. (Or alternatively, the expenses must include all the people for a substantial portion of the organization, such as an entire agency or service-delivery arm.) People with this misconception have usually been exposed only to ABC/M models or systems that are used for calculating the total costs of a product or service-line—for *strategic* purposes—to determine pricing under a full-cost recovery policy or, in some cases, to measure total profitability.

In actual practice, however, the vast majority of ABC/M is applied to subsets of the organization for the *operational* purpose of process improvement rather than revenue enhancement and profit margin increases. An example of a subset is an order processing center or equipment maintenance function. These ABC/M models and systems are designed to reveal the cost structure to the participants in the primary department and related secondary areas.

However, the ABC/M principles apply. With ABC/M's cost assignment view, the cost structure is seen from the orientation of how the diversity and variation of the function's outputs cause various work activities to happen—and how much. The costs of the work activities in the ABC/M model are also revealed as they relate in time and sequence.

Remember, activities *belong* to the processes. However, it is ABC/M's powerful revealing of the costs of various types of outputs that serves as a great stimulant to spark discussion and discovery. For example, when an order processing center learns that the cost per each adjusted order might be roughly eight times more than the cost for each error-free or adjustment-free order, that gets people's attention. This result happens even if the order entry process has been meticulously diagrammed, flowcharted, and documented.

With the flexibility of commercial ABC/M software, the technology now enables consolidating some, and usually all, of the local *children* ABC/M models into the enterprise-wide *parent* ABC/M model. The local ABC/M model data are used for tactical and operational purposes, often to improve productivity. In contrast, the consolidated enterprise-wide ABC/M model is often used for strategic purposes, since it helps focus on where to look for problems and opportunities. Also, enterprise-wide models are popular for calculating full cost recovery and profit margin data at all levels, including channel-related and customer- and service-recipient-related profit contribution layers.

An Example of a Local ABC/M Model

Figure 4-22 illustrates a template timesheet input form for a local ABC/M model of a typical purchasing function. Consider for this example that the sole interest of this portion of the organization is to understand how different types of suppliers create and cause varying levels of costs—both the obvious, such as from the purchasing department, and the hidden tangential costs from other departments. For purchasing departments, an increasingly popular exercise is to continuously evaluate and grade their suppliers. This use of a local ABC/M model provides excellent metrics to assist in supplier ratings.

Figure 4-22 includes *all* the expenses of any department or group of people who may have any involvement or are affected by the purchasing process. The magnitude of the cost impact on each department may be large or small. For the departments and functions outside the formal purchasing department, the specific work is described using the verb-adjective-noun grammar of ABC/M. All the work of those employees not related to the purchasing process, regardless of what they do and why, is simply lumped together as a single activity (e.g., "do all the *other* work").

In some cases, the headcount of one of these tangential groups of workers may be many orders of magnitude greater than the number of employees in the purchasing department itself. As a result, for example, if a large tangential group records as low as a 5% activity rate against the purchasing department account, this yields a significant amount of traditionally hidden or usually non-quantified costs. In the time sheet shown, the full-time equivalent (FTE) headcount related to the purchasing process is 20.5 (i.e., $1,025,000/$50,000) even though the purchasing department has only ten employees.

The cost math on the timesheet input form consequently first computes a total cost for all the employees, but then carves out only those activity costs that are related to the purchasing process. In the community of professional purchasing managers, this total cost has been referred to as the total cost of

FIGURE 4-22 An ABC/M Timesheet for a "Local" ABC/M Model

Work Activity Time Sheet		annual salary & benefits costs =			$ 50,000
Dept	activity	Number of employees	%	TCO $	other $ (per capita)
Purchasing		10			
	process blanket purchase orders		10%	$ 50,000	
	process unique purchase orders		30%	$ 150,000	
	negotiate deals		10%	$ 50,000	
	process returns to suppliers		20%	$ 100,000	
	troubleshoot product problems		5%	$ 25,000	
	resolve problems & disputes with suppliers		25%	$ 125,000	
Inspection		10			
	resolve inbound problems		20%	$ 100,000	
	Do other Core work		80%		$ 400,000
Receiving		10			
	process supplier paper work		20%	$ 100,000	
	Do other Core work		80%		$ 400,000
Production planning	reschedule opperations -- supplier-caused	5	10%	$ 25,000	
	Do other Core work		90%		$ 225,000
Operations	idle or wasted time -- supplier-related	100	5%	$ 250,000	
	Do other Core work		95%		$ 4,750,000
Sales	Explain late shipments -- supplier-related	20	5%	$ 50,000	
	Do other Core work		95%		$ 950,000
		155		$ 1,025,000	$ 6,725,000
			total =	$ 1,025,000	
	NOTE: $525,000, which is over 100% of the Purchasing Department's expenses, are usually "hidden" supplier-related costs.				

ownership (TCO). The first part is the direct purchase price of the product or service-line printed on the supplier's invoice. This form is like a block of marble for a sculptor. After the non-TCO costs are excluded, like the finished sculpture, the costs that remain are pure TCO.

Revealing the Differences in Costs of Cost Objects (Outputs)

Figure 4-23 illustrates how a local ABC/M model can aid learning. Discovery comes from tracing and assigning the activity costs from all the functions to their cost objects. In the case of our purchasing department, the various activities will usually trace activity costs disproportionately into various types of processed purchase orders or directly to different types of suppliers. Note in the figure that the different types of suppliers consume different quantities of the different types of purchase orders (using a cost object cost driver), so 100% of the TCO costs are ultimately traced to suppliers.

In Figure 4-23, only two types of purchase orders were segmented, a standing blanket order versus a traditional unique purchase order. However, by imagining a dozen or more types of purchase orders, you can get a much better idea of how ABC/M traces and accumulates the costs into various suppliers. The learning benefit for employees comes in particular from the combination of (1) seeing the work activity costs that reflect non-conformance, such as to "process customer returns," and (2) defining cost objects that require different amounts of work effort.

Revisit Figure 4-7 shown earlier in this chapter. It argues quite clearly for the inclusion of the local ABC/M model in the parent consolidated model. The supplier-related costs are reassigned into the specific products and service-lines purchased. By folding these costs into the costs of products and service-lines, these very same costs then provide for accurate profit margin reporting—for product and service-lines and for customers. Remember that the customers also consume a unique mix of products and service-lines, as demonstrated in this figure.

As with the tracing of product-sustaining costs (i.e., non-unit, non–batch-related volume consumption relationships), do not worry about which driver measures to use to trace an intermediate cost object. Remember that most of the accuracy, from the final cost object's perspective, was achieved by the segmentation assignment. Therefore, applying an "evenly assigned" or "volume-based" activity driver measure would be acceptable under most conditions and still achieve reasonable accuracy.

FIGURE 4-23 Tracing Obvious and "Hidden" Supplier-Related Costs

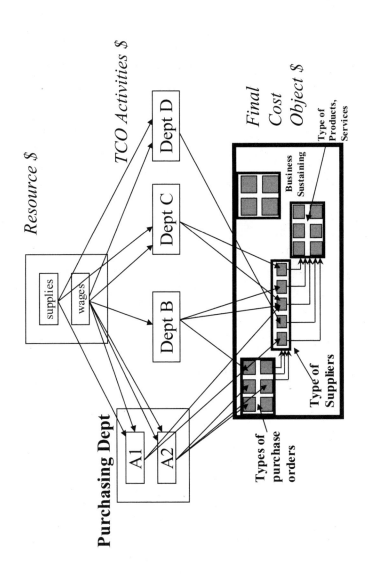

In one sense, the impact is as if a specific product normally sourced from multiple suppliers will now have its single product cost uniquely segmented into multiple costs (e.g., as if a vendor-specific suffix number is added to the part number.) The idea is not to further complicate the inventory cost accounting system to track these costs (e.g., LIFO, FIFO). However, for industries such as foods and pharmaceuticals, unique traceability of cans, boxes, bottles, and so on is needed for regulatory compliance reasons. Local ABC/M models are sort of similar, but after each cost is segmented and reassigned, the cost object costs can be combined. Then, these average costs—no longer broad-brush but now useful—can be applied for decision-making.

Applications of Local ABC/M

Most ABC/M data are applied locally. Examples, such as for the purchasing process, are limitless. Whenever you have people and equipment doing work where the outputs have diversity, then a local ABC/M model can be constructed.

The objective of local ABC/M models is not to calculate full cost recovery or the profit margins of products, service-lines, and customers. The objective is to compute the diverse costs of outputs to understand better how they create complexity that adds to the organization's core cost structure.

An interesting application is in a marketing, recruiting, or promotion department—employees who are trying to generate new or continuing inbound orders. They may be trying multiple avenues, such as newspapers, radio, television, tradeshows, websites, billboards, and so on. The costs for advertising placements are different and so might be the results in terms of success (including any additional differences in the type of sale, recruit, etc.). This is an ideal case for an ABC/M calculation to determine the costs versus benefits of all the channel combinations, and to then rank them according to return on spending.

There are thousands of similar applications of ABC/M. Some refer to the application of local models as activity-based management (ABM), an earlier term for ABC/M, because the uses of the ABC/M data are more operational than strategic. I like to view local ABC/M models as analogous to an orchestra conductor in rehearsal—first working with the violins, then the trumpets, then all the string instruments, then all the brass instruments, and finally with the entire orchestra in a live concert. The combined orchestra represents a consolidated parent ABC/M model, with local models rolled up into a parent model, and then performing as a repeatable and reliable system.

SUPPLY CHAIN MANAGEMENT AND E-COMMERCE: WHERE DOES ABC/M FIT IN?

In this section we will look at some of the dramatic changes wrought by recent and accelerating technological developments. No one is immune. Business, commerce, government—indeed, society itself across the globe—are being transformed by a system of high-speed communication without boundaries. ABC/M will play a critical role in helping organizations adjust to this revolution.

THE INTERNET IS CHANGING EVERYTHING

The Internet is clearly the revolution of the 21st century. Many deem its future impact on society to be greater than the changes that came from the telephone, highway systems, and even electricity. We are all becoming digital citizens in a global networked society.

Some e-commerce experts attempt to distill the impact of the Internet into a single profound sentence. Some describe it as an opportunity for people to join communities of common interest without boundaries or borders. Others view it as the ultimate network across which data, voice, and video communications are carried. Some see the Internet as the expansion of a more mobile information society where individuals have universal access to their work and personal data, accessed not only from a home base but from wherever they may be sitting, standing, or traveling.

A Fundamental Increase in Consumer Power

My simplistic reduction is that the Internet is shifting power from the seller and service provider to the buyer—irreversibly. This is a one-time event occurring in our lifetime. The ability of the buyer to access incomprehensible amounts of data using search engines to seek out products and services is now unlimited. Buyers have access to sellers and service providers for transactions and purchases 24 hours a day 7 days a week (i.e., "24x7") via the supplier's website host server. Further, the buyers' increasing demand for unique requirements will likely force suppliers and service providers to respond with increasing flexibility. This may add costs to suppliers and service providers; it will also add competitive pressure from alternative sources. It should come as no surprise that, when I refer to suppliers and service providers, I am including government agencies as well. The Internet will further accelerate increasing overlap among public and private sector organizations.

Ironically, both private and public entities are assisting in the shift of power to buyers and service-recipients. Government organizations are providing vast amounts of information about their products and services via their websites. In the commercial arena, teenagers already perform exhaustive searches to identify the exact make and model of an item they want; then they locate a cheap source from which to purchase the item. Adults are learning to do this type of research too. The buyer has access to a much greater market than ever before. In a word, the Internet is a gift to buyers, taxpayers, and service-recipients everywhere.

The consumer who benefits from this power shift will not only be the taxpayer or the end-consumer shopping at a retail store. Purchasing and requisition agents within business and government will also enjoy an upper hand over their suppliers. This is the new business-to-business (B2B) economy or government-to-business (G2B) environment.

Buyers and service-recipients are already exhibiting new capabilities to determine for themselves broader ranges in terms and conditions with their suppliers. They can compare and contrast features of products and services offered by competing or alternative suppliers. To complicate matters, suppliers and service providers are finding that consumer and taxpayer expectations are rising faster than some can deliver. Consumer and taxpayer tastes, preferences, and expectations are not static. Many buyers base their standards on their last best-service experience. The bar rises constantly. Government service providers cannot hide behind the excuse that they are somehow different from alternative providers.

Some argue that e-commerce is not as major an event as the media are presenting it. They see e-commerce as simply streamlining the matching of resources to customers and service-recipients. But, in a single punctuated change, the Internet is removing substantial transaction costs, including those from intermediary organizations like wholesalers and distributors. And, although e-commerce may be considered other than a major transformation since the market exchange behavior will continue to exist as it has for centuries, change will be much quicker and more dynamic. In any event, the Internet will continue to shift power toward consumers, taxpayers, citizens, and service-recipients.

An additional pressure on suppliers from buyers and users of services is a shift in the source for competitive advantage. Government is not always a monopoly, and users have the option to use commercial suppliers. Business strategists all agree that differentiation is a key to gaining a competitive advantage. Today, many service-lines are becoming commodities. By definition, there is no competitive edge to suppliers in offering them. If government offers a new service, commercial organizations are adept at offering the same service. Hence, if the differentiation for service-lines is being reduced or totally neutralized, then there must be a shift from service-line differentiation to value-added service differentiation to individual users, or at least to different segments of users. The result is that additional power is shifted from suppliers to buyers and users.

How Can Suppliers Counter This Power Shift?

Suppliers and service providers must now react more quickly than ever before. Call centers, taxpayer services, and customer support functions have become integral for suppliers and service suppliers—and these services come with new costs not present in old government and business models.

A major consequence of the shift in power to buyers is that tremendous pressure is placed on suppliers and service providers to offer more value at competitive prices. They will no longer be able to protect a niche market or to bank on large or long-lasting profit margins, as they did in the past.

How can suppliers and service providers, such as government agencies, counter this power shift? One option is to alter their service-recipient and customer behavior to minimize the power shift, but that option has some obvious limitations. Perhaps a more fruitful course is for trading partners along the supply chain to mutually measure and remove the unnecessary costs that they create among themselves. This means identifying mutually beneficial projects at the supplier and receiver trading partner interface to remove unnecessary work and costs. Each trading partner can gain much better insight into the true and relevant costs for their products, service-lines, inventory, freight, and channels, as well as for the various segments of their service-recipients and customers. This endeavor has been greatly aided by major advances in profit contribution reporting and analysis, which equates to full cost recovery and margin management.

The focus of this section will be on the supply chain for physical products, including food and commodities. However, as many organizations add services to their products to enhance their value, it takes only a little imagination to extend the supply chain to pure service providers as well. This section also describes the role that ABC/M is now playing and will increasingly play as the Internet, e-commerce, and supply chain management mature.

Options for the Public Sector

Imagine that an organization has completely and successfully reengineered itself and become lean and agile, not anemic. Further, imagine that it has streamlined its business processes and workflows, and then it discovers that its directors, governance bodies, and clients are demanding an even better and higher level of performance. What are this organization's options? Across-the-board cost cutting and employee layoffs may no longer be an acceptable option without risking rapid deterioration in customer service and eventual decline in demand for service. If service-recipients have no choices, then their increasing displeasure can only lead to more complaints and damage to the service provider's reputation.

One possibility for the government agency, if feasible, is to raise prices to increase funding. In some cases, an extra fee or surcharge may be applied, such as for renting a special campsite in a park. However, in some situations or markets, small price increases can lead customers to delay their purchase or to switch to competitors, alternatives, or substitutes. All these outcomes lead to less demand for the services.

Another possibility for the government agency is to abandon headache products, service-lines, channels, or customers. These are service-recipients with special demands, such as special rubbish disposal handling, and they disproportionately consume the scarce government resources that could be serving all the other less demanding service-recipients.

Countervailing actions first require the government to properly and accurately measure costs caused by the various types of service-lines, channels, and service-recipients. Where fees or service charges are applicable, measuring revenues is not a problem, but measuring costs is. ABC/M solves that problem. With knowledge of who or what is not fully recovering the costs (e.g., profit contribution margins), the government agency can more intelligently rationalize what to change and which types of service-lines or service-recipients to drop or at least discourage. Pruning and dropping products and customers is not easy and is fairly emotional.

Another less draconian option may be available to public sector organizations (as it is to other service providers). They can alter the behavior of their trading partners. Through collaboration, persuasion, or creation of incentives for one's suppliers and/or customers, fewer demands on work can be placed on the organization's employees. The newly freed-up time of employees—plus their associated operating expenses—can then either serve new service-recipients and customers or handle increased service levels from existing customers. (Alternatively, the service provider's employees can be transferred to where they might be needed elsewhere in the organization.)

New Thinking Needed Across the Board

Technology is no longer an inhibitor for suppliers and service providers to economically capture true costs and test potential scenarios under which the impact of shifts in demand may exceed resources. Commercial ABC/M software can model the costs and compute the math. What organizations now face is more of a thinking problem. They must really understand their assumptions about used and unused capacity and about fixed and variable costs as well as the implications of each assumption.

The option of altering the behavior of their trading partners is not commonly pursued because many organizations haven't yet adequately considered it. Most organizations are habitually inward-focused and concentrate on how they should manage their internal costs. They do not adequately understand how much of their cost structure is in fact a consequence of the collective suppliers' (and service-recipients') demands-on-work. Costs measure effects. The thought of influencing outside agencies to behave differently to lessen the organization's employee workload and costs is often outside the realm of many organizations' thinking. Supply chain management will force organizations to truly understand their *inter-organizational* costs. To understand inter-organizational costs, one has to measure them.

Altering trading partner behavior requires trust among suppliers and customers. Businesses have historically been wary of releasing information to trading partners, even when that information will aid mutual understanding. And one place where disclosure is needed is regarding an organization's cost structure. Yet, many organizations mistrust their own cost data and certainly are loath to share. While understanding true and actual costs is not the whole solution, it is a critical first step toward improving efficiency and competitive position.

MEASURING SUPPLY CHAIN COSTS: ABC/M TO THE RESCUE

There are many popular prescriptions for success in managing the supply chain. One model distills into four success factors: customer differentiation, low-cost provider, effective asset utilization, and flexibility. An organization's departments usually attempt to optimize all four factors. The supply chain manager's contribution to this optimization is to make effective decisions about distribution network and warehouse planning and to develop logistics alternatives. Trade-off analysis will become increasingly critical for supply chain managers. For example, "Should we expand our warehouse space 25 percent? Or should we bypass the distribution centers and ship direct?" Those two alternatives require specific information about the pick, pack, and delivery costs for specific products, freight routes, carriers, and customers. Traditional cost accounting data do not capture sufficient information to make such a comparative analysis easy. They are not designed to accommodate "what-if" analysis.

As organizations have begun to adopt "process-based" thinking, they are recognizing the greater importance of managing their outputs, in contrast to just managing their hierarchical, stove-piped functions. Business processes create and deliver value for service-recipients and customers as the work outputs traverse organizational boundaries. Ideally, value is added every step along the way. Unfortunately, in some steps costs are added, but not much value. Continuously improving planning software tools assist in the process of matching customers with resources. ABC/M mirrors these execution systems with excellent cost data visibility and the cost drivers that cause costs. Some of the ABC/M data are applied within the ERP and planning tools for optimizing schedules and delivery routes.

In a very broad sense, individual supply chains (of products and services) are competing against *other* supply chains for the same consumers' limited discretionary time or spending money and for their keener sense of value. As shown in Figure 4-24, today's supply chain contains redundancies, waste, and low value-added costs.

Where applicable, future competition will increasingly place importance on high retention rates for existing service-recipients and customers. This applies to some government agencies too. Competition will focus on addressing the needs of supply chain customers and their end-consumers located at the end of the chain. Sustained loyalty from service-recipients and customers is now touted as a key organizational objective.

The Need for "Extended Enterprise"

Regardless of where a service provider or government agency is located in its supply chain, one can view *each* trading partner participating in the

FIGURE 4-24 Components of the Supply Chain

The traditional supply chain is a patchwork of centuries-old business practices fraught with redundancies and inefficiencies. Plus, there is great tension between the supplier's sales people and the customer's purchasers.

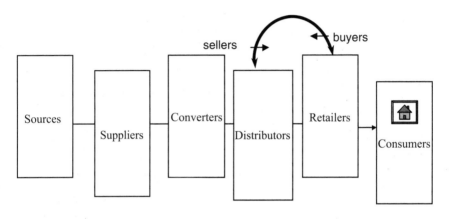

supply chain as having a vested interest in a reasonably high level of productivity and effective performance by *all* the other participants in the chain. By working together in a collaborative way, the trading partners can behave as *an extended enterprise*. They must perform together as if they were *one organization*. It will no longer be a what-is-good-for-me-is-bad-for-you era of business. Instead, it will be "one team . . . one mission." The pipeline across all the suppliers in the chain becomes the inventory, including the information related to the inventory. Speed is becoming the rule of business.

As shown in Figure 4-25, the supply chain leverages information technology to perform as a *value chain*. With improved communications and less uncertainty, buffer stock inventory is reduced everywhere. Buffer stock was traditionally used to protect suppliers from their unreliable suppliers and from unpredictable surges in demand from customers. But "demand-pull" methods plus better forecasting have changed the ways producers produce goods. Advanced planning and scheduling systems (APS) with powerful simulation logic are permitting more material throughput and workflow with

FIGURE 4-25 Information Connects the Supply Chain

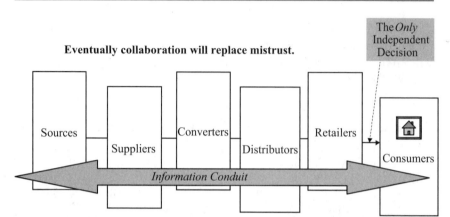

As the "conduit" becomes seamless to the consumer, buffer stock inventory disappears and forecasting demand becomes more important than execution.

less waste. Risk and uncertainty are sliding to the side, taking inefficiency with them and allowing higher customer service levels.

Today, each participant, and each step it performs, will be increasingly scrutinized for the *value* added to the process. Weak performance will lead to removal from the chain.

Trading partners routinely create costs for each other. These costs are usually not intentional but are presumed to be just part of doing business or engaging in transactions. As an example, a customer requests that one of its suppliers deliver goods or services five days per week. What would occur if the customer could get by with deliveries or service-calls on only three days per week? The effect would be that the change in the customer's ordering habit would save the supplier considerable time and effort. In another example, consider a purchasing agent who is required to physically examine and process a supplier's paperwork. What if that administrative paperwork could be handled electronically (or reduced, or not even required)? The effect would be that *both* parties might save time and effort.

Close observation of the supply chain reveals opportunities for significant cost savings. The potential service-level improvements and cost reductions attributable to more efficient supply chains are enormous.

Another large component of cost savings will be realized on the avoided costs of brick-and-mortar physical facilities required to store inventory. And part of these savings is the associated indirect costs of carrying inventory along with the avoided misspendings (i.e., write-offs for commercial companies) on excess and obsolete inventory.

Some of the cost savings will result from discarding bad habits. In the past, buyers would deliberately over-forecast demand so that suppliers would over-produce. The motive for this practice was to drive prices down while reducing the risk of shortages. This kind of behavior leaves lots of unnecessary inventory with high carrying costs all around the world. Then if the slack in the product pipeline runs out, suppliers waste additional energy scrambling to replenish their products. A more synchronized, continuous flow of materials and work outputs, like a frictionless plane, can be more economical in many situations. It wastes less energy, equating to lower costs. Digital exchanges will be so dependent on information that misleading data from the buy-side or sell-side will not be tolerated.

But an even larger component of cost savings will be generated from the current supply chain by eliminating redundant communication and information exchanges via more powerful and intelligent software connecting the buy-side and sell-side information technology infrastructures. Much of the non–value-added time within the supply chain is spent in the "front office" of the order cycle. New and better information technology, in the form of high-speed networks and standards, is the enabler that will facilitate quicker, more accurate information exchanges between the parties essential to the procurement and movement of goods within the supply chain. Non-essential, non–value-added information exchanges will be eliminated, or at least minimized.

ABC/M data will be used to identify the opportunities, assess the investment justification, and measure the post-realization of the savings.

Mutual Trust Brings Mutual Cost Savings

How can some of the redundancies and excesses within the supply chain be eliminated? One way to encourage collaboration between trading partners is for each partner to better understand how it affects the others' cost structures. Better yet, consider the benefits if trading partners could credibly measure the cost impact that they create among themselves. Reliable measures can foster better communications, analysis, and understanding about how trading partners might *collectively* reduce costs.

A dilemma is *measuring* the relevant costs, be they inter-organizational or intra-organizational. As I've stated many times, the fund accounting and general ledger accounting system, although very useful for posting bookkeeping transactions to various accounts, is *structurally deficient* for reporting costs in a format useful to managers and employee teams for decision support. In addition, many organizations simply do not apply the appropriate assignment methodologies for tracing resource expenses into costs (e.g., they do not use drivers used in ABC/M) and do not have adequate analytical application software (such as ABC/M and OLAP).

The relevance to supply chain managers of the new visibility provided by ABC/M-generated costs and their related insights becomes apparent when one appreciates the types of decisions that suppliers and service providers must make. Managers are routinely asked to base decisions on and report using costs by territory, commodity, channel, method of sale, class of trade, order size, stock keeping unit (SKU), delivery method, route, carrier type, terms of sale, type of service-recipient, and so on. These many and diverse costs ultimately are consumed by service-recipients and customers.

ABC/M becomes a vehicle to measure how *all* those different costs are individually consumed by *each* service-recipient or customer. As a bonus, ABC/M computes the costs of the *intermediate* work elements and outputs throughout the value chain. It provides the detailed cost information to support contribution analysis and assess trade-offs. There will be continued and increasing pressures to understand the cost implications of merchandising, storage, space, purchasing, inventory investment, product handling, freight, discounts, and allowances—for products and for service-recipients and customers.

In summary, as trading partners better measure and understand how they create costs for each other, they can begin thinking about how to help each other reduce their collective costs. Trust in others must be well placed. Collaboration leads to high-fidelity relationships.

Although ABC/M reflects for an organization how its trading partners—both suppliers and customers—create and shape its cost structure, ABC/M as practiced is usually treated with an inward-looking focus. That is, improvement opportunities tend to be in the category of "What can we change about ourselves and our *internal* processes?" ABC/M should be used for its outward-looking capabilities as well. Indeed, the pressures for improvement to the entire supply chain costs are now forcing organizations to look outside their four walls at the *entire* value chain. Figure 4-26 illustrates

FIGURE 4-26 SCM is a Value-Add "Chain of Chains"

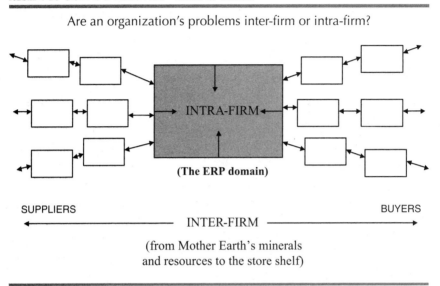

Are an organization's problems inter-firm or intra-firm?

INTRA-FIRM

(The ERP domain)

SUPPLIERS

BUYERS

INTER-FIRM

(from Mother Earth's minerals
and resources to the store shelf)

how the supply chain includes multiple trading partners both upstream and downstream. Organizations must consider their linkages across the chain, consider their interdependencies, and cooperate in reducing inefficiencies and costs.

As the B2B, B2G, and G2B buyers and sellers better understand their relationship at their interfacing touchpoints, improved workflows based on joint technologies will generate benefits. They will also tighten the relationship and improve retention of service-recipients (or at least improve the satisfaction of hostage recipients).

The elegance of ABC/M is that it combines all the costs—upstream costs, production costs, and downstream costs. Inevitably, costs spanning all the supply chain organizations will require understanding in order to simulate and test the effect of proposed changes on overall supply chain costs. The invisibility of costs (also referred to as the lack of cost transparency) and the reluctance of trading partners to share cost information represent significant hurdles for evaluating supply chain performance. ABC/M data remove the blindfolds and create the visibility and transparency that the supply chain trading partners need to make their chain realize its full profit potential.

THE CRITICAL ROLE OF ABC/M

The ABC/M cost assignment network accurately computes supplier-related, channel-related, and customer-related costs by tracing and accumulating how they uniquely consume work activities in relative proportions. When all participants in the chain have ABC/M data, they then can see the uniquely computed profit margins for all the specific supplier, product, channel, and customer combinations. ABC/M's assignment structure, extremely sensitive to segmenting all the diversity, makes it possible to deliver these data.

Figure 4-27 illustrates how the ABC/M cost assignment network traces profitability among various sales and distribution channels apart from products. Supply chain management, and the introduction of so-called virtual networks and webs, is making decisions regarding where to squeeze or push channel costs trickier.

Unfortunately, the sad truth is that many of the trading partners across the supply chain have archaic and poor product and service-line cost allocation practices. In addition, most have no repeatable or reliable cost assignment methods for their expenses from distribution, sales, and customer management functions. Therefore, their cost assignments of all the resources are incomplete. Consequently, even if suppliers disclose their specific product and service costs, from which profit margins can be derived, the calculated costs are likely to be bogus or at least have uncertain error. This means that all the suppliers' products and services are probably over- or under-costed within their own cost accounting system. For government entities, this means their reporting system probably over- or under-counts against full cost recovery.

Any changes that are mutually beneficial should yield a reduction in time and effort, resulting in increased capacity to be redeployed or eliminated.

When inter-organizational costs are better understood, opportunities will surface to restructure according to which trading partner is more efficient at performing an activity. Redundancies can be eliminated. "Functional shift-ability" can be deployed to determine which trading partner should do what specific work activities. Relative final costs are usually transparent to the

FIGURE 4-27 Measuring Channel Costs and Profitability

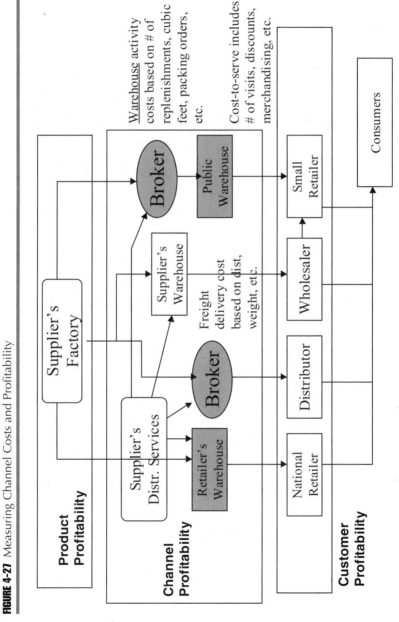

service-recipient or consumer at the end of the value chain. And, in many cases, consumers are simply interested in low cost.

WHO BENEFITS FROM THE COST SAVINGS?

When cost savings are indeed generated and realized, who benefits? How are the cost savings to be shared? This will always be a thorny problem. ABC/M will not provide the answer, but it will at least provide incontestable data to illuminate the discussion.

From a supplier's perspective, there are three potential beneficiaries from improvements and cost savings: (1) the supplier itself, (2) the supplier's direct customer, and (3) that customer's customers all the way through to the chain's end-consumers. The last beneficiary could potentially be you or me in the form of a consumer benefiting from a lower price. But for that to occur, the upstream groups of trading partners will have consciously agreed to a no-profit-impact arrangement where any change in their costs is identically matched with a change in price. In practice, the incremental savings "pie" from productivity improvements would likely be split in various portions among the chain's trading partners and their customers.

Predictably, the profit motive of each trading partner will make the sharing of cost savings an awkward experience. ABC/M data can lessen the debate but cannot stop greed and aggression. The more proficient each trading partner is with its ABC/M system, the more practical these discussions can be. It is important that an organization's "back office" execution systems perform well in fulfilling customer orders, but the "front office" may be even more critical. In other words, organizational effectiveness is necessary but not sufficient. In the end, the satisfaction of the customer and service-recipient is essential. Bottom line: Regardless of whether you are a government agency, where pricing and profits may be less meaningful, or a commercial organization, where cost behavior matters, understanding not only your own organization's cost structure but those of your trading partners as well is increasingly critical.

> **"We do not know a truth without knowing its cause."**
> —Aristotle (384–322 B.C.), Greek philosopher, Nicomachean Ethics, Book I, chapter 1

> **"Science is facts. Just as houses are made of stones, so is science made of facts. But a pile of stones is not a house, and a collection of facts is not necessarily science."**
> —Henri Poincare, French scientist, Value of Science (1904)

Chapter 5

Using ABC/M Attributes to Assess Quality and Value

"The great enemy of truth is very often not the lie—deliberate, contrived, and dishonest—but the myth—persistent, persuasive, and realistic. Too often we hold fast to the clichés of our forbears."

—John F. Kennedy, 35th President of the United States, commencement speech, Yale University, 1962

"Every individual endeavors to employ his capital so that its produce may be of greatest value ... He intends only his security, only his own gain ... By pursuing his own interest, he frequently promotes that of society more effectively than when he really intends to promote it."

—Adam Smith, English economist, *The Wealth of Nations* (1776) Volume II, book IV, chapter 2

P UBLIC SECTOR ORGANIZATIONS need to distinguish among work activities that are:

- Not required at all and can be eliminated (e.g., a duplication of effort)
- Ineffectively accomplished and can be reduced or redesigned (e.g., due to outdated policies or procedures)
- Required to sustain the organization (i.e., work that is not directly caused by making products or delivering services but cannot easily be reduced or eliminated, such as building security
- Discretionary and can be eliminated (e.g., annual employee picnic)
- Directly related to core activities (i.e., making products or delivering services)

ABC/M systems provide for distinguishing these work activities either by incorporating them into a cost assignment structure (i.e., organizational sustaining cost objects) or by tagging their costs as an overlay (i.e., attributes). Revisit Figure 3-6 to note how attributes address the third question related to activity analysis.

ATTRIBUTES ENERGIZE ABC/M COST DATA

Organizations have very few insights about how their individual costs—for products, service-recipients, or business processes—vary

167

among themselves aside from the *amount* of the cost. Traditional cost accounting methods do not provide any way for individual costs to be tagged or highlighted with a *separate dimension of cost* other than the *amount* that was spent. An example of the range of one tag that can be scored against activities is "very important" vs. "required" vs. "postponable." Tags are a popular way of measuring how much value-added is contained in the costs and where it is located.

In short, traditional accounting simply provides racked-and-stacked numbers. The problem is that, aside from the cost amount or bolding or italicizing the print font, one cannot differentiate one cost from another. This is true whether one is examining resource expenditures or their calculated costs of activities, processes, and final cost objects (i.e., workflow outputs, service-lines, or service-recipients). *Attributes* solve this money-level-only limitation of traditional costing. One can think of attributes as offering many other dimensions to segment costs that are different from absorption costing's single dimension, which only reflects variation and diversity consumption of cost objects such as outputs, products, service-lines, and service-recipients.

Attributes in no way affect the calculation of ABC/M costs. Attributes are user-defined, unlimited in number, and often subjectively assigned. Attributes can be used as a grading method to evaluate the individual activities that contribute to a process output's goods or services. ABC/M attributes allow managers to differentiate activities from one another even if they are equal in the amount of costs.

The Analyst's Dream

Some practitioners of ABC/M believe that it is the use of attributes that really brings power to ABC/M analysis. This implies that the attributes information may be more important than the traced and assigned cost data that are so fundamental to what ABC/M is doing—calculating the unique costs of work activities and their consuming outputs. In contrast to ABC/M's objective reporting of the facts, attributes take the ABC/M data an additional step by making the data very *suggestive* of what actions to take. Attributes have been referred to as the "air conditioning" for ABC/M.

With attributes one is no longer just tracing or adding up costs as an accounting exercise. They serve an alternative purpose: differentiating among the costs that reside within outputs, such as standard service lines and/or customers, or within business processes. The differentiating is based on something other than the amount of costs.

Monetary information *alone* about the cost amount of an output, product, or service line does not necessarily convey what to do or how to improve. Just knowing the amount of costs may not be sufficient to analyze the results and make judgments. You may want to know more about various types of cost, too; types and attributes are synonymous. Beyond relative magnitude, the activity monetary costs can be *further* differentiated into user-defined categories to facilitate managerial analysis. Without this additional differentiation, the activities will all look the same except for their description and dollar amount.

ABC/M attributes are frequently scored and graded against the work activities. The number of different attributes is unlimited, but many organizations settle in on their favorite half-dozen or so. Key examples include the level of importance and level of organizational performance. The quality management community uses attributes to calculate the cost of quality (COQ). Figure 5-1 illustrates the three popular COQ categories for grading work activities. Categories themselves can be branched into sub-categories for more refined reporting.

FIGURE 5-1 ABC/M's "Attributes" Can Score and Tag COQ Costs

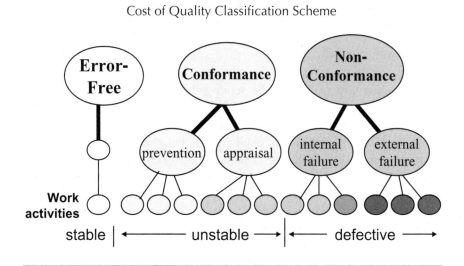

Cost of Quality Classification Scheme

Category 1 in this graphic means a good and stable process. Category 2 has quality-related costs because the process is not sufficiently stable to trust it, so you must inspect and test. Category 3 has quality-related costs because something is already defective or does not conform to specifications defined for or by the service-recipient. With rigor like this, quality teams can pursue stronger improvement programs and shift their time and emphasis away from documentation and reporting to taking corrective actions.

Multiple activities can be simultaneously tagged with these grades. And, of course, the money amount trails along, first at the work activity level and then traced into the cost objects or into the processes to which the activities belong. Attributes can also be directly tagged on resources as well as final cost objects, but tagging activities is the more popular.

We will further discuss how ABC/M supports quality management in the next major section of this chapter.

The Popular Attributes

Advanced, mature users are masters at employing ABC/M attributes. A popular attribute involves scoring activities along their "high vs. low value-adding" scale. The idea is to *eliminate* low value-adding activities and *optimize* higher value-adding activities, thus enabling employees and managers to focus on the worth of their organization's work. Employees can see which work really serves customers and which activities may be considered wasteful. Focus and visibility are enhanced because people can more easily see where costs are big or small and also which costs can be changed or managed in the near term. Scoring costs with *attributes* invokes action beyond just gazing at and analyzing costs.

In the early days of ABC/M, the scoring choices for this specific attribute were limited to either "value-added (VA)" or "non–value-added (NVA)." This simple either/or choice created problems. First, it was a personal insult to employees to tell them that part or all of what they do is non–value-adding— employees are not really happy to hear that. But even more troublesome, the restrictive nature of this scoring method can lead to unresolvable debates. For example, take the activity "expedite orders" to prevent a tardy delivery of a service to an important service-recipient. Is this value-added or non–value-added work? A solid argument can support either case. It is better to simply replace the VA vs. NVA label with a different set of words that scale along a continuum and better describe levels of importance (e.g., critical, necessary, regulatory, or postponable.)

Regardless of what type of scale you use to score or grade value, the objective is to determine the relevance of work or its output to meeting customer and shareholder requirements. The goal is to optimize those activities that add value and minimize or eliminate those that do not. Here are some tips, but by no means hard rules, for classifying value attributes.

High value-adding activities are those that:

- Are necessary to meet customer requirements
- Modify or enhance purchased material or product
- Induce the customer to pay more for the product or service
- Are critical steps in a business process
- Are performed to resolve or eliminate quality problems
- Are required to fulfill customer requests or expectations
- If time permitted, you would do more of.

Low value-adding activities are those that:

- Can be eliminated without affecting the form, fit, or function of the product
- Begin with the prefix "re" (such as rework or returned goods)
- Result in waste without commensurate value
- Are performed due to inefficiencies or errors in the process stream
- Are duplicated in another department or add unnecessary steps to the business process
- Produce an unnecessary or unwanted output
- If given the option, you would do less of.

Another popular attribute scores how well each activity is performed, such as "exceeds," "meets," or "is below customer expectations." This reveals the *level of performance*. Multiple activities can be simultaneously tagged with grades for two or more different attributes. As an option, activities can be summarized into the processes to which the activities belong. Using two different attributes along the process view allows organizations to see, for example, whether they are very, very good at things they have also judged to be very unimportant—and whether they are also spending a lot of money doing those unimportant tasks!

Note how suggestive attributes are. Figure 5-2 illustrates the four quadrants that result from combining the attributes for performance (vertical axis) and importance (horizontal axis). In the case just described as being good at something unimportant, it is obvious that the organization should scale

FIGURE 5-2 ABC/M's Attributes Can Be Suggestive of Action

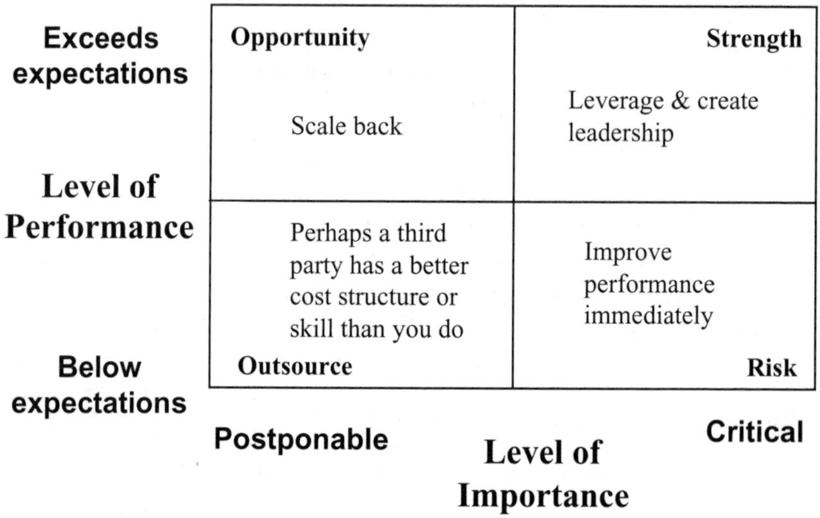

Level of Performance		
Exceeds expectations	Opportunity Scale back	**Strength** Leverage & create leadership
Below expectations	Perhaps a third party has a better cost structure or skill than you do Outsource	Improve performance immediately **Risk**
	Postponable	**Critical**
	Level of Importance	

back and spend less on that kind of work. These activity costs would be in the upper-left quadrant.

Although most attributes are subjectively scored or graded by managers and employees, when the scores are grouped together, the subjectivity begins to become directionally reliable (presuming there was no bias in the scoring of every single attribute). As a result, the attributed costs introduce an emotionally compelling force to consider taking actions, as in the example above.

Here are a few tips related to ABC/M attributes:

- Keep the definitions concise.
- Allow employees to develop the classifications—and, more importantly, to classify (or distribute) their own activities with the attributes.
- Be clear that attributes are tagged to activities—not to the people who perform the work.
- Constantly ask, "Can the high value-adding activities be done more quickly or at a lower cost?"

- Determine if low-value adding activities can be eliminated or at least minimized.

Some analytical types of people are uncomfortable with any form of sub-jective grading and prefer rigorous rule-based methods to determine which attribute score is applicable. In this area, they can lighten up and just go with the flow. Yes, the scorings may come from some snap judgments of employ-ees and other process participants. But the resulting view of the costs is just a starting point for asking more questions. Don't make the data collection effort too large an obstacle.

Since in ABC the activity costs will "pile up" into their final cost objects, and the attribute costs can tag along, one can get another view of attributes now located in the outputs. Figure 5-3 illustrates an individual product or service line that is losing money in an environment where fees or prices are charged for usage. The product's or service-line's revenues are below its

FIGURE 5-3 Attributes Accumulate in Cost Objects Too

ABC/M allows numerous "attributes" to grade each activity that then trace into products. Attributes are used in multi-dimensional cost analysis.

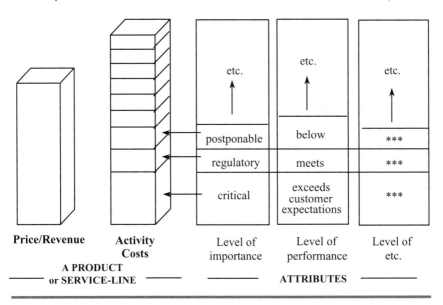

costs. It becomes apparent that as low-value added costs are removed, the financial loss (or under-recovery) for this product or service-line is reduced. The lower product or service-line costs would reflect the improvements.

Here is another way of thinking about this. When attributes are tagged to activities, each cost object will consume multiple grades of a select attribute. As a result, the cost objects will reflect different blends relative to each other. An analogy would be the different gallonage (cost amount) of different colored paint (an attribute's different score) being poured (activity driver) into an empty paint can (cost object). As each empty can is filled, the color shade of paint will be different, even if the cans are filled to comparable levels (same amount of cost).

In this way, attributes can reveal a different mix of value or performance. For example, there can be a major difference between two products with roughly the same unit cost. That is, one color of paint may cost $50.00 per gallon, with $15.00 of that total coming from a dozen activities scored as "below expectations" performance. Another color may also be $50.00 per gallon, but with only $5.00 of that total coming from two "below expectations" activities. Armed with this information, the product managers of these colors now have more insights to adjust their products' costs by adding or lowering services or price. In this way, the attributes are being used as in benchmarking to compare and contrast—and then to focus.

Attributes make ABC/M data come alive to some people. And when the attributed ABC/M data are exported into on-line analytical processing (OLAP) software and executive information system (EIS) tools, they can have a very stimulating impact on users.

APPLYING ABC/M ATTRIBUTES FOR QUALITY MANAGEMENT

Although leaders in business, commerce, and government have strived for excellence through the ages, quality management has come into its own only in recent decades. More recently it has evolved into the Six Sigma methodology. In the effort to gain competitive edge in both foreign and domestic markets, senior managers have been forced to focus on increasing customer satisfaction while reducing costs. This era has spawned a raft of quality enhancement programs, most prominently Total Quality Management (TQM).

A Renewed Emphasis on TQM

There are and will continue to be endless debates about which management techniques matter and are effective—and which don't matter. The prevailing consensus is, however, that strategy and mission are essential; after strategy and mission are defined by senior management, the core processes take over to execute the strategy. The core processes are now accepted as the mechanism for delivering the *value* defined by the strategy. Time, flexibility, quality, service, and cost are all derivatives of the business process. They are inextricably braided and should not be addressed in isolation from one another.

A simple equation for value is Value = Performance/Cost, where Performance loosely refers to the right type of results aligned with the organization's strategy. With this math, Value increases if the numerator goes up or the denominator goes down.

In some ways, executives feel boxed in, given that the amount of resources available is usually budget-constrained. They are realizing that achieving their strategic goals will require clear visibility and relentless management of their costs. TQM (in conjunction with ABC/M) will be essential for managing these costs.

21st Century COQ: Technology Meets Relevance

Some of the deficiencies of the past that prevented TQM from realizing its greater potential are being solved by attention to:

- Linkage of TQM data to enterprise data
- Customer-driven requirements for quality and satisfaction
- Cost pressures to minimize costs of quality (COQ), including costs related both to conformance and non-conformance
- Integration of problem-solving methodologies with fact-based data

A vision is emerging that links TQM to supply-chain management and e-commerce (B2B). As the digital economy evolves, there will be an absolute need for transactional accuracy. E-commerce communications are obviously intolerant of the most minor errors.

In addition, a force that has historically pushed an interest in quality has been competition. And this force continues. For government agencies, the pressure comes from the threat of privatization or outsourcing. Senior managers are attracted to a process that concurrently improves customer satisfaction and reduces costs relative to competitors or alternative sources.

TQM can be viewed as an approach to gaining and sustaining a competitive lead.

Why is Traditional Accounting Failing TQM?

One of the obstacles affecting TQM initiatives (and other initiatives as well) has been shortcomings of the financial accounting field. Part of the problem is the traditional emphasis of accounting on external reporting requirements. Fortunately, contributions from the balanced scorecard movement are helping reduce the focus on these "lagging indicator" financial result measures. The balanced scorecard is placing greater emphasis on non-financial "leading indicator" performance measures. This topic is covered in Chapter 6.

Part of the problem is the accountants themselves and their dependence on a flawed financial accounting system. This book appeals to the accountants to understand their role in the collection, validation, and reporting of information better. As mentioned several times, cost data in the traditional format (e.g., salaries, supplies, depreciation) are structurally deficient for decision support, including measuring COQ. The accounting community has been slow to understand and accept this problem.

It will become increasingly important for the quality professional to focus on the quality of cost as well as the cost of quality. That is, it is as important to ensure that any money spent on the organization produces that money's equivalent in value for the customer and taxpayer as it is to measure how much money is lost due to poor quality. This is a before-investment view in contrast to an after-the-fact view.

With this introduction to the background and issues related to the quality movement, the next sections discuss issues related to measuring the financial dimensions of quality.

WHY INTRODUCE FINANCIAL COSTS TO ANALYZE QUALITY?

To some, it is intuitively obvious that better management of quality ultimately leads to goodness, which in turn should lead to the improved financial health of an organization. Perhaps some of these same people have difficulty imagining a bridge of linkages that can equate quality improvements to exactly measured costs. They operate with a faith that if you simply improve quality, good things—such as happier service-recipients and greater productivity—will automatically fall into place.

Other types of people prefer having fact-based data and reasonable estimates with which to evaluate decisions and to prioritize spending. These types of people do believe in quality programs, but in complex organizations with scarce idle resources, they prefer to be more certain that they know where it is best to spend the organization's discretionary money.

Some quality managers have become skeptical about measuring the costs of quality (COQ). They have seen increasing regulations and standards, such as the ISO 9000 series, where installing any form of COQ measurement was perceived as more of a compliance exercise to satisfy documentation requirements to become "registered" than a benefit to improve performance.

Some perceive quality and cost as an investment choice implying a tradeoff decision. This thinking presumes that achieving better quality somehow costs more and requires more effort. This is not necessarily true. If quality programs are properly installed, productivity can be improved while also raising customer satisfaction. These two combined eventually lead to a more effective and better performing organization.

The broader notion of quality is well beyond classic TQM as simply being conformance to standards. For producers, it is no longer enough just to make and deliver quality goods and services. The deliverer must be a quality organization as well. The intent of Six Sigma is to refocus on economics as the driver of quality improvements.

The trick to realizing the benefits from Six Sigma is identifying the vital few projects that will have the impact to keep the organization on its path to Six Sigma. Six Sigma TQM projects are like the stocks in an investment portfolio: They must produce returns. Specific cost savings or productivity improvements are assigned by senior management, and "black belt" projects are defined to achieve the goals. Qualified employees are intensively trained as black-belt project managers. These individuals are next assigned several black-belt projects. The organization then relies on the black-belt managers and programs to achieve the results and realize the savings.

In simple language, TQM can be thought of as involving all employees, and occasionally trading partners, in continuous improvement through teamwork. The universally accepted goals of TQM are lower costs, higher revenues, delighted customers, and empowered employees.

Almost every organization now realizes that not having the highest quality is not even an option. High quality is simply an entry ticket for the opportunity to even exist to provide services or to compete if your customers have choices for sources. Attaining high quality is now a must. Anything less than high quality will lead to an organization's terminal collapse. In short, high quality is now a presumed prerequisite for an organization to continue to exist. The stakes have gotten much higher.

HOW DO YOU CATEGORIZE DIFFERENT QUALITY COSTS?

To some, quality costs are very visible and obvious. To others, quality costs are understated. They believe that much of the quality-related costs are hidden and go unreported.

There are *hidden* financial costs beyond those associated with traditional, obvious quality costs. Examples of obvious quality-related costs are rework costs, excess scrap material costs, warranty costs, or field repair expenses. These are typically costs resulting from errors. Error-related costs are somewhat easily measured *directly* from the financial system. Spending amounts are recorded in the accountant's fund accounting or general ledger system using the "chart-of-accounts." Sometimes the quality-related costs include the expenses of an entire department, such as an inspection department that arguably exists solely as being quality-related. However, as organizations flatten and de-layer and employees multi-task more, it is rare that an entire department focuses exclusively on quality.

The *hidden* poor quality costs are less obvious and more difficult to measure. For example, a hidden cost would be those hours of a few employees' time sorting through paperwork resulting from a record-keeping or reporting error. Although these employees do not work in a quality department that is dedicated to quality-related activities, such as inspection or rework, that portion of their workday was definitely quality-related. These costs are not reflected in the chart-of-accounts of the accounting system. That is why they are referred to as being *hidden* costs.

Providing employee teams with visibility of both *obvious* and *hidden* quality-related costs can be valuable for performance improvement. Using the data, employees can gain insights into the causes of problems. The hidden and traditional costs can be broadly categorized as:

- **Error-free costs**—Costs unrelated to planning of, controlling of, correcting of, or improving of quality. These are the did-it-right-the-first-time (nicknamed "dirtfoot") costs.

- **Costs of quality (COQ)**—Costs that could disappear if all processes were error-free and if all products and services were defect-free. COQ can be subcategorized as:
  - *Costs of conformance*—Costs related to prevention and predictive appraisal to meet requirements.
  - *Costs of non-conformance*—Costs related to internal or external failure to meet requirements, including defective appraisal work. The distinction between internal and external is that internal failure costs are detected prior to the shipment or receipt of service by the service-recipient or customer. In contrast, external failure costs usually result from discovery by the service-recipient or customer.

An oversimplified definition of COQ is the costs associated with avoiding, finding, making, and repairing defects and errors (presuming that all defects and errors are detected). COQ represents the difference between the actual costs and what the reduced costs would be if there were no substandard service levels, failures, or defects.

Simple examples of these cost categories for a magazine or book publisher might be as follows:

- *Error-free*—"First time through" work without a flaw
- *Prevention*—Training courses for the proofreaders or preventive maintenance on the printing presses
- *Appraisal*—Proofreading
- *Internal failure*—Unplanned printing press downtime or corrections of typographical errors
- *External failure*—Rework resulting from a complaint by a service-recipient or customer

In principle, as the COQ expenses are reduced, they can be converted into budget surpluses or spent on higher value requirements.

Let's revisit Figure 5-1. It illustrates how "attributes" can be tagged or scored into increasingly finer segments of the error-free and COQ subcategories. Attributes are tagged to individual activities for which the activities will have already have been costed using ABC/M. Hence, the subcategory costs can be reported with an audit trail back to which resources they came from. Each of the subattributes can be further subdivided with deeper "indented" classifications.

Since 100 percent of the resource costs can be assigned to activities, then 100 percent of the activities can be tagged with one of the COQ attributes—the activities have already been costed by ABC/M. The attribute groupings and summary roll-ups are automatically costed as well.

Life would be nice in an error-free world, and an organization's overall costs would be substantially lower relative to where they are today. However, just like an individual's natural body fat and cholesterol levels, all organizations make mistakes and errors. They will always experience some level of error. This is human nature. However, the goal is to manage mistakes and their impact. COQ simply serves to communicate fact-based data—in terms of money—to enable focusing and prioritizing.

As previously mentioned, unless an entire department's existence is fully dedicated to one of the COQ subcategories or coincidentally an isolated chart-of-account expense account fully applies to a COQ category, then most of the COQ spending is hidden. That is, the financial system cannot report those costs.

A danger exists if only a fraction of the quality-related costs are measured and their amount is represented as the total quality costs—this is a significant understating of the actual costs. And, unfortunately, there are as many ways of hiding quality costs as there are people with imagination. Organizations that hide their complete COQ from themselves continue to risk deceiving themselves with an illusion that they have effective management. Activity-based cost management is an obvious approach to make visible the missing COQ amount of spending.

Benefits from Including Total Expenditures When Measuring Quality

There are several benefits from starting the measurement by assuming a 100 percent inclusion of the total expenditures, and then subsequently segmenting those expenses between the error-free costs and the quality-related COQ:

- **Reduces debate**—With traditional COQ measures, people can endlessly debate whether a borderline activity is a true COQ, such as scrap produced during product development that may arguably be expected. By including such a cost as COQ, it may inflate a measure that is of high interest. By excluding it, that expense melts away without any visibility into all the other total expenditures of the organization. It can be tempting for controversial costs to be excluded as a quality-related cost category. By starting with the 100 percent expenditure pool, *every* cost will fall into *some* category and always be visible. Each type of cost can always be reclassified later on, as people better understand how to use the data.

- **Increases employee focus**—By developing classifications into which all costs can be slotted, organizations should focus much less on their methods of measurement and much more on their organization's problems and how to overcome them.
- **Integrates with the same data used by the governing authority**—When traditional and obvious COQ information is used, only portions of the total expenditures are selected for inclusion. This invites debate about arbitrariness or ambiguity. However, when the 100 percent total expenditures are included, the COQ plus error-free costs exactly reconcile with the same data used by executive management, the governing authority, or—for commercial organizations—the board of directors. There is no longer any suspicion that some COQ has been left out or that the COQ data are not anchored in reality. By starting with 100 percent expenditures, the only debate can be misclassification, not omission.

The capture of COQ can be further refined if it is worth it for the organization.

COQ: Both Good and Poor Quality

Some equate quality-related work activities only with problems and reactionary efforts by employees to fix things. But with COQ, additional quality-related work activities (e.g., inspection) that are not directly associated with poor quality are included as part of the broad COQ category. In short, one can think of COQ's costs of conformance work as *good* quality COQ and the costs of non-conformance as *poor* quality COQ. However, both good and poor COQ when combined are costs of quality that may not be incurred at all in a perfect world. In short, prevention and appraisal costs are worth measuring.

This broader picture of COQ provides much greater visibility and thereby ensures that the quality management projects and programs are efficiently run. That is, including the costs that are intended to prevent potential problems can ensure that there is not overspending too far beyond the spending required to satisfy the service-recipient or customer. It is natural for organizations to be interested in failure-related costs. These usually attract the most attention. But prevention and appraisal costs are not that difficult to identify and report, and they should not be excluded from the visibility of managers.

When making decisions, the universally popular costs-vs.-benefits test can be applied with COQ data. If either subcategory of COQ is excessive, it draws down profits for commercial companies or draws down resources in government agencies that could have been better deployed on higher value-added activities elsewhere.

GOALS AND USES FOR THE COQ INFORMATION

An organization should not invest its time in constructing a COQ measurement system if it is destined to be just another way for some employees to spin numbers. The bottom line message is: Don't start measuring COQ information if you won't use it!

In short, the uses of a COQ measurement system can include (1) favorably influencing employee attitudes toward quality management by quantifying the financial impact of changes, and (2) assisting in prioritizing improvement opportunities. The premise for even bothering to implement COQ is based on the following logic:

- For any failure, there is a root cause.
- Causes for failure are preventable.
- Prevention is cheaper than fixing problems after they occur.

If you accept the premise that it is always less expensive to do the job right the first time than to do it over, then the rationale for quality management and using COQ to give a quality program concrete and fact-based data should be apparent:

1. Directly attack failure costs with the goal of driving them to zero.
2. Spend time and money in the appropriate prevention activities, not fads, to effect improvements.
3. Reduce appraisal costs according to results that are achieved.
4. Continuously evaluate and redirect prevention efforts to gain further improvement.

Figure 5-4 illustrates the direction for which quality-related costs can be managed. Ideally, all four COQ cost categories should be reduced, but one may initially need to prudently increase the cost of prevention in order to

FIGURE 5-4 Driving COQ Downward

ABC/M supports quality initiatives by allowing "ownership" of the process a level below departments—with work activities.

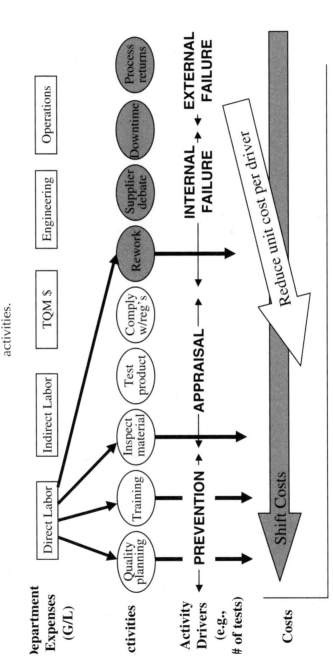

dramatically decrease the costs of and reduced penalties paid for nonconformance. This makes COQ more than just an accounting scheme; it becomes a financial investment justification tool.

A general set of corrective operating principles is that as failures are revealed, for example via complaints from service-recipients, the root causes should be eliminated with corrective actions. A general rule-of-thumb is that the nearer the failure is to the end-user, the more expensive it is to correct. The flip side is that it becomes less expensive—overall—to fix problems earlier in the business process. As failure costs are reduced, appraisal efforts can also be reduced in a rational manner.

Figure 5-5 illustrates the midway point of a fictitious manufacturer's COQ as nonconformance-related costs are displaced by conformance-related costs.

The figure illustrates a more desirable end goal for our fictitious manufacturer. Not only are nonconformance costs significantly reduced, but the level of prevention and inspection costs, which some classify as non-value added, are also reduced. The $20,000 of COQ has been reduced by $12,000, to $8,000. The reward for this good work has meant more requests for orders and higher sales without any changes in manpower. The error-free costs have risen by the same $12,000, from $80,000 to $92,000.

Next we will discuss how the COQ can be measured.

QUANTIFYING THE MAGNITUDE OF THE COSTS OF QUALITY

Now comes the hard part. Regardless of what the intended purpose for the quality-related data will be and regardless of how precise or accurate the data need to be to meet that purpose, at some point in time you have to come to grips with quantifying the COQ. And that means collecting, validating, and reporting the data.

COQ Measurement System

The more formal *COQ measurement system* provides continuous results. In contrast to a one-time assessment, it requires involvement by employees who participate in the business and administrative processes. More importantly, these employees need to be motivated to spend the energy and time, apart from their regular responsibilities, to submit and use the data.

Commercial ABC/M software products were designed for frequent repeated updating. For such a COQ system to be sustained longer-term, the

FIGURE 5-5 COQ Histograms—Before and After

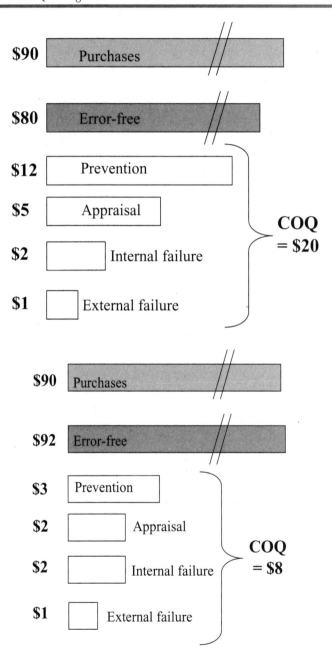

FIGURE 5-6 Typical Examples of Cost of Quality Components

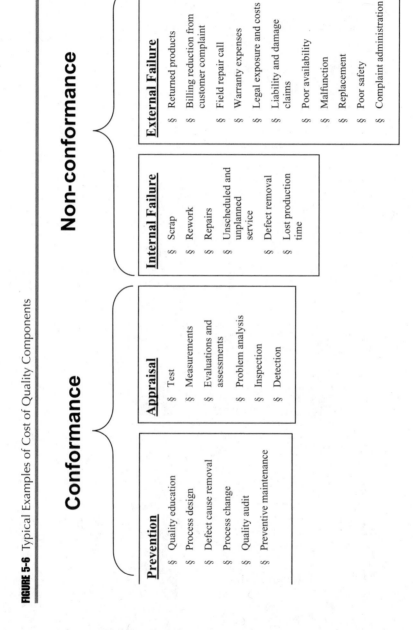

Conformance

Prevention

§ Quality education

§ Process design

§ Defect cause removal

§ Process change

§ Quality audit

§ Preventive maintenance

Appraisal

§ Test

§ Measurements

§ Evaluations and assessments

§ Problem analysis

§ Inspection

§ Detection

Non-conformance

Internal Failure

§ Scrap

§ Rework

§ Repairs

§ Unscheduled and unplanned service

§ Defect removal

§ Lost production time

External Failure

§ Returned products

§ Billing reduction from customer complaint

§ Field repair call

§ Warranty expenses

§ Legal exposure and costs

§ Liability and damage claims

§ Poor availability

§ Malfunction

§ Replacement

§ Poor safety

§ Complaint administration

system requires senior management's support and interest as well as genuinely perceived utility by users of the data to solve problems.

Continuous COQ measurement systems require a greater amount of effort, expertise, and maturity. Many organizations underestimate the maturity requirement. It is advisable that the organization gradually implement its system through a combination of: (1) measuring selected and local areas where relatively higher benefits are more likely to be realized, and (2) starting at more summarized levels of data before decomposing the levels of detail to the more granular work task level. The level of detail should only be relatively greater in the areas where there are anticipated opportunities. The levels of depth and detail can be raised or lowered as problems arise and recede following resolution.

Decomposing COQ Categories

In effect, the technique for calculating a reasonably accurate COQ is to apply ABC/M and ABC/M's attribute capability. Figure 5-6 reveals a list of categories for work activities that are one additional level below the four major categories of COQ. Each of these subcategories can be tagged against the ABC/M costs. This provides far greater and more reliable visibility of COQ without the great effort required by traditional cost accounting methods.

> **"Man, at bottom, is not entirely guilty, since he did not begin history, nor entirely innocent, since he continues it."**
> —Albert Camus, Algerian-born French novelist, *Notebooks I* (1935–42)

Chapter 6

Performance Management Using Strategy Maps and the Balanced Scorecard

"A new scientific truth does not triumph by convincing its opponents and making them see the light, but rather because its opponents eventually die out, and a new generation grows up that is familiar with it."
—Max Planck, physicist who was originator of the Quantum Theory,
The Philosophy of Physics (1936)

"Those who cannot remember the past are condemned to repeat it."
—George Santayana, Spanish-born American philosopher,
The Life of Reason (1905–06)

F YOU DO an Internet search with a search engine like Google or Yahoo for "performance+based+government," you may be surprised by the large number of hits. Performance and accountability are now mainstream practices in government, as explained in Chapter 1. But there is confusion about the new term *performance management*. Are organizations defining it too narrowly—as simply better strategy, budgeting, and control? It is much more than that. And how does ABC/M apply to it? And how do such concepts as the balanced scorecard fit with it? This chapter will clarify these issues.

With performance management, governments can proactively manage their organizational performance and programs by analyzing and predicting performance in order to optimize effectiveness, by calculating true costs and efficiency, by adjusting resource utilization, and by monitoring performance by using current and accurate information. They can use accurate and current performance information to develop and justify budgets. They can also promote a culture change to one that widely accepts and adopts performance management as a discipline.

Agencies can expect to improve program execution by focusing on communication of results, performance optimization, insights on where to adjust priorities and resource allocations, cost reduction via cost analysis and management, and collaboration to collectively improve performance. They can consider the ability to predict performance and do what-if analyses.

ORGANIZATIONAL DIRECTION, TRACTION, AND SPEED

Direction, traction, and speed. When you are driving a car, you *directly* control all three. You can turn the steering wheel to change direction. You can downshift the gears to go up a steep hill to get more traction. You can step on the gas pedal to gain more speed.

Senior executives who manage organizations do not have *direct* control over results and outcomes. Executives can only achieve improvements by influencing other people—namely, their managers' employee teams. Employees do not always do what you tell them to do. And sometimes they do the opposite of what you tell them to! This is a major frustration for the executive team. The team is usually very capable at defining a good strategy. Its frustration is to successfully execute the strategy.

The fallout of this problem is career impacting. Evidence from the commercial sector indicates that it is a tough time to be a chief executive. Surveys by Chicago-based employee recruiting firm Challenger, Gray & Christmas, Inc., repeatedly reveal increasing rates of job turnover at the executive level compared to a decade ago.[1] In complex and overhead-intensive organizations, where constant redirection to a changing landscape is essential, the main cause for executive job turnover is the failure to execute the strategy. High officials in government cannot avoid similar pressures and consequences.

There is a big difference between formulating a strategy and executing it. What is the answer for executives who need to expand their focus beyond cost control and toward value creation and other more strategic directives? How do they regain control of the direction, traction, and speed of their organization? Performance management (PM) provides managers and employee teams at all levels with the ability to move like a laser beam toward the senior team's defined strategy.

One cause for failure to implement the strategy is that managers and employee teams typically have no clue what their organization's strategy is. Most employees, if asked, cannot articulate their organization's strategy. The implication of this is significant. If managers and employee teams do not understand their organization's strategy, how can the executive team expect employees to know how what they do each week or month contributes to

---

[1]Webber, Alan; "CEO Bashing has gone too far;" USA Today; June 3, 2003; p. 15A

the achievement of the strategy? Employees can effectively implement a strategy only when they clearly understand the strategy and how they contribute to its achievement.

Further, a strategy is never static; rather, it is dynamic and based on a constantly changing environment. When executives adjust and shift their strategy, they find that their employees typically continue to perform without much change. The massive inertia of the existing and usually unchanging measures forces employees to continue to do what they have been doing in the past. A change in direction may not happen despite the executives' proclamations and appeals to managers.

The executives are not particularly interested in employees just getting better at what they have been doing. They want employees to change their priorities. Getting people to focus on the right things is much more important than improving on things that don't matter. Everyone recognizes the saying "What you measure is what you get." Measures drive behavior.

Performance management resolves these problems by communicating strategy to employees in a way they can understand and by aligning the behavior of the workforce with the strategy using carefully selected metrics—and much more. It is important to include managerial accounting information, enhanced with ABC/M principles, as one of the components of the performance management portfolio. It adds the language of money to support decisions that may be imbalanced without considering true costs and the visibility to what causes them.

WHAT IS PERFORMANCE MANAGEMENT?

A simple definition of *performance management* is "the translation of plans into results—execution." It is the process of *managing an organization's strategy*. The good news is that performance management is not a new concept or methodology that everyone has to learn. It is simply the integration of existing improvement methodologies, like Six Sigma or balanced scorecards, that managers and employee teams are already familiar with (or at least have heard of). The problem has been that most organizations implement these in isolation of each other. It is as if the project teams operate in parallel universes. Performance management links multiple methodologies. Most organizations were doing performance management many years before it became the new buzzword. What is different is that, with PM, the puzzle pieces of multiple improvement methodologies can be combined for synergy to accelerate achieving higher value. Everyone has known that the pieces fit together, but no one has had the puzzle box cover to see the complete picture.

PM is sometimes confused with a human resources and personnel system. It is much more encompassing. PM describes the methodologies, metrics, processes, software tools, and systems that manage the performance of an organization. PM is overarching. It cascades down from the highest level executives through the organization and its processes. From the top desk to the desktop. To sum up its benefit, it enhances broad cross-functional involvement in decision-making by providing tremendously greater visibility with accurate, reliable, and relevant information—all aimed at executing an organization's strategy.

To minimize anyone's confusion, no single PM methodology exists. PM spans the complete management planning and control cycle. Think of it as a broad end-to-end union of solutions including three major purposes: collecting data, transforming and modeling the data into information, and web-reporting it to users and decision-makers. Many of PM's component methodologies have existed for decades or have become recently popular, such as lean management. Some of PM's components, such as activity-based cost management, are partially or crudely implemented in many organizations. PM refines them so that they work in better harmony with PM's other components. Early adopters have deployed parts of PM, but few have deployed its full vision.

The term "knowledge management" is frequently mentioned in business articles. It sounds like something an organization needs, but the concept is somewhat vague and does not offer any direction for improving decisions. In contrast, the main thrust of PM is to make better decisions that will be evidenced, and ultimately measured, by outputs and outcomes.

MANAGEMENT'S QUEST FOR THAT ELUSIVE MAGIC PILL IMPROVEMENT PROGRAM

Executive management's greatest challenge is in communicating its strategy to its workforce. An integrated suite of methodologies and tools—the PM solutions suite—provides the mechanism to bridge the business intelligence gap between the executive team's vision and employees' actions.

Many organizations, however, jump from improvement program to program hoping that each new one may provide that big, elusive, step in organizational improvement. However, most managers would acknowledge that pulling one lever for improvement rarely results in a substantial change—particularly a long-term sustained change. The key to improving is integrating and balancing *multiple* improvement methodologies.

As mentioned, PM tightly integrates the organizational improvement and analytic methodologies that managers and employees are already familiar with. These include strategy mapping, balanced scorecards, costing (including activity-based cost management), budgeting, demand forecasting, and resource capacity requirements. These methodologies fuel other core solutions, such as supply chain management (SCM), enterprise risk management, and human capital management (HCM) systems, as well as Six Sigma. Admittedly, it is quite a stew, but the methodologies and solutions all blend together.

In the end, organizations need top-down direction setting and guidance with bottom-up execution. PM makes this happen by converting plans into results. PM integrates operational and financial information into a single decision-support and planning framework. And based on a common database platform, it provides one version of the truth rather than disparate, inconsistent data that annoy both employees and the people they serve. Simply put, PM helps an organization understand how it works as a whole.

THE ROLES OF STRATEGY MAPS AND THE BALANCED SCORECARD

Leadership's role is to determine strategic direction and motivate people to go in that direction. However, senior executives are challenged and usually frustrated when it comes to cascading their strategy down through their organization. Executives and management consultants have hailed the balanced scorecard as the new religion to resolve this frustration. It serves to communicate executive strategy to employees and also to help navigate direction by shaping the alignment of employees and their priorities with the strategy. The balanced scorecard bridges the substantial gap between the raw data spewed out from operations transaction–based systems, such as its enterprise resource planning (ERP) or a comparable purpose system, and the organization's strategy. In addition, it provides immediate and visual feedback through graphical dashboards that display differences between actual performance and the targets set by management.

Despite much publicity about the balanced scorecard, the strategy map intended to precede the development of the scorecard is considered to be much more important. Sadly, some organizations neglect the important step of creating a strategy map, so they wind up monitoring what they *can* measure rather than what they *should* measure. Strategy maps serve as a guide with signposts and guardrails, enabling leadership to motivate people. Strategy maps explain high-level causes and effects with if-then logic, helping executives choose the best strategic objectives followed by the supporting projects and action items that will help the company attain them.

PERFORMANCE MANAGEMENT IS AN ITERATIVE PROCESS

Similar to the popular plan-do-check-act (PDCA) iterative cycle made popular by W. Edwards Deming, the famous quality improvement expert, performance management also has an iterative cycle. As Figure 6-1 illustrates, you can imagine performance management as a wheel with three arcs: focus, communicate, and collaborate. The figure also shows how fact-based managerial accounting data and operational data provide input to the performance management wheel.

1. **Focus**—The process of managing strategy begins with *focus*. You never have enough money or resources to chase every opportunity. You have to think in terms of being continuously limited in terms of scarce and precious resources and time, so focus is key and strategy yields focus. In this important initial step, senior management, drawing on its vision and mission, defines and continuously adjusts its strategy. Next, by mapping cause-and-effect relationships with its strategy map, senior management defines strategic objectives and higher impact action steps and projects that will achieve those objectives. Organizations can ideally turn big goals into small, manageable projects that can actually be accomplished.

   The first step in this translation is to create a set of vision-based strategic themes that will bridge the gap between the existing state of operations and the desired state. These themes then set priorities and organize the work of the organization. By focusing on critical areas, everyone can identify the true sources of failure, as well as the best practices that lead to future success. The *strategy map* is the key tool for communicating the strategy.

2. **Communicate**—The process of managing strategy continues with *communication*. The key is for senior management to articulate its strategy

FIGURE 6.1 The Performance Management Framework

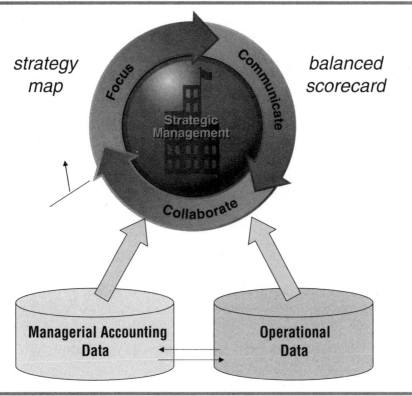

to employees in a way they can understand. Along with articulating strategy comes the all-important feedback to employee teams. The balanced scorecard is the key tool for feedback on how well the strategy is being achieved and for taking corrective actions. Monitoring the dials is not enough. The dials must be moved.

Think of scorecards as the drive gears of the strategy map. Think of scorecards as having carefully selected and defined indicators and measures, each weighted to reflect their relative level of importance. Think of scorecards as a set of chainlinks of the strategy map's strategic objectives, where each chainlink uses if-then relationships with leading and lagging measures to drive work efforts to align with the executive team's mission and vision. If properly implemented, a scorecard enables all employees and managers to be able to quickly answer a powerful question: "How am I doing on what is important?" By integrating, distributing, and analyzing enterprise-wide information, an organization gains the power to act on this information.

3. **Collaborate**—The process of managing strategy ends with *collaboration*. By providing strategy understanding and ongoing feedback, the organization taps into the collective knowledge of its employees and unleashes each person's potential. E-mail discussion threads, generated directly from the scorecard, can be created for faster consensus and truly make executing strategy everyone's job. Employees do not need to wait for instructions from their hierarchical managers above them, but rather can actively make decisions. Collaboration in this sense is all about collective dialog.

Ultimately, executives can move beyond the traditional practice of focusing on backward-looking results by using scorecards and strategy maps to focus on their organizations' strategic objectives in the areas of learning, growth, innovation, process, and service levels. They can focus on leading indicators, measured during the period, that ultimately result in the organization's performance in terms of outcomes.

WORK ACTIVITIES AND THEIR COSTS ARE FOUNDATIONAL TO A PERFORMANCE MANAGEMENT SYSTEM

A major benefit of PM is that when everyone gets the same facts, they generally reach the same conclusions on how to act.

What makes today's PM systems so effective is that work activities—what people, equipment, and assets do—are the foundations of PM reporting, analysis, and planning. These work activities are the keys in defining the actions and projects essential for meeting the strategic objectives constructed in the strategy maps and measuring the outcomes highlighted in scorecards. Activity-based cost management (ABC/M) systems are used to accurately measure work activities, such as process costs, output costs, and service levels. ABC/M applies its data for operational cost management—with a subset of ABC/M's measures serving as key performance indicators (KPIs) used in the balanced scorecard.

The term *performance management* is now widely accepted by the IT research analyst firms, who proclaim that combining the components of PM in a unified approach makes more sense than pursuing and operating individual methods in isolation. PM helps to orchestrate an organization's priorities and efforts to improve its alignment with its strategic objectives, resulting in better direction, traction, and speed—and most importantly, sustaining improved performance longer term. PM provides managers and employees with the power to know how to act proactively, before events occur or proceed so far that they demand a reaction.

THE QUEST FOR A COMPLETE SOLUTION USING BUSINESS INTELLIGENCE

Organizations that are enlightened enough to recognize the importance and value of their data often have difficulty in actually *realizing* that value. Their data is often disconnected, inconsistent, and inaccessible because it results from too many non-integrated single-point solutions. These organizations have valuable, untapped data that is hidden in the reams of transactional data they collect daily. Unlocking the potential information trapped in mountains of data has been, until recently, a relatively difficult task to accomplish effectively.

Fortunately, innovation in data storage technology is now significantly outpacing progress in computer processing power, heralding a new era in which creating vast pools of digital data is becoming the preferred route. The pools of data are then coupled with powerful data mining and analytical solutions, including predictive analytics, since making decisions for the future has become more important than reacting to reported measures of the past. This type of functionality has been named by the information technology research firms *business intelligence*. It is based on locating transactional data and other information from disparate data sources into a central repository, typically called an *integrated information platform*, and then applying powerful statistical and filtering analytics to support decision-making.

Rising specialization, complexity, and value-adding services cause the need for more, not less, PM. Despite the impact that technology and more flexible work practices and policies have on continuously changing organizational structures, without ongoing adaptation the correct work at acceptable service levels will not get done. All employees must have some accountability to manage for improved results. Somehow their collective performance must be coordinated. Creating a united and sustained performance is a challenging part of management. PM aids in accomplishing this goal.

HOW DO YOU KNOW IF YOU ARE PERFORMING WELL?

Let's now dig deeper to understand how to design and deploy strategy maps and balanced scorecards.

One of the mysteries of the workplace continues to be how to support a manager's claim, "We did well last quarter." The normal follow-up question is "How do you know?" Organizations have a sea of collected data, but struggle making sense of it all. Organizations are generally data rich and information poor. Attempts are being made to fix this with data warehouses and number crunching software. But are those technologies simply bandages and medications, or are they a real cure?

When a manager states, "We did well," how can anyone detect if the *entire* organization benefited from whatever that department did when it supposedly "did well?" How does management know how much of that department's work and outcomes advanced the organization toward realizing its strategy, and how much was errant work on less relevant pursuits or pet projects?

One way to answer these questions is to improve the organization's measurement system itself. As discussed, strategy maps and scorecards are excellent tools in the quest for a strategy-supporting measurement system that links to operations and tactics. These are management tools that establish strong relations between the vital areas of the strategy and the organization's measures.

Strategy maps are like geographical maps that visually aid in understanding how one gets from point A (the present capabilities, organization, and focus of the enterprise) to point B (the future, desired capabilities, organization, and focus), as laid out in the executive team's vision, mission, and strategy plan. Scorecards are like a pilot's cockpit, enabling managers and employee teams to navigate and steer to the destinations. Scorecards without strategy maps may lead to failure. How do you know if what was measured as KPIs reflected the strategic intent of the executive team? That is, when scorecards are built and reported in isolation, there is no direct linkage to strategy. As its name suggests, a scorecard contains the key and relevant performance measures. A scorecard is like the coxswain of a racing boat crew who periodically shouts critical information to the rowers. The scorecard's critical role is that it puts the KPIs in the context of the strategy.

Strategy maps and scorecards go hand in hand. Once created, they embody the strategic intent of the executive team and communicate to employees and managers both the strategic objectives the organization intends to meet as well as the critical KPI measures of success for attaining those objectives—be they strategic, tactical, or operational measures. A way to think of this is that the organization's vision and mission statement answer the question, "Where do we want to go?" whereas the strategy map and scorecard answer, "How are we going to get there?" Through continuous reporting of the actual scores against the KPI targets, an organization is kept on track. Some of the KPI measures, strategic or operational, lend themselves to monitoring from an activity-based cost management (ABC/M) system. ABC/M as a supplement to populate scorecards with measures will be discussed later in this chapter.

WHAT IMPEDES ORGANIZATIONAL PERFORMANCE?

Why is it that so many organizations exhibit so much energy but never seem to get much traction? And why is it that those few organizations that get traction seem to drift off course from their strategy? Four problems are:

1. **Lots of energy, but poor traction.** Employees often spin their wheels without much to show for their work. I genuinely believe that most employees do show up at work to put in a good day's effort. But it is not usually clear to them what priorities are most important.
2. **Poor alignment.** As earlier described, few if any employees truly know and understand what their organization's strategies are, as defined by their senior management. As a result, increasingly empowered employee teams may be selecting the wrong projects to work on, despite their good intentions.
3. **Too many measures and wrong measures.** Organizations often monitor the wrong measures. Also, they typically judge employees by monitoring their results with too many measures, several of which are outside the employees' influence and control. How fair is it for you or your team to be judged by measures that are affected by the performance of others? Scorecard principles suggest minimizing employee team mea-

sures to roughly three or four at the most—only the vital few measures, rather than the trivial many.

4. **A focus on historical financial budget measures.** Performance information is typically reported too late, is too financially weighted, and is not predictive. Most measurement systems foster reactive behavior, often focusing on cost variances with budgets and funding appropriations. Employees and managers are swamped with too many after-the-fact measures that inadequately summarize too much information.

The evolving management philosophy of the balanced scorecard[2] has immediate appeal because of its fundamental message: Excessive focus on financial budget cost variances is unbalanced because *nonfinancial* measures influence eventual outcomes. Many organizations monitor and analyze their financial results with much more energy than they put into understanding the influencing metrics that lead to those financial results. Nonfinancial measures, such as those that monitor the satisfaction and service levels of the people the organization serves, deserve more attention.

Organizations need more nonfinancial measures reported *during* the period, not *at the end* of the period. This type of measure is popularly called a *leading indicator* measure; if leading indicators are promptly reacted to, there is enough time to favorably change the outcome of the strategic objective(s) they influence and, eventually, the financial results. In this sense, these leading indicator measures are predictive measures of imminent results.

POOR ALIGNMENT OF STRATEGIES WITH MEASURES

The mantra for using scorecards is simple: "How am I doing on what is important?" This question should ideally be answerable at every level of the organization—from the operational teams to managers to directors up to the individuals responsible for governance. Note that this important question has two components:

> *How am I doing* guides people with feedback on what work to do more and better or to do less of.
>
> . . . *on what is important* points toward what is important to attain the strategy. What's important has been predetermined.

---

[2]Robert S. Kaplan and David P. Norton, *The Balanced Scorecard: Translating Strategy into Action* (Boston: Harvard Business School Press, 1996).

One of today's organizational problems is the disconnection and absence of alignment between *local* measurements of things a manager or employee can control or influence and the subsequent *organizational* results. Figure 6-2 reveals how dysfunctional measures create undesirable behavior and results. It illustrates the problem with a symbolic "wall of disconnects" that prevents the existing measures from aligning with the vision and strategy. The example in the figure is of a purchasing department. If you motivate the purchasing function to purchase the lowest price supplies, equipment, and services, the purchasing function may look good, but other departments may end up having problems. You did not necessarily eliminate costs, but rather shifted costs elsewhere. Worse yet, you may have increased total costs. Strategy maps and a scorecard system remove this wall by selecting the few KPIs that point like vectors toward the organization's vision, mission, and strategy.

FIGURE 6-2 Goal Non-congruency and Misalignment

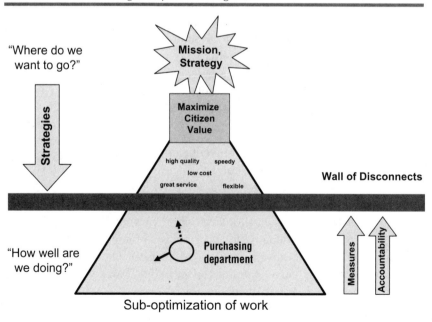

The original idea for the balanced scorecard was introduced by Professor Robert S. Kaplan and Dr. David Norton, who recognized the problems and issues described in this chapter. However, their thinking introduced additional order and structure to this procedure when they described dependencies *among* the groupings of strategic objectives. They called these groupings "perspectives" and described a hierarchal sequence to be visually viewed in the strategy map where accomplishing strategic objectives in one perspective contributes to the success of accomplishing the strategic objectives in the dependent perspectives—kind of like pointing energy force fields. The sequence of the hierarchy is important because it begins at the base with people—the soft side of managing an organization—and using cause-and-effect relationships moves up through the processes people perform, ultimately realizing the high level vision and mission that the senior management team is tasked to define for the organization's strategic direction.

The original four popular perspectives were defined for commercial, profit-making companies. However, with a slight modification, the same principles can apply to government and not-for-profit organizations. The four perspectives are:

1. **Financial**—Profit and investment return results.
2. **Customer**—Customer satisfaction and needs attainment.
3. **Internal core business process**—Efficient and effective execution.
4. **Innovation, learning, and growth**—The "soft" side measures describing new product and service development as well as people development and learning. Another way to think of this perspective is as enabling assets, including not only people but also equipment, technologies, and brand power.

The first perspective, financial, inherently contains lagging measures. The other three perspectives, which collectively are the horsepower for value creation and yielding outcome results, are each individually comprised of both lagging and leading indicators for each strategic objective. A leading indicator is a measure that has a causal effect on time-lagging indicators. Leading indicators are valuable to track because merely sanctioning and reporting them serves to drive behavior—which is the intent. Think of leading indicators as cumulatively adding power to the alignment and achievement of the overarching strategic objective.

STRATEGY MAPS PROVIDE CONTEXT FOR THE SCORECARD

The sequence of Kaplan and Norton's four perspectives makes reasonable sense. However, some organizations have added additional perspectives (such as one for safety, health, and environment). Some organizations have used the multi-stage assessment framework used for selecting winners of the prestigious Malcolm Baldrige award, and in Europe some use the European Foundation for Quality Management (EFQM) framework for European Quality Award. The important point is to place strategic objectives in the context of a framework.

Let's continue with the Kaplan and Norton framework. The top perspective (the financial perspective for commercial companies) is the beneficiary of meeting the strategic objectives in the three perspectives beneath it. The bottom perspective, the learning and growth (or enabling assets) perspective, is the most foundational, not unlike the foundation for a house.

An effective way to understand a strategy map is to visualize a hypothetical example. Figure 6-3 illustrates a generic strategy map for a commercial

FIGURE 6-3 A Generic Strategy Map

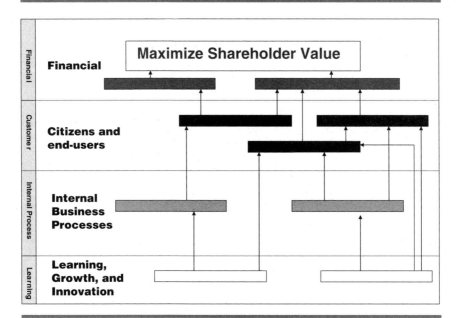

company. Each node in the network represents a strategic objective. The figure includes if-then linkages where the paths drive, or at least contribute to, the outcome of the strategic objectives above them—those energy force fields.

An interesting question that is routinely asked is "Where is the organization's *strategy* defined and located on the strategy map?" The simple answer is that it does not appear. Why not? The reason is that the connected network of the strategic objectives is equivalent to the strategy! Strategic objectives suggest the actions that an organization must complete—or at least make much progress toward completing—or the core processes to excel at in order to achieve the organization's *mission*, which in turn would realize its *vision*. The role of the strategy map is to communicate to employees and managers the direction the executives wish the organization to go. In short, the strategic objectives collectively are the strategy!

Figure 6-4 illustrates a modification for public sector organizations. Maximizing community value replaces maximizing shareholder wealth. Also, the

FIGURE 6-4 A Public Sector Strategy Map

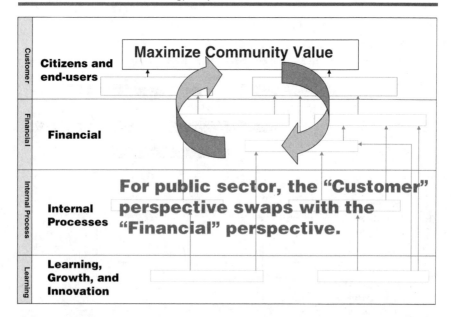

financial view is switched with a citizen/stakeholder view. This reflects the relatively higher importance of outcomes.

WHO SHOULD DEFINE AND CONSTRUCT THE STRATEGY MAP— EXECUTIVES OR EMPLOYEES?

There are two approaches to implementation:

1. A somewhat dictatorial approach, in which a top-down strategy map is cascaded down and deployed at all levels of the organization with little modification, to ensure strategy-aligned behavior and make everyone aware of the larger picture.
2. A decentralized approach, in which each business group or function can adapt to encourage buy-in and foster in employees a sense of belonging and involvement.

The culture of an organization should influence which approach the implementation goes toward; the best approach lies between these two extremes. Figure 6-5 shows who should be responsible for which components of constructing and operating the strategy map and scorecard system. Do not get the impression this is an us-versus-them game. A key determinant of successful scorecard implementations is employee involvement.

FIGURE 6-5 Who Is Responsible for What?

1st Quarter						
	Strategic Objective	Identify Projects, Initiatives, or Processes	Measure	KPI Target	KPI Actual	Comments/ Explanation
Executive Team	X			X		
Managers and Employees		X	X		their score	X
					<----- period results ----->	

A scorecard is more of a *social* tool than a technical tool

As Figure 6-5 shows, the executives must initially construct the strategy map in order to derive the themes (ultimately the strategic objectives) and their interconnections. The employees then select the appropriate measures they believe will best report progress toward achieving the strategic objective. The executives' next role is to approve the measures and, more importantly, assign a target. The target should be set with a Goldilocks spirit of not too high or too low—both are demoralizing—but just right. It should be achievable so that measurable progress can be made. During each reporting period, the employee teams try their best to achieve the key performance indicator (KPI) target. Finally, the employee team, or alternatively the KPI owner accountable for the measure, explains why the score hit, exceeded, or fell short of the KPI target and whether the difference was within typical and acceptable variation (to prevent unnecessary and often wasteful oversteering) or truly an outlier worthy of corrective action.

As a rule, each strategic objective should be restricted to the KPI measures for the action programs or business processes that will be key to accomplishing it. A KPI should answer the question "What is an excellent quantitative measure that would communicate how well the strategic objective is being met?" by considering the action step or business process aimed at the strategic objective. Do not confuse this step with *choosing* the specific *target* score for each KPI measure. Each KPI target score level or amount should pass the test of "If we were doing well in accomplishing the associated strategic objective, this would be the level or amount of this metric."

COLLECTING THE ACTUAL KPIS, DISPLAYING SCORES, AND COMPARING TO TARGETS

This step is mechanical. You could expand Figure 6-5 to include a row labeled "the computer," since today almost all data can be extracted from existing data files already collecting operational data. In short, actual KPI measures are collected and inserted into the scorecard. Figure 6-6 displays a screenshot of a strategy map and some of the associated meters, often referred to as *dashboards*. The screenshot comes from one of the leading analytical software vendors, the SAS Institute Inc. (www.sas.com).

The actual scores displayed in the dashboards of a scorecard are populated with data imported from an organization's operational systems. The differences between the *actual* KPI scores and the *target* KPI scores are calculated and displayed, usually with a meter. Regardless of which side of

FIGURE 6-6 Meters and Dashboards Provide Feedback

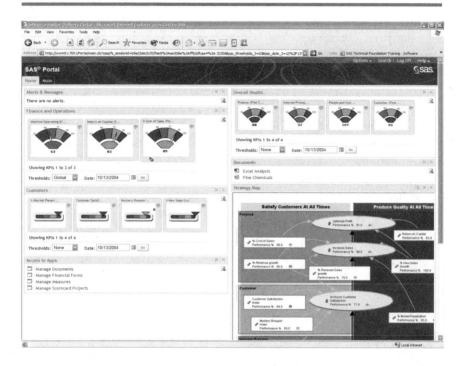

the KPI meter a score difference lands on, it is implicit that a favorable score positively contributes to accomplishing the strategic objectives that, when achieved, guide and speed the organization toward realizing its vision and mission.

These types of signals and alert messages that monitor real-time trends assure managers and employee teams that if something is likely to happen that will exceed a pain threshold, they will be notified beforehand.

Note that at this point in constructing the scorecard system, the scorecard is not yet being used to measure and score *actual* data against the predetermined target scores. That step happens when the actual results are imported into the scorecard from operational systems and compared to the target KPIs. Then, that important question, "How am I doing on what is important," can be answered by managers and employee teams.

CASCADING MEASURES TO PROVIDE EMPLOYEES LINE OF SIGHT

Selecting appropriate KPI measures is more art than science. The key is to associate each KPI measure with action plans, manageable projects, and the core process to excel at. Strategy maps bring science to the art of selecting measures. A good set of KPI measures will balance competing forces such as short-term versus long-term priorities or internal needs versus external needs (those of service-recipients and suppliers). After the high-level measures are selected based on the if-then dependencies in the strategy map, lower-level KPIs can be identified that will influence the higher-level KPIs. This is referred to as *cascading measures*.

Figure 6-7 visually reveals the cascading of a top-level strategy to a front-line action by exhibiting KPI measures as a proxy for those projects or core process that will contribute to achieving the strategic objectives. The KPI measures can be thought of as an overlay to the strategic objectives in the strategy map. Reporting the KPI targets and their actual scores ensures that managers and employees share a common focus on the executive team's strategy. At the top of the figure is where the high-level KPI measures (X,Y,

FIGURE 6-7 Shift of Cascading Measures

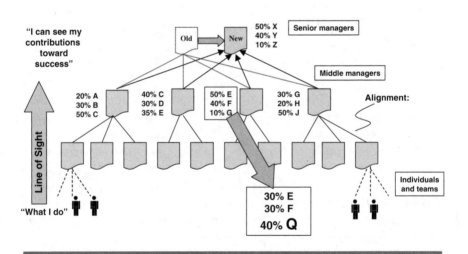

and Z in the figure) reside for the executive team. Below them are the next level of managers with their own KPIs. Continuing downward, each layer of managers (and ultimately employee teams) has its own operational measures, all of which are linked with influencing the KPIs above them. Because these lower-level measures align with the higher-level measures, if the employee teams are scoring favorably to their KPI targets, the collective work efforts will lead to achieving the overall strategy.

Note in Figure 6-7 how an employee can have a line of sight on how what he or she does can affect other performances that eventually affect the achievement of the strategic objectives. Employees can therefore see how what they do contributes to their organization's success. If management is bold, it will allow the employee teams to view how co-workers are also contributing to success.

Remember that a strategy is dynamic, never static, requiring adjustments as the environment changes. With a properly cascaded strategy map, changes in strategy can quickly be mirrored in the measurement system. That is, as the senior management shifts strategic direction, then with new strategic objectives, existing KPIs will be dropped and new ones created. With advanced commercial software, the same KPIs may apply, but their weighting for performance evaluation can be shifted. For example, following an announced strategy shift by the executive team, the same three KPIs for a strategic objective might shift in percentage terms from 50-25-25 to 10-30-60—the same 100% but with shifted emphasis.

Think of the KPIs as the drive gears to the strategy map's strategic objectives and its action plans or processes.

Figure 6-7 illustrates this dynamic effect. When the senior managers shift strategy, one or more of the employee team's vital few measures can be added or removed, yielding the current, more applicable measures. Then the weightings of each KPI can be reweighted to put a new emphasis on what is newly important. That is, when senior management shifts to the new strategy, not only do the high-level weightings change, but also in one case in the figure KPI measure Q replaces measure G. This does not mean that measure G is now unimportant. It simply means that measure Q has now become relatively more important. Remember that the desire is to have the vital few measures. This type of adjustment can be made throughout the scorecard.

Rebalancing the weightings by modifying the coefficient percentages that reflect importance is comparable to an airline pilot slightly adjusting the aileron flaps on an airplane's wings to slightly alter the airplane's course.

Replacing an old measure with a new one is more intense—like banking the airplane left or right. In summary, with a properly cascaded scorecard, changes in strategy should result in new initiatives (or existing ones escalated in importance) and quickly be mirrored in the measurement system. Remember, a scorecard is a social system, and you get what you measure.

Many of today's commercial software programs for strategy maps and scorecards are web-enabled from a server rather than residing independently on employee computers. Web-enabled scorecards with traffic light and alert messages as visual aids add timely communications and discussion threads among managers and employees. That is, Web-enabled scorecards allow employees to *actively* write e-mails and record notes directly *from* their scorecard system rather than external to it. This way they can immediately investigate problems, focus on key needs, and *actively* take corrective actions to improve their scores. With scorecard feedback that is Web-enabled for e-mail and discussion threads, the dialogues are focused and associated in the context of the strategy. The concept of *context* is important. It elevates this methodology well above traditional management by objectives (MBO) and spreadsheet performance reports.

ABC/M CALCULATED RESULTS PROVIDE A SUBSET OF KPIs

Activity-based cost management systems are an excellent source of data to use in a performance management scorecard system. ABC/M accelerates information-enabled focus and productivity improvement primarily by providing fact-based data. As earlier described, ABC/M's repeatable and reliable data can be used to both assess past progress and support future decisions.

To be clear, ABC/M is *not* the measurement system. Rather, the *output* of ABC/M can be an important additional *input* to the performance measurements in a scorecard system along with the non-financial KPIs. The presence of ABC/M data can stimulate greater numbers of actions and decisions.

Most executives and managers have very little insight about their outputs—not only about the obvious products and standard service lines that they deliver to external service recipients, but also about the internal outputs of the work done within their organizations.

Outputs are not simply the work activities that employees perform. They are descriptions of the results *after* the activities have been performed; in other words, they are the outputs of work. A collection of outputs leads to outcomes—products, services, and the like.

So where does activity-based cost management fit in? ABC/M does a great job tracing resource expenses to all sorts of internal outputs. This does not mean that the work processes producing these outputs are unimportant. It simply means that many people react more to the visibility of output costs than they do to the process costs to which the work activity costs belong.

In short, when unit costs are trended or internally benchmarked to be compared with other unit costs, employees and managers gain more insight. With benchmarks, organizations can deduce if they might have a best or worst practice. Per-unit-of-each costs should not only be included in the scorecard's financial perspective, but should also appear in the other perspectives as well. While unit costs represent dollar figures, they are much more like a representation of the equivalent resources consumed by the unit measure, in this case stated in terms of money.

To ensure that team leaders and employees are working on projects today that will move the organization toward its strategic objectives in the future, everyone needs timely, fact-based information that helps them see which projects are impacting the budget and contributing to the organization's desired outcomes—and which projects, however well-intentioned, are not. ABC/M provides valuable insight far beyond the general ledger and helps executives make sure they are doing well on those activities that directly lead to improved traction, increased organizational agility, and better results.

Certainly, ABC/M is not a prerequisite for designing and using a performance management scorecard system. But the introduction of ABC/M data can populate the scorecard framework with robust and high-octane information that can give executives, managers, and employees an idea of how well the organization is aligned with its strategies right now and how this information will influence outcomes down the road.

MEASURES ALIGN EMPLOYEE BEHAVIOR WITH THE STRATEGY

Many factors impede organizational performance. The impediments can be removed if employees better understand their organization's strategy and the key initiatives chosen to achieve that strategy. The impediments are definitely removed by selecting the correct performance measures. In these ways, employees can more clearly view how the work they do contributes to their organization's results. Measure things that people can influence.

I think of strategy maps and scorecards as enabling employees to move together like a flock of birds or school of fish. It is amazing how mother nature provides the instinctive navigational ability so that hundreds of birds in a flock can fly in formation with such synchrony. Up, down, left, right—all together, as if they were one tightly tethered unit. Imagine viewing employees of a typical organization in motion. I see some colliding and others straying away from the pack as if they've lost their bearings. Strategy maps and scorecards can keep all employees in formation.

THE PERFORMANCE MANAGEMENT FRAMEWORK FOR VALUE CREATION AND RESULTS

One of the most ambiguous terms in discussions about business and government is *value*. Everybody wants value in return for whatever they exchanged to get value. But whose value is more important and who is entitled to claiming it? Customers and end-users conclude that they receive value if the benefits received from purchasing a product or service meet or exceed what they paid for it (or the time put into it, if the service is free). With regard to a government agency's governance body, they may believe if the investment return to operate the organization they are responsible for is less than overall benefits to the community or taxpayers, then the governance body, if acting socially responsibly, should take actions to reverse such an imbalanced value situation. A fundamental principle in social economics is that the benefits of an investment or program should exceed the costs. Value to employees may be tied to compensation and satisfaction.

Three groups believe they are entitled to value: citizens and end-users, the governing body, and employees. Are they rivals? What are the trade-offs? Is there an Adam Smith–like invisible hand controlling checks and balances to maintain an economic equilibrium so that each group gets its fair share? Are some groups more entitled to receiving value than others?

A PICTURE OF PERFORMANCE MANAGEMENT OPERATING AS AN INTEGRATED SYSTEM

Figure 6-8 illustrates the interdependent methodologies that comprise performance management for a government organization. Before reading the explanation of the figure, first ask yourself: what are the most important words in any of the boxes or ellipses?

The answer depends on who you are. If you are the organization's executive team, the most important words must be "Strategy, mission." The pri-

FIGURE 6-8 Performance Management Framework

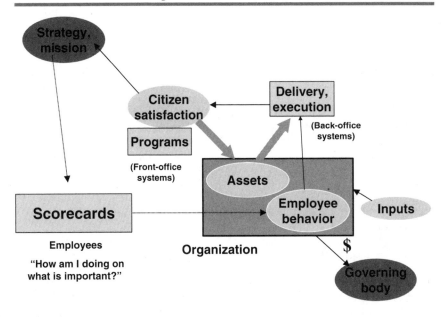

mary job of executives is to define and constantly adjust their organization's strategy as the environment changes. That is why they are paid high salaries and reside in large corner offices. However, after the strategy definition is complete and maintained as current, then the core processes take over, with competent process owners held accountable to manage each one.

Most readers might think that "Citizen satisfaction" is most important. Citizen satisfaction encompasses four customer-facing trends. Increased focus on:

1. End-user retention, because increasingly they have options to seek services elsewhere and there are relatively lower costs to retain them than seek new ones, because you already service them.
2. The source for citizen value, because of a shift due to neutralized advantages from commodity-like services to value-adding service differentiation to end-users.
3. Micro-segmenting of citizens to focus on their unique preferences, rather than mass one-size-fits-all services.

4. Internet's shift in power from service-providers to citizens and end-users, due to their increased ability to comparison shop and seek knowledge.

It's easy to conclude that a focus on citizens and end-users is critical.

In the figure, the two ultimate mega-core business processes possessed by any organization on the planet are represented by the two thick arrows. The two arrows are (1) take an order or assignment, and (2) fulfill an order or assignment. When stripped to its core, this is what *any* organization does. The two arrows are universal. Can you name an organization that doesn't receive tasks and then attempt to execute them? The figure reveals that the field of information technology (IT) has named the support systems for these two mega-processes as *front office* and *back office* systems. Other IT systems serve as components in managing the value chain.

The citizen-facing front office systems are citizen relationship management information systems and program management. This is also where work order management systems reside. The back office systems are where the fulfillment of orders, process planning, and execution reside—the world of enterprise resource management (ERP), comparable operational systems, and Six Sigma quality initiatives. The output from this execution box is the product, service, or mission intended to meet the needs of the citizen and end-user. Imagine the three arrows continuously circulating counter-clockwise. To the degree that this cycle is producing satisfactory (or preferably bringing delight) to the citizens at an appropriate level of funded spending, then the governance body in lower right ellipse are happy that the organization is doing its job.

The need to satisfy citizens and end-users is the major input into senior management's "Mission, strategy." As earlier described with strategy maps and scorecards, when the executive team adjusts its strategy it may add or abandon some key performance indicators (KPIs) or adjust the KPI weightings for various employee teams. As the feedback is received from the scorecards, all employees can answer a key question: "How am I doing on what is important?" With analysis for causality, corrective actions can then occur. And note that the output from scorecards does not stop at the organization's boundary, but it penetrates all the way through to influence the employee behavior. This in turn leads to better execution.

AN AUTOMOBILE ANALOGY FOR PERFORMANCE MANAGEMENT

All organizations have been doing performance management since well before it was labeled as such. It can be argued that on the date an organization was first created, it immediately was managing (or attempting to manage) its enterprise performance by offering products or services and fulfilling requests for citizens and end-users.

If you will, imagine an organization at its start-up as a poorly tuned automobile. We would observe the consequences of unstable methods and processes: unbalanced wheels, severe shimmy in the steering wheel, poor timing of engine pistons, thick power steering fluid, and mucky oil in the crankcase. Take that mental picture and conclude that any physical system of moving parts with tremendous vibration and part-wearing friction dissipates energy, wasting fuel and power. At an organizational level, the energy dissipation from vibration and friction translates into wasted expenses and poor service levels. The greater the waste and the poorer the service, the more the governance body will be disappointed with the organization.

Now imagine an automobile with its wheels finely balanced and well lubricated. That is, now imagine the full potential of performance management, where the strategy is managed well and where data is digitized and transformed for analysis and good decision-making. The performance management framework (i.e., the automobile) remains unchanged, but the governance body is happy. No vibration or friction.

Well, that's how good performance management integrates the multiple methodologies of the performance management portfolio of components and provides better decision analysis and decision-making that aligns work behavior and priorities with the strategy. Strategic objectives are attained, and the consequence is satisfaction among citizens, end-users, and the governing body.

ABC/M data, a key component in performance management, permeates every single element in this scenario to help balance the competing values between service levels for citizens and budgeted resources made available to governing bodies. ABC/M itself is not an improvement program or execution system, unlike several other systems in the figure, such as Six Sigma or an ERP system. ABC/M data serve as a discovery mechanism and an enabler for these systems to support better decision-making, as described in this book. Performance management provides the framework to model all of these important relationships. We know that an organization's various programs and improvement methodologies are interdependent and connect, but organizations struggle with how they do it.

Is my Figure 6-8 the best diagram to represent the performance management framework for a government organization? I do not know. It is my diagram, and professional societies, management consultants, and software vendors have their own diagrams. Perhaps a business magazine or web portal can have a contest where diagrams are submitted and voted on by readers. But the key point is that performance management should not be defined narrowly as "better strategy, budgeting, planning, and control." Clearly, it is also about balancing sometimes competing values.

ACCOUNTABILITY AND TRANSPARENCY: YOU CAN'T HAVE ONE WITHOUT THE OTHER

Accountability means responsibility of a government program to deliver a service or product—to the public. The responsibility relies on both effectiveness and efficiency of delivering that service or product. Government programs are put in place for a purpose—if that purpose is not clear, or the effectiveness of the program is not clear, the program may face scrutiny and slashed budgets.

To hold an entity accountable means that the effectiveness and efficiency must not only be determined, but communicated—this is where transparency comes in. Transparency is delivering the performance and financial results to the public—so all stakeholders are aware, including the public. For Federal agencies in the U.S., transparency includes providing insightful reporting with explanatory information to the president's administration, Congress, OMB, and GAO. The public has the right to know how its tax monies are being spent; it also have a vested interest in realizing the *value* that is delivered to it, the customer. Therefore, performance and financial results should be made available, or transparent, to all these constituents. If you do not have transparency, then accountability is not being enforced— and the benefits and purpose of accountability are not optimized.

"There are two levers for moving men—interest and fear."
—Napoleon Bonaparte, Corsican Emperor of France, quoted in
Emerson's Representative Men

"We made too many wrong mistakes."
—Yogi Berra, US Baseball Hall of Fame athlete, quoted after his team, the
New York Yankees, lost the 1960 World Series

Chapter 7

Activity-based Budgeting: Myth or Reality?

Contributor: Mike Tinkler, Synerma, www.synerma.com

"They say that knowledge is power. I used to think so, but now I know that they mean money."
—Lord Byron, English poet, *Byron's Letters and Journals,* edited by Marchand

"Money, which represents the prose of life, and which is hardly spoken of in parlors without an apology, is, in its effects and laws, as beautiful as roses."
—Ralph Waldo Emerson, "Nominalist and Realist (1844)," Essays and Lectures (New York: Literary Classics of the United States, 1983), p. 578

WE NOW HAVE a better approach to forecasting the location and level of resources and budgeted expenditures. This approach, called activity-based budgeting (ABB), recognizes that the need for resources originates with a demand-pull triggered by customers or end-users of the organization's services and capabilities. In contrast, traditional budgeting tends to extrapolate the level of resource spending for each spending line item from spending levels of past periods, and then adds a small percentage increase to allow for monetary inflation. In the traditional approach to budgeting, the budget process starts with the current level of expenses. A problem with budgeting this way is that the past is not a reliable indicator of the future.

Many of today's managers correctly believe that the budget should flow backwards from the outputs. Activity-based budgeting (ABB) in effect does flow backwards. ABB assists in logically determining what levels of resources are truly required to meet the future demands placed on the organization.

In the 1980s, financial planners—particularly in the U.S. federal government—actually experimented with a precursor to ABB. It was called zero-based budgeting (ZBB). Managers' instincts then were similar to what they are today. Managers suspected it might be better to imagine a budgeting process where each department begins its budget thinking with a clean slate—as if it were just

---

Portions of this chapter are adapted with permission of the McGraw-Hill Companies from Gary Cokins, *Activity-Based Cost Management: Making It Work.* © The McGraw-Hill Companies, Inc., 1996.

starting up new and staffing the department from scratch. In other words, what resources would a department need next year if it had no idea what it had last year?

However, timing is everything when it comes to major changes in management techniques—and the timing was not right in the 1980s for ZBB to be successful. Cost pressures were not as significant then as they are today. In addition, software modeling tools and validly measured activity driver cost rate data were hard to come by. Those conditions have now changed for the better. Many organizations have had their ABC/M system implemented and routinely recalculated for several years. The more advanced and mature ABC/M users have already constructed models that depict their cost structure and cost behavior reasonably well. The timing and conditions are now suitable for change.

In the late 1990s, the more mature and advanced ABC users increasingly began using their calculated activity costs, as well as unit cost rates for intermediate work outputs and for products and services, as a basis for estimating costs. Popular uses of the ABC data for cost estimating have been for calculating customer order quotations and for make-or-buy analysis. The ABC data also were being recognized as a predictive planning tool. It is now becoming apparent that ABC data have tremendous utility both for examining the as-is, current condition of the organization and for achieving a desired to-be state.

BUDGETING: USER DISCONTENT AND REBELLION

Why is interest in activity-based budgeting (ABB) increasing? Simply put, many people have problems with the annual budget process, and not just because they are not getting approval for the funding they want. They are disturbed by the budgeting process altogether. There is great cynicism about budgeting as well as an intuitive sense that a better way to budget exists.

Often, a substantial change in management technique is born of a combination of dissatisfaction with current methods and a vision of what a replacement method could look like. For the launching of ABB, both conditions are present.

Why are managers and employees cynical about the annual budgeting process? They find that the process is too long, too detailed, and excessively burdensome. In addition, they view budgeting as a political game that usually results in some departments being over-funded while others labor on as have-nots. Many workers in this latter group toil without relief. Through organizational downsizing, senior management has often removed the bodies but not taken out the work! Across-the-board cuts in manpower, some of the slash-and-burn variety, are likely to cut into the muscle in some places while still leaving excess capacity in others. Figure 7-1 provides some sarcasm about traditional budgeting in the form of a check-the-box survey.

Thankfully, there is a vision of what a better way of budgeting looks like—ABB. But ABB is better for what purpose and for whom? Fundamentally, we

FIGURE 7–1 A Quiz: Check the Boxes.

Our budgeting exercise . . .

- ☐ is a death march…with few benefits.

- ☐ takes 14 months from start to end.

- ☐ requires two or more executive tweaks at the end.

- ☐ is obsolete in two months due to re-orgs or competitor moves.

- ☐ starves truly needed spending with excess funding elsewhere.

- ☐ caves in to the loudest voice and political muscle.

- ☐ rewards veteran sand baggers who are experts at padding.

- ☐ is over-stated from the prior year's use-it-or-lose-it spends.

- ☐ incorporates last year's inefficiencies into this year's budget.

- ☐ provides lifetime security for our budget analysts to perform variance analysis with all the subsequent forecast updates.

- ☐ focuses much less on "*what* should we be doing?" and much more on "*how much* we are doing what we did?"

- ☐ de-motivates managers when targets are too easy or too tough.

- ☐ could get better results if managers signed fewer POs.

- ☐ is a trap for the young and naïve who have yet to learn how to negotiate to pad and sandbag for the unexpected.

Reprinted by permission of the McGraw-Hill Companies from Gary Cokins, *Activity-Based Cost Management: Making It Work.* © The McGraw-Hill Companies, Inc., 1996.

need to understand what purpose a budget serves. Most people think that a budget is a set of predetermined spending limits put in place so that if all departments roughly spend what was allotted to them, then the estimated total spending for the organization will be reasonably achieved. In this way of thinking, the purpose of a budget is as a control tool, not an analytical and allocation tool. Don't exceed your spending limit, or you'll get your hand slapped by the accounting police: "You took two more airline flights than planned. Explain why."

However, the broader purpose of budgeting should be to predetermine the level of resources that will be required, such as people, material, supplies, and equipment, to achieve an expected or desired amount of demand for employee services—meaning demands for their work. ABB advocates are interested in the notion of resource requirements as being the result of budgeting, not the starting point. ABB advocates want to be able to first estimate oncoming customer and management demands, and second estimate the supply of resources, in terms of cost, that will be needed to match the work demands. In short, ABB advocates want to reverse the traditional budget equation and start with the expected outcomes, not with the existing situation.

Criticisms abound about the use and development of budgets. Some organizations are saying they want cost management, not budget management. In fact, they believe their organizations will never "budget manage" their way to cost management.

With hindsight, we now realize that the fund accounting and general ledger systems, as well as their derivative budgets, are a mirror of the organization chart, not of the business processes. Yet the processes are what actually deliver value to service recipients and customers. And worse, the budget has no visibility into the "content of work." Moreover, it has no provisions for logically determining how external or internal cost drivers govern the natural levels of spending caused by demands on work from those cost drivers. Traditional budgeting is done more by push than pull.

Here are further observations about traditional budgeting, some of which appeared in the survey quiz:

- Today's budget process takes an extraordinarily long time, sometimes over a year, during which the organization often reshuffles and resizes. In addition, customers and competitors usually change their behavior, for which a prudent reaction often cannot be accommodated in the budget.

- Low cost is a dependent variable; low costs are the result of doing things well. You cannot budget your way into low-cost operations. Budget management and cost management are not synonymous.
- Allocating resources based on the loudest voice, the greatest political muscle, and the largest prior-year budget is no longer a valid way to manage resources.
- The annual budget is steeped in tradition in some organizations, yet the effort of producing it heavily outweighs the benefits it supposedly yields.
- Budgets are useful for organizations that are stable and in which senior managers do not trust their organization to spend money intelligently. Both of those conditions are invalid today.
- Many companies confuse budgeting (spending control) with financial planning (forecasting). Computer models today can forecast the expected outcomes of all sorts of assumption-based scenarios without the need for a formal budget exercise. Organizations should experiment more with financial simulators before they spend the hard dollars.
- Budget should reflect strategy. Strategies should be formulated at two levels. First, the diversification strategy level asks, "What should we be doing?" Second, the operational strategy level asks, "How should we do it?" Unfortunately, most of the effort is on the latter question, and companies get preoccupied with simply finishing the budget—and the budget by that time may be disconnected from the strategy.
- Often the budget is revised midyear or more frequently with forecasts. After a new forecast, an excessive amount of attention is given to analyzing differences between the budget and the forecast—all the differences. These analyses include budget to forecast, last forecast to current forecast, actual to budget, actual to forecast, and on and on.
- Often the budget numbers that roll up from lower- and mid-level managers mislead senior executives because of sandbagging (i.e., padding). "Use it or lose it" is standard practice for managers during the last fiscal quarter. Budgets can be an invitation to some managers to spend needlessly.
- Budgets do not identify waste. In fact, inefficiencies in existing practices are often baked into next year's budget. Budgets do not support continuous improvement.

In response to the rising awareness that current methods of budgeting are flawed, leaders are moving away from silo planning to process-based thinking and enterprise-demand planning. According to a study in the late 1990s by the CPA firm PricewaterhouseCoopers, the average large company spent 110 days developing an operational budget—every year! Public sector organizations likely devote a similar amount of time to creating a budget. And the budget is typically wrong the day it is frozen. A better way to budget will consolidate what is today an extremely fragmented and disjointed exercise.

SOME PERSPECTIVES ON COST ESTIMATING

In the description in Chapter 4 of the six significant advances of ABC/M, applying ABC/M data for cost estimating was the fifth advantage. Chapter 4 further explained that conventional costing, including ABC/M, takes a historical view of time and experience. It is akin to a cost autopsy. The management accountant basically strives to segment how *past* resource expenditures either directly trace or are fairly allocated to final cost objects. But all decisions, by definition, affect the *future*. Advanced, mature users of ABC/M data have moved on to applying their ABC/M data to predictive planning purposes, budgeting, and evaluating what-if scenarios.

Figure 7-2 expands Figure 1-2 and illustrates that the true focus of managerial accounting is ultimately on making better decisions about future resource levels. And, as already mentioned, decisions always affect what occurs in the future. An organization's total resources are ultimately what are being managed. The figure shows that organizations try hard to manage their level and types of resources in the context of present and future demands. But the key is to make better decisions—for the future. The figure illustrates how ABC/M provides a resource as well as an output view. These are the calculated costs of activities, processes, and outputs.

ABC/M substantially improves on simplistic and broad-averaging cost allocations to reflect true consumption patterns. In the historical view, ABC's correct application of absorption costing has added visibility to both "the work" and to the "outputs" of the work. (Note that in this view "the work" costs also belong to the processes. As will be described, process simulation software tools are already taking advantage of this link to absorption costing tools.)

The figure reveals that despite the fact that activities belong to processes (which is the time-based view), when activity costs are translated into outputs, employees and management teams are provided insights and inferences. Now comes a critical point. The figure illustrates that when historical

FIGURE 7-2 Validating the Inferences

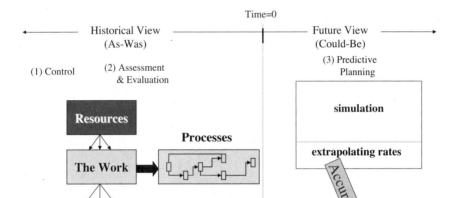

information from the past is applied to the future, it may not be sufficient for that information only to be suggestive as to what actions to take. The information must also be accurate. That is, it must reasonably reveal the level of resource spending for the outcomes. In other words, based on inferences as well as cost estimates that may use the ABC/M activity driver rates and estimates of driver volumes, extrapolated costs may require further adjustment and validation to ensure that the predicted resources are in fact a valid amount. As we will see shortly, ABB provides for that validation. And under some conditions, the use of simulation technology will improve an ABB-derived cost estimate by providing even higher accuracy.

ABC/M AS A SOLUTION FOR ACTIVITY-BASED PLANNING AND BUDGETING

Although many organizations recognize the problems with traditional budgeting and acknowledge their dissatisfaction with it, few have taken action to fix matters. But ABC/M provides hope. Activity-based planning and budgeting (ABP/B) is an approach that can help to fix the broken budgeting process. It is a more recent development than ABC/M, but in some cases it may produce more dramatic results. ABP/B calculates the future level of resources and capacity required to meet forecasts of the demands that are expected to be made on an organization. ABP/B uses cost and consumption rates derived from a calculated ABC/M model from relatively recent past periods. ABP/B is the forward-looking view of an organization's costs.

Why are we using the term "Planning and Budgeting" rather than just "Budgeting," and now substituting the acronym "ABP/B" for "ABB"? The difference is subtle but significant and will be explained below.

Activity-based costing mechanics effectively model the resource consumption rates and patterns of an enterprise on a cross-functional basis that focuses on work activities. Hence, ABC/M-type budgets can be regenerated at periodic intervals based on estimates of the quantities of activity drivers in combination with the precomputed historical consumption rates for the activity drivers. In a nutshell, ABP/B can be looked at as ABC in reverse: instead of allocating resource costs to activities and activity costs to cost objects, ABP/B starts with the demand for cost objects (products and services), calculates the work (activities) required to produce those cost objects, and then moves to determining the level of and type of resources needed to perform the work, in terms of salaries and other expenses.

ABP/B is basically doing resource capacity planning. Measurements of capacity utilization will increasingly be adopted for use in managing resources, in the manner that one might manage weight or cholesterol level. ABP/B will not be the end-all but will truly measure the behavior of the lean organization. In this sense, ABP/B will serve more as a gauge or altimeter for how well an organization's actual spending is tracking or is in sync with its *required* spending level.

From a government budgeting perspective, the beauty of this backwards calculation to objectively determine a "correct" level of resource spending is that it shifts the focus from the inputs (how much are we going to spend on salaries, travel, professional services) to the process (what activities are in our process), and more importantly, to the outputs (what services are we providing) that cause the need for inputs. The ABP/B reverse calculation establishes the logical linkage shown below:

> the demand for services → the work that the demand generates → the resources that the work consumes → the funding required to acquire the resources

This is radically different from the traditional budgeting approach described earlier in this chapter, that looks at how much was spent in the previous year and then adjusts this amount upwards or downwards by a target percentage (e.g., a 2% increase or a 10% decrease). ABP/B's logical linkage provides the basis for a more rational dialogue at all levels between what we might call resource providers (politicians and senior managers) and resource requesters (middle managers). Here's what this dialogue might look like:

> Resource provider: "You're getting 10% less money next year."
>
> Resource requester: "Then I can only satisfy 90% of the demand for my services. What about the other 10% of my clients?"
>
> Resource provider: "You still have to provide services to all your clients. You need to cut the inefficiencies in your process."
>
> Resource requester: "I've already looked at all the activities in my process and eliminated or reduced those that don't add value. My process is already efficient."
>
> Resource provider: "Then maybe we need to look at whether all of your clients really need your services. Maybe we should change the responsibilities that you have to the public."

This dialogue could then continue in a number of directions, including examining the priority of the services being provided compared to other services, whether the lowest possible prices are being paid for resources, whether the right resources are being used, and so forth. The point is that, with ABP/B, the impact of the cut can be documented and discussed. Whether a dialogue like the above will actually occur is another question, of course, but at least the information will be available to facilitate it.

The dialogue also points out another advantage of activity-based approaches described earlier in this book. Attention is paid to the process and to the work activities that make it up. Process improvements can be made by eliminating low value-added activities, by eliminating duplication, by reorganizing the process, by using information technology enablers, and so on.

In addition to focusing on external demand for services, ABP/B can take into account the internal demands that operational or program departments place on the technical and administrative support departments. As examples, this is the demand for IT services, for financial services, for training, for recruiting, for procurement services, and for facilities and accommodations. The demand for these support areas is derived from the impact of the external demand on the operational areas. Looking at this internal demand can help to develop a healthy customer-supplier relationship between the operational departments and the support departments.

HOW ABP/B WORKS: AN EXAMPLE

Let's look at a simple example, taken from a human resources department that provides services to its internal clients.

Figure 7-3 is a high-level view of what an activity-based planning model might look like for the staffing and recruiting section of an HR department. The first thing that would be done would be to model the activities performed in the section. In our example, these activities are internal competitions, transfers, and acting appointments. In real life, there would be several more and the activity model would need to be more detailed—internal

FIGURE 7-3 Sample Activity-based Planning Model

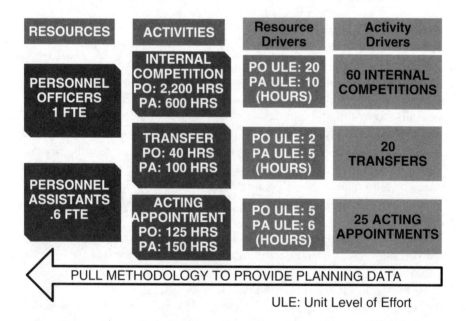

RESOURCES	ACTIVITIES	Resource Drivers	Activity Drivers
PERSONNEL OFFICERS 1 FTE	INTERNAL COMPETITION PO: 2,200 HRS PA: 600 HRS	PO ULE: 20 PA ULE: 10 (HOURS)	60 INTERNAL COMPETITIONS
	TRANSFER PO: 40 HRS PA: 100 HRS	PO ULE: 2 PA ULE: 5 (HOURS)	20 TRANSFERS
PERSONNEL ASSISTANTS .6 FTE	ACTING APPOINTMENT PO: 125 HRS PA: 150 HRS	PO ULE: 5 PA ULE: 6 (HOURS)	25 ACTING APPOINTMENTS

← PULL METHODOLOGY TO PROVIDE PLANNING DATA

ULE: Unit Level of Effort

competitions might have 10 or 15 sub-activities. The modeling would be done in modeling workshops where the participants would be the people who actually do the work.

Once the activities have been established, the next step, which would also be done in the modeling workshop, would be to determine the resource drivers, or unit levels of effort (ULE). The ULE is the average time that it takes to perform an activity once. The ULEs for various activities are established through discussion among the people who do the work. The participants may disagree with each other on the exact time it takes to perform a task, but a consensus is arrived at. Establishing ULEs is not a stopwatch study or time-and-motion analysis of the sort performed by industrial engineers in the 1920s, but the results are accurate enough and they can be validated later.

In addition to the time required to do an activity, the category of staff that does the work is also identified. In our example, we have personnel officers (POs) and personnel assistants (PAs), and an internal competition takes 20 hours of a PO's time and 10 hours of a PA's time.

The next step is to obtain a forecast of the expected demand for services in the coming budget period, usually the next fiscal year. Since HR is an administrative support department, its demand is derived from the needs of the other departments in the organization, both operational and support. It would need to poll these departments to find out what recruiting they expect to do, for example. In addition, it would probably do some projections based on past experience. In order for this to work, the rest of the departments have to complete at least the first pass at their planning, so that they can provide an initial feed to HR, and as their plans evolve they need to keep HR updated.

Once the volume of demand is established (for example, 60 internal competitions), the number crunching begins. The ULEs are multiplied by the forecasted demand for each activity and for each category of staff. In Figure 7-3, 60 internal competitions with a ULE of 20 hours for a personnel officer means that 1,200 hours of personnel officer time is required for this activity. This same operation is repeated for all the cost objects, activities, and resources. Adding all the requirements for a category of staff and dividing by the number of productive hours in a year gives the total number of full-time equivalent resources (FTEs) required for that category.

Take another look at Figure 7-3. The personnel officer can expect that, in the coming year, she will spend 1,200 hours on internal competitions, 40 hours on transfers, and 125 hours on acting appointments. Added up, this is

1,365 hours, or approximately one year of productive full-time employment. You might expect the number of hours in a year to be closer to 2,000, but the key word here is productive, so that means that annual leave, statutory holidays, sick leave, other leave, breaks, and personal time are subtracted from the total hours available in a year to give the productive hours. Obviously, this calculation will differ from organization to organization and requires some analysis in each case.

Having established that we need one personnel officer and .6 of a personnel assistant for staffing and recruiting, the other functions of HR, such as labor relations, performance evaluations, pay and benefits, and classification, can be addressed using a similar process in order to determine HR's total staffing requirements for each category of personnel. In addition, we can look at other resource requirements based on the activity model, such as accommodations, travel, professional services, and procurement services.

ABP/B AND CAPACITY

The model has now given us a quantification of the resource requirements based on the forecasted demand for services. We can now turn these quantities into budget dollars, but first we need to do a capacity check, determining and validating that the quantity and type of existing resources currently available are sufficient to meet the future requirements. In other words, do we have too much or too little capacity? Suppose we have built, validated, and calculated the HR department's planning model for the coming fiscal year and have come up with the following results:

Section	Resources required (FTEs)	Resources available (FTEs)	Over- (Under-) Capacity
Staffing and recruiting	5	3	(2)
Labor relations	2	3	1
Performance evaluations	4	2	(2)
Pay and benefits	3	3	
Classification	3	4	1
HR Department Total	17	15	(2)

On an overall basis, the HR department needs two more FTEs, while two sections are overstaffed and two are understaffed. These variances can be resolved in a number of ways:

- To the extent that skill sets allow for this, people can be transferred from an overstaffed section to an understaffed one. For example, it might be possible to transfer 1 FTE from classification to staffing and recruiting.
- It might be possible to transfer staff into or out of HR.
- Overtime, casual (i.e., temporary contractor) staff, and consultants can be used to deal with shortages.
- As a last resort, for changes that are significant and permanent, employees can be hired or terminated.

In real-life situations, the solution is often a combination of the above. Regardless of the strategy, these capacity management issues need to be resolved before moving on to the next step—activity-based budgeting.

The top portion of Figure 7-4 shows a conceptual overview of the activity-based planning process that we have just described. This is known as the "pull" methodology, because we have pulled the forecasted demand for products and services back through the activity model to determine the resources required to meet the demand.

Incidentally, readers with a manufacturing background may have noticed a strong resemblance between activity-based planning and material requirements planning (MRP), a widely-used manufacturing planning tool. You can look at activity-based planning as MRP applied in a service industry context. In Gary Cokins' first book on ABC/M, *An ABC Managers Primer*, he referred on page 47 to what we have called ABP/B here as ARP (activity requirements planning).

MOVING FROM ACTIVITY-BASED PLANNING (ABP) TO ACTIVITY-BASED BUDGETING (ABB)

The next step after planning is to turn the quantified requirements into dollar amounts. For salaries, which are usually the major part of public sector expenditures, we do this by applying salary rates to the FTEs that were the result of the planning process. Other resources, such as travel and professional services, can be similarly dollarized by using rates and prices.

When we have converted all the resource requirements into dollar amounts, we have created input that can be documented in a conventional budget by nature of expense (i.e., expense account) and responsibility center. We need to combine these "recurring" expenses with other one-time non-recurring resource expense data (e.g., a project), and we'll look at how that

FIGURE 7-4 Activity-based Planning Is Driven by Consumption Forecasts

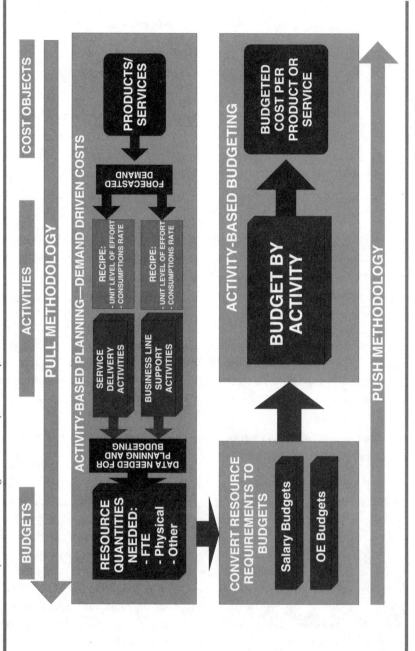

can be done in the next section. The big difference here is that the budget amounts are solidly based on the demand for cost objects and the work load required to produce or deliver the demand.

With activity-based budgeting, though, we can go beyond the conventional budget. We can use the relationships that we established in activity-based planning—between resources and activities and between activities and cost objects—to "push" the budget down to activities and from there into cost objects. This is actually the same process as activity-based costing in its historical descriptive view, but we are using budgeted resource expenses instead of actual resource expenses downloaded from the general ledger. Accountants would refer to the numbers derived from the process as *pro forma* numbers—projected costs.

Some organizations that have sufficiently large uncertainty in accurately estimating the key independent variable, the future demand, apply the same ABP method on a quarterly basis. This is referred to as rolling financial forecasts. (Some commercial companies have questioned the usefulness of an annual budget altogether. They have proposed a radical approach: Abandon the annual budget, and replace it with rolling financial forecasts and other expense forecasting methods that are described later in this chapter. More about this approach is at the website of the Beyond Budgeting Round Table, www.bbrt.org.)

The ability to look at budgeted activity costs and service costs is a major leap forward for public sector organizations. Often, one of the first reactions from managers when they see the budgeted activity costs is, "It costs us that much to do THAT??!!" This type of realization can lead to a deeper examination of low value–added activities and to questioning of their purpose or cause. Having budgeted activity costs can also bring an added dimension to process improvement initiatives like Kaizen and Six Sigma by allowing an organization to focus attention on the high-cost activities whose elimination or improvement can yield the highest benefits. And if ABB is implemented alongside ABC, the ability to compare actual and budgeted activity costs can give new meaning to cost variance analysis and financial performance measurement.

Knowing the budgeted cost of services is a key element of performance-based management initiatives in the public sector. If full or partial cost recovery (i.e., charging fees for services) is one of the objectives, many agencies or jurisdictions require that the charging organization (i.e., the service provider) determine the costs of these services and make this information available to users of the services. While service costs can be determined retrospectively with ABC, it makes a lot more sense to use next year's expenses and calculated costs (ABB) to determine what to charge next year.

TOP-DOWN FUNDING VERSUS BOTTOM-UP BUDGETING

What if the ABP/B process produces a result that is not feasible in terms of available resources? Perhaps there has been a top-down decision from the political level of the government organization that the funding available to the organization will be frozen at last year's levels or that budget increases will be restricted and limited to a specified percentage. In these circumstances, the total funding envelope for the organization is determined in advance and this total envelope is then allocated down through the branches and divisions of the organization, sometimes on an arbitrary, politics-driven basis. How can the fundamentally bottom-up process that is ABP/B be reconciled with these constraints? The answer is to make adjustments through what is known as a closed-loop planning and budgeting process.

Figure 7-5 shows how these adjustments can be integrated into the resource planning and budgeting model. This figure draws on excellent research by the activity-based planning and budgeting special interest group of the Consortium of Advance Management—International (www.cam-i.org) that resulted in the book *The Closed Loop: Implementing Activity-Based Planning and Budgeting.*

The first step is to do activity-based planning to determine resource requirements (people and other resources) and compare the required resources to available capacity. If a shortage or excess exists, management has three potential ways to bring capacity back into balance:

1. As we have already shown, management can adjust capacity by adding staff on a permanent or temporary basis, purchasing equipment, requesting overtime, or reducing staff.
2. Efficiencies can be introduced either by reducing the time required to perform activities, eliminating activities, or increasing the services produced by the process. Another approach is to reduce service levels, which usually has the impact of reducing resource requirements.
3. It may be possible to adjust demand by some sort of rationing process that restricts access to the services and filters out low priority or unnecessary demand. Preventive education is another way to reduce demand.

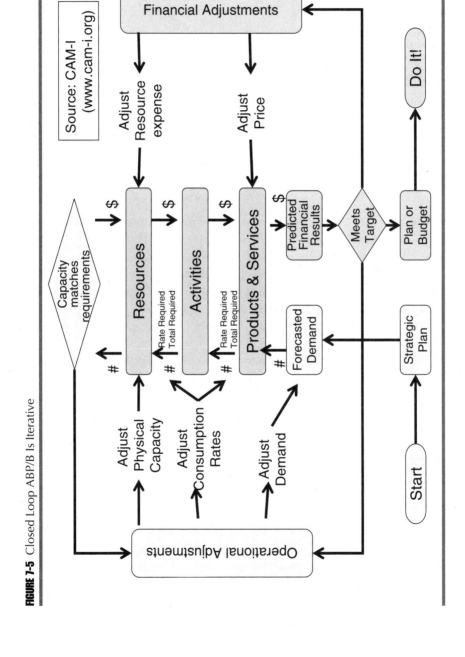

FIGURE 7-5 Closed Loop ABP/B Is Iterative

The extent to which these adjustments can be made within a single budgeting cycle may be limited, but they should nevertheless be addressed. Adjusting demand may have political consequences that need to be carefully considered as well.

Once a balance has been achieved between capacity and demand, activity-based budgeting will show the financial resources required, or the amount of funding necessary to meet the demand. If this is greater then the financial resources available, managers have two options for adjustment:

1. If some of the expenses are recovered by charging user fees for services, user fees (prices) can be raised. Care is required here. If demand is elastic (sensitive to changes in price), increased fees may result in a reduction in volume that more than offsets the price increase.
2. If possible, resource expenses can be adjusted by renegotiating salary levels or the purchase prices of other resources.

This process is more delicate in an environment that emphasizes performance while funding is simultaneously reduced. Managers at all levels need to be sure that senior decision-makers, including elected or appointed officials, are continually informed of the impact that some of these adjustments may have on performance. Performance expectations may need to be adjusted as well. If they are not, holding managers accountable for the same performance objectives they had at a higher funding level when resources are being reduced may be grossly unfair.

This process of reconciling the top-down and the bottom-up approaches to resource planning is critically important, since there will always be top-down pressures. The reality is that public sector organizations will always have spending goals or constraints. It's naïve to think that, just because resource requests are more thoroughly and logically justified, they will automatically be granted. But this doesn't mean that ABP/B should be abandoned. In fact, as we have just seen, it provides an excellent tool for reconciling the bottom-up model to the overall constraint.

WHAT COMES FIRST—ABC OR ABP/B?

ABC was developed before ABP/B, and is probably a more familiar concept for most managers. Thus, an organization that is getting started with activity-based approaches might have a tendency to implement ABC first. Then, once the system has settled down and stabilized, it moves to ABP/B.

However, in the public sector this might not be the best strategy. While public sector organizations need to know actual costs by activity and cost object, this need may not be as pressing as it is in the private sector. Of greater concern to public sector managers is how to justify their annual or special funding requests, or, if they are setting user fees for services, what the total and unit-level costs of those services will be in the future.

Activity-based planning and budgeting responds more effectively to these concerns than ABC, so implementing ABP/B and then moving to ABC makes sense. After the ABP/B is implemented, the activity model for ABC is relatively easy to develop.

STRATEGIC RESOURCE PLANNING AND BUDGETING (SRPB)— TAKING IT UP A NOTCH

Activity-based planning and budgeting is a powerful tool, but it has one serious failing from a resource planning perspective: it doesn't take all expenses into account, as the astute and experienced reader may already have noticed. For example, what about the non-recurring projects that are carried out in most organizations (and are the basic business of some organizations)? What about the expenses that are inherent in the organizational structure or are incurred to provide the physical and technological infrastructure? Can we talk about budgeting without taking these expenses into consideration?

In order to include these expenses in a budgeting process that applies the same basic principle of providing a logical underpinning for annual funding requests, a technique known as strategic resource planning and budgeting (SRPB) has been developed.

SRPB begins with the basic premise that all costs have a cost driver. A cost driver, described in Chapter 2, is basically something that causes a cost to be incurred, the *raison d'être* for the cost.

SRPB categorizes all costs according to their cost driver and applies different budgeting techniques to each category. It also provides a means to relate these costs to the strategic objectives of the organization.

The Four Drivers

SRPB classifies costs into four basic categories according to what drives them:

- Demand-driven costs
- Project-driven costs
- Structure-driven costs
- Decision-driven costs

These categories, as we shall see, cover all the expenses in the organization. A resource planning and budgeting model that addresses them all will produce comprehensive budgets.

Because of the differences between these four cost categories, it makes sense to use different planning and budgeting processes for each one of them. We can then pull the results together into an integrated resource budget. Figure 7-6 provides an overview of this process.

Once the four categories of costs have been covered, an integrated and comprehensive budget can be prepared for the entire organization and presented in multi-dimensional views: by cost-driver category, by nature of expense, and by responsibility center.

The added dimension of cost-driver categories can provide information to managers in a format that they have not seen before. Reporting by each of the cost-driver categories can give managers a new perspective on their total resource requirements and provide them with insight on how easy or difficult it will be for them to adjust resources.

Another advantage to using cost-drivers is that doing so diverts attention and discussion from the sometimes misleading and confusing categories of fixed and variable, direct and indirect expenses.

Demand-Driven Costs

Demand-driven costs are what we have been talking about throughout this chapter. They are triggered by an event such as an application from the public or some other form of request for services. This trigger then sets in motion a series of activities (a process) that are designed to satisfy that demand. These are the high-volume, transactional processes that are found in most organizations. As we have already seen, demand can be internal as well as external. Activity-based planning and budgeting is the technique of choice for analyzing these demand-driven costs.

Project-Driven Costs

In addition to the ongoing transactional processes generated by internal or external demand, most organizations have a number of projects underway at any point in time. These could be systems development projects, facilities

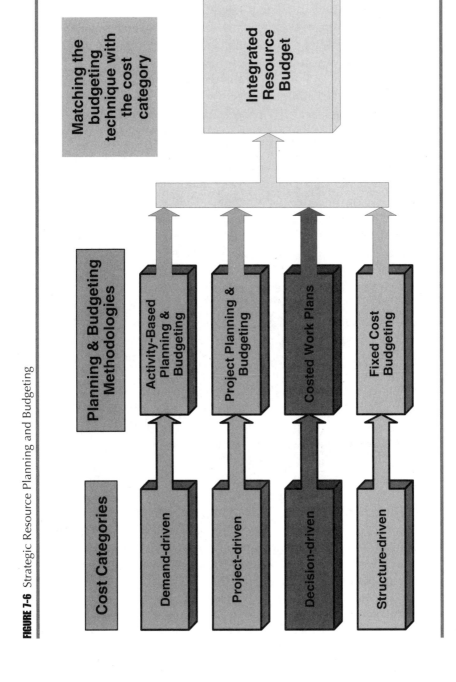

FIGURE 7-6 Strategic Resource Planning and Budgeting

expansion projects, training program development projects, or new product development projects, to name a few possible examples. They may also result from government-wide initiatives. They frequently involve people from various sectors of the organization in addition to the core project team. The impact of these projects on the workload of these non-core participants is frequently not taken into account in determining resource requirements, and this is one of the causes of project delays and even project failure.

For organizations that are mainly geared to engineering, auditing, consulting, and systems development and implementation, projects are the main mode of operation.

The resource planning and budgeting technique for project-driven costs is, quite simply, project planning and budgeting. This is a mature, well-documented planning discipline and is promoted and supported by organizations such as the Project Management Institute (www.pmi.org), which accredits project management professionals (the PMP designation) and maintains the Project Management Body of Knowledge. For the purposes of SRPB, having the same level of detail that the project managers have in their project plans is not necessary. What is necessary is to get summary information from each project.

Since project planning and budgeting may be more focused on the project life cycle than on the annual planning cycle, and since projects frequently straddle two or more fiscal years, the challenge may be to report project-driven cost information on a fiscal year basis.

The information that is needed from the project plans is similar to what is generated from the activity-based planning model. In fact, a project can be viewed as a structured set of activities with a driver volume of 1, since they occur only once in the fiscal year. The level of effort for each project activity is analogous to the unit level of effort (ULE). What is needed for SRPB purposes are the resource quantities that the project will consume in the coming fiscal year, including person-days (which can then be converted to FTEs), consulting services, travel, and software. The resource quantities are then converted to dollars by nature of expense (i.e., general ledger expense account) and integrated into the overall budget. As is the case for operating departments, the project may generate internal demand for the support areas such as human resources and contracting.

Structure-Driven Costs

In addition to costs from processes and projects, all organizations have structure-driven costs. These are associated with the capacity required to deliver the services and support the projects. Structure-driven costs fall into three main categories:

1. **Management structure costs:** These are basically the salaries and other expenses associated with the organization structure, from the chief executive officer down to the director or manager level. These expenses only change when the organization structure changes and they can be regarded as a special type of capacity cost.
2. **Technology structure costs:** These are the expenses of the information technology and telecommunications infrastructure, including both hardware and software. Only the fixed portion of these expenses is included as a structure-driven cost, since the variable costs for workstations, landlines, and cell phones is calculated as part of the FTE-driven costs in activity-based planning and budgeting.
3. **Physical structure costs:** These expenses include the costs of the physical accommodations needed to provide the products or services, as well as the vehicles and equipment that may be required.

The budgeting approach for these expenses is traditional fixed cost budgeting, a technique familiar to financial planners. Once the budget for this cost category has been determined, it too can be integrated into the overall budget.

Decision-Driven Costs

Decision-driven costs are found in almost every organization, to a greater or lesser extent. In the past, these expenses have sometimes been called discretionary expenses, since management has some leeway in deciding on how much should be spent. However, we have avoided that term, since it downplays the importance of these expenses in contributing to the achievement of the organization's mission and mandate.

This cost category is found in areas such as communications and outreach, employee assistance plans, research, and corporate planning groups. All of these areas may be of great importance to the organization, but they are not subject to a cost formula and they do not have an inherent structure. Different levels of expenditure will be associated with different levels of contribution to desired outcomes and strategic objectives; management decides on the combination of expenditures and outcomes it can best afford. In times of budget constraints and cuts, these may be the first expenses to be affected, often to the long-term detriment of the organization.

Budgeting for decision-driven costs is best accomplished through costed work plans. Costed work plans provide a more structured, organized approach to planning these expenses. They are basically tables that are organized with the following column headings:

- Major activity
- Activity
- Person-days
- Salary expenses
- Other expenses
- Expected results
- Contribution to strategic objectives

Once again, we are framing the plan in terms of activities, so that we are still in the realm of activity-based approaches. The function may include some project-driven and demand-driven costs, and these can easily be incorporated into the costed work plan. The work plan can also be prepared to show what could be achieved with two or three different levels of funding, giving management options for the decision-making process.

Compliance-Driven Costs

Another type of cost is worth mentioning: compliance-driven costs. This is not a separate cost category. These costs may be found embedded within each of the other four categories and they should be flagged and summarized (using ABC attributes). They represent the costs of compliance with legislation, whether it is specific legislation that governs the department or agency or general government-wide legislation and policy to which the organization must conform. The significance of these costs for planning purposes is that, unlike decision-driven costs, they are non-discretionary. If they are reduced or eliminated, the organization runs the risk of sanctions from regulatory agencies or central audit authorities.

A Second Look at Closed Loop ABP/B

Figure 7-7 expands the closed loop approach discussed above and illustrated in Figure 7-5 to include all of the cost-driver categories of strategic resource planning and budgeting.

FIGURE 7-7 Closed Loop Strategic Resource Planning and Budgeting (SRPB) Information Flow

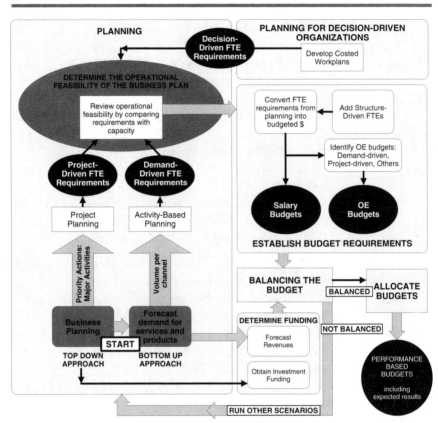

It is a much more complex process, but the principles and the adjustment strategies are basically the same. For the non-demand-driven costs, these adjustment strategies would include:

- Slowing down or deferring implementation of projects
- Scrutinizing structure-driven costs to identify and eliminate chronic over-capacity
- Reducing decision-driven costs, while continuing to work toward key objectives

The Link to Strategy and to Performance Management

Figure 7-8 provides an overview of how SRPB is linked to strategy and to performance measurement.

- Strategic planning and scorecarding will have a major impact on processes, projects, and decision-driven activities. SRPB can provide strategic planners with a powerful tool to view the cost impact of different strategic initiatives or changing performance targets.
- Demand forecasting will be a critical input to planning for demand-driven costs.
- The long-term technology plan will feed into the next fiscal year's projects and will also determine expenditures on the technology infrastructure.
- Ongoing organizational design activities will set the management structure and the associated expenses.
- Capacity planning will determine the physical structure expenses.

SRPB also provides the link to performance reporting and measurement. Here, again, we are suggesting that different feedback mechanisms are appropriate to each category of costs. We are getting away from blanket reporting by nature of expense and by cost center.

For demand-driven costs, using the actual costs generated by an ABC system to calculate cost variances by activity and by cost object is an excellent way to provide information for cost control and performance measurement. Dynamic ABM is a tool that can be used to split a total variance into its volume and performance components, which is essential if managers are to be held accountable only for what they can control. The costs and their cost variances from plan or budget can also feed into performance measures that would be part of a scorecard.

For project-driven costs, simple reporting of actual against budgeted costs by activity will be sufficient.

For structure-driven costs and decision-driven costs, reporting of actual costs against budget by nature of expense and responsibility center is the best approach.

FIGURE 7-8 Strategic Resource Planning and Reporting

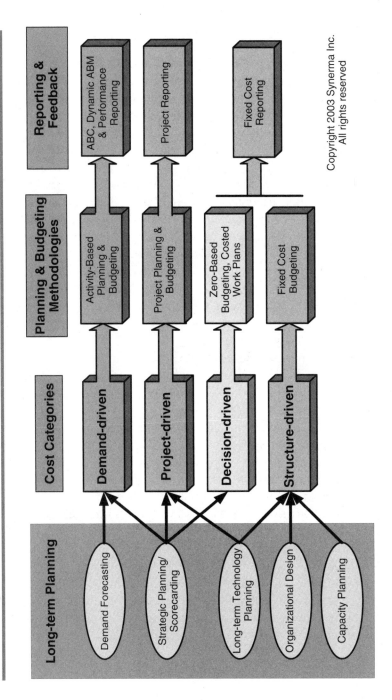

IMPLEMENTATION CONSIDERATIONS

Activity-based planning and budgeting and strategic resource planning and budgeting present major implementation challenges. The implementation process needs to be carefully thought-out and well managed.

This fundamentally different approach to resource planning and budgeting is a big shift in the management culture. Change-management techniques such as education, consultation, participation, and communication are essential to the process.

There is a need to move forward with some caution, ensuring that buy-in is obtained from all levels of management, starting at the top but including middle managers and front-line managers. Having a project champion from an operational area would send the important message that switching to ABP/B and SRFB is not just another accounting exercise.

It is very important to start off with a planning or project definition phase. The main deliverable of this phase is a project charter that confirms the project objectives and scope, presents the approach and methodology, defines roles and responsibilities, and presents plans for implementation, communications, and performance measurement.

The project team should be selected with care and should include members from finance, operations, and IT (if software is being implemented). It may be advisable to include outside consultants, if additional expertise and manpower are needed.

Most major implementations start with a pilot project. The choice of the pilot department (or process) is important. A balance must be found between a pilot department that is large enough so that the results will be credible to the rest of the organization, yet small enough so that the results of the implementation will be available fairly quickly. The management of the pilot department must be receptive to the new approaches and willing and able to cooperate in the effort. Starting with an operational department rather than a support area may be best.

The software question needs to be addressed early in the process. The first issue that will come up is "Why can't we just implement ABC/M and ABP/B in Excel?" The answer is that, while Excel may be adequate for simple implementations and is very useful for data gathering during the model building phase, an Excel-based ABC/M and its extended ABP/B are difficult to maintain over the long term and totally unsuitable for more complex, enterprise-wide implementations.

Only three or four software solutions on the market can handle ABP/B. The software evaluation and selection process should be carried out prior to the pilot project, so that the software can be used during the pilot. The ideal situation would be a rental or loan of the software for the pilot, but this may not be possible.

Another issue with SRPB, as far as software is concerned, is that much of the process has been and can continue to be carried out with traditional financial planning and budgeting software, often in the financial planning and budgeting module of ERP systems. The financial planning staff is usually comfortable with this software and may want to continue using it. If this is the case, ensuring that the ABM software is compatible and that the interface is carefully designed are important.

ABP/B provides a clear vision of what better budgeting looks like. As early adapters of ABP/B work out the bugs and glitches and demonstrate that ABB assists organizations in achieving competitive advantage, widespread use of ABP/B will be inevitable.

This chapter has presented a dramatically new approach to resource planning and budgeting. The value added of this approach, in terms of the ability to secure adequate funding to deliver on performance targets, to manage resources, and to report to management, is enormous. Even though the initial implementation effort is far from trivial, the payoffs in the medium and long-term make it all worthwhile.

> **"Every idea is a source of life and light which animates and illuminates the words, facts, examples, and emotions that are dead—or deadly—and dark without them. Not to engage in this pursuit of ideas is to live like ants instead of men."**
> —Mortimer J. Adler, American philosopher, quoted in
> *Saturday Review*, November 22, 1958

Chapter 8

A Framework for Balancing and Integrating Cost, Performance, and Risk Management

Contributor: Martin Croxton, Bearing Point, www.bearingpoint.com

"That men do not learn very much from the lessons of history is the most important of all the lessons of history."

—Aldous Huxley, *Collected Essays* (1959)

"We need to learn how to use our resources in both warfighting and in the support area to do our business more efficiently. In that regard, we're like any other agency or private-sector business. We're under constant pressure to spend money wisely and be good stewards of the taxpayer's money."

—Admiral Archie Clemens, U.S. Navy Pacific Fleet Commander, March 20, 2000

RECENT HIGH-PROFILE CORPORATE DEBACLES in the U.S., like Enron, Barings, and WorldCom, as well as the terrorist attack of September 11, 2001 and the controversial response in 2005 to Hurricane Katrina, have resulted in the implementation of regulatory or statutory mandates such as the Sarbanes-Oxley Act and the Patriot Act. Organizations are striving to implement an enterprise risk management (ERM) system and its associated processes to address these requirements and avoid future disasters. A comprehensive framework for balancing and integrating cost, performance, and risk management does not currently exist. ABC/M can contribute to balancing and integrating these concepts.

Not many people in the United States would disagree that the world fundamentally changed on September 11, 2001. A new perspective on the vulnerabilities of our open society to attacks on our own soil came sharply into focus. Unprecedented changes in the structure, mission, and funding of many governmental organizations followed. How were these decisions made? Are resources being managed effectively and efficiently in the ongoing global effort against terrorism? One would hope that these decisions, as well as those that follow in future years, are made with due consideration to the concept of risk rather than out of mere expediency. To facilitate effective risk-based decision-making, good definitions of risk and risk management frameworks are needed. Managers will need to know how risk should be factored into decisions related to areas of public service, including the obvious ones of the national defense and homeland security apparatus. Managers also need to know deficiencies in their current approaches to risk management. Ultimately what are needed are new and innovative ideas for combining performance and risk management approaches to support strategic planning and resource management decisions.

RISK AND RISK MANAGEMENT—DEFINING OUR TERMS

Despite the fact that contending with risk may be more art than science, substantial volumes are dedicated to the study and application of the scientific aspects of risk. Many frameworks and techniques have been developed in an attempt to make considerations of risk less random and more comprehensive. They support a perception that there are strong cause-and-effect linkages between our decisions and outcomes, and that we have an ability to effectively manage complex security situations to the successful conclusions that we desire.

Risk is a nebulous term. One dictionary states that *risk* is "the possibility of injury, damage, or loss; dangerous chance; hazard."[1] Risk has a negative connotation; it is something to avoid. The closely related term *chance*, however, is defined more positively: "an unpredictable event or accidental happening; a risk or gamble; an advantageous or opportune time or occasion; opportunity."[2] So applying the term *risk* in the context of *chance* leads to an enlightened view that "risk is a subjective judgment, the product of the likelihood and consequence of some future and uncertain event."[3] Liotta and Lloyd define risk is as "the gap between desired ends (national security objectives) and available means (strategy and forces)."[4] This definition introduces the concept of resources—and ultimately leads to a need to understand expenses and costs for capacity and capability.

Because risk is so inseparable from goals, organizations should not merely acknowledge the possibility that a risk event will actually occur, but instead

---

[1]*The New Webster Encyclopedic Dictionary of the English Language*, 1980 ed., (Consolidated Book Publishers, Chicago), p. 726.

[2]Ibid, p. 136.

[3]Ronald E. Ratliff , "What Is Uncertainty? And What Is Risk?", U. S. Naval War College, *National Security Decision Making, Decision Making and Implementation Selected Readings, Volume One*, Jan 2004, p. 2.

[4]P. H. Liotta and Richmond M. Lloyd, "The Strategy and Force Planning Framework," *Strategy and Force Planning, Fourth Edition*, (Naval War College Press, Newport, RI, 2004), p. 13.

should actively manage risk. Risk management is a process that involves identifying risks, treating them in a manner that reflects the organization's risk appetite, and providing reasonable assurance regarding the achievement of the organization's strategic goals.

In the U.S., the most widely known and employed risk management framework is the COSO model. COSO stands for the Committee of Sponsoring Organizations of the Treadway Commission. The commission, originally created in response to the savings and loan debacles and other corporate finance scandals in the 1980s, brought together professional business associations, academics, financial advisory services firms, and private sector institutions to study the problem and develop a solution that had broad appeal and applicability. The result was a high-level risk management framework that could be used to help organizations better understand and enhance their individual systems of internal controls and thus avoid or prevent strategic, financial, operational, compliance, and reputation-related disasters.

The initial COSO report, *Internal Control—Integrated Framework*, was published in 1992. It was updated in 2004 because of heightened concerns about the state of risk management due to a new generation of financial disasters (Enron, WorldCom, Tyco, etc.) These failures shattered investor confidence and threatened our nation's economic stability. COSO's updated publication, titled *Enterprise Risk Management—Integrated Framework*, was released in September 2004. It rests on the underlying premises that "every entity exists to provide value for its stakeholders," and that the central challenge for leaders is "to determine how much uncertainty to accept as [the organization] strives to grow stakeholder value."[5] According to the publication, a clear linkage exists between strategy, risk management, and performance management, as evidenced by the following passage: "Value is maximized when management sets strategy and objectives to strike an optimal balance between growth and return goals and related risks, and efficiently and effectively deploys resources in pursuit of the entity's objectives."[6]

Leaders can employ the COSO framework to "help an entity achieve its performance and profitability targets, and prevent loss of resources . . . [or]

---

[5]COSO, *Enterprise Risk Management—Integrated Framework, Executive Summary*, 2004, p. 1.
    [6]Ibid, p. 1.

help an entity get to where it wants to go, and avoid pitfalls and surprises along the way."[7]

Another risk management framework is the Control Objectives for Information and Related Technology (CobiT) model. Produced by the Information and Systems Audit and Control Association (ISACA), it is an adaptation of COSO. CobiT outlines a comprehensive control model of information technology in support of business processes.

The foundational premise of CobiT is that "in order to provide the information that the organization needs to achieve its objectives, IT resources need to be managed by a set of naturally grouped processes."[8] The model classifies 34 control processes into four domains: planning and organization, acquisition and implementation, delivery and support, and monitoring. It also defines seven criteria for information, and outlines guidance that "provides the structure that links IT processes, IT resources, and information to enterprise strategies and objectives."[9]

COSO and CobiT present unique risk management guidelines, perspectives, and points of emphasis, but leave it to each organization to determine how to implement them. Areas that remain ripe for further advancement are measurement, integration with other key managerial considerations, and reporting. According to one source, "While . . . [there] are sophisticated measures for financial risk, measures do not yet exist for nonfinancial risk. Since many of the events in the nonfinancial risk area are random, it is difficult to build models that offer predictability."[10] This presents a distinct challenge for implementation of risk management within the defense and security environments.

RISK MANAGEMENT IN THE DEPARTMENTS OF DEFENSE AND HOMELAND SECURITY

Risk management has taken on increased importance in the defense and security establishments in the aftermath of 9/11. One indication is that the

---

[7]COSO, *Internal Control—Integrated Framework, V. Framework*, 1992, p. 3.

[8]IT Governance Institute, *CobiT Framework, 3rd Edition*, released by CobiT Steering Committee and the IT Governance Institute, Jul 2000, p.6.

[9]Ibid.

[10]Thomas L. Barton, William G. Shenkir, Paul L. Walker, *Making Enterprise Risk Management Pay Off—How Leading Companies Implement Risk Management*, (Financial Times/Prentice Hall PTR, Upper Saddle River, NJ, 2002), *Ch. 8 Conclusion*, p. 222.

last *Quadrennial Defense Review Report* (*QDR*) contains a chapter dedicated to the subject. The chapter begins, "Managing risk is a central element of the defense strategy. It involves balancing the demands of the present against preparations for the future consistent with the strategy's priorities."[11] The *QDR* goes on to indicate that a risk management structure will be used to assess tradeoffs between ends (objectives) and means (resources).

The Department of Homeland Security is no less enamored with risk. In fact, it is being compelled to use a risk management approach as the basis for distribution of security assistance funds. This recommendation was formalized in *The 9/11 Commission Report*: "Throughout the government, nothing has been harder for officials—executive or legislative—than to set priorities, making hard choices in allocating limited resources. . . . Homeland security assistance should be based strictly on an assessment of risks and vulnerabilities."[12]

The assumption is that a combination of assessments can help government leaders make better decisions in supporting defense of the homeland. However, while progress is being made to include risk concepts in managerial thought processes, the truth is that both departments' approaches to risk management are presently deficient. Merely assessing risks for a "one moment in time" snapshot every few years will not truly accomplish the aims of risk management; nor will doing so meet the expectations of our nation's citizens. It will take additional effort to make the vision of using the frameworks to measure risk and manage the implementation of departmental strategies a reality.

FILLING THE RISK MANAGEMENT GAP

The difficulties and deficiencies encountered by Defense and Homeland Security are not uncommon. Many organizations struggle with similar issues. In part, this is because only in the past several years has risk gained attention and been considered a core management concern rather than a separate and secondary financial function. Thus, risk is still maturing as a management concept. While the risk management frameworks are typically robust and

---

[11]*Quadrennial Defense Review Report*, Department of Defense, U.S.A., Sep 30, 2001, *VII. Managing Risks*, p. 57.
[12]*The 9/11 Commission Report*, "What To Do? A Global Strategy," Dec 2004, p. 395–396.

sophisticated, they do not proscribe managerial measurement, integration, and reporting requirements. They focus on assessing risk and defining risk mitigation plans, but lack sufficient guidance on how to implement a solution to routinely measure and track the cost and performance characteristics of risk-based decisions. This will undoubtedly improve over time and with experience.

Fortunately concepts, tools, and methodologies are available that, when coupled with a comprehensive risk management model such as COSO, can help address the gaps. Those I consider to be most useful—the balanced scorecard (BSC), performance logic models (PLMs), and activity-based cost management (ABC/M)—are often components of an organization's control and performance management system infrastructure. Integrating these performance management tools with risk management frameworks offers the possibility of a managerial system that promotes internal control in tandem with alignment of resources, risk responses and mitigation efforts, and organizational objectives.

PLMs promote disciplined thinking and communication about alignment. PLMs typically are process oriented rather than organization oriented, and are used to visually reflect the linkage between desired outcomes, outputs, activities, and resources. To better understand the process view is why ABC/M is essential for measuring costs. This is because ABC/M focuses on the work activity costs that *belong* to horizontal processes in time-sequence rather than on the organizational cost center where the expense was spent from. Risk-based thinking is needed to answer the why (risk assessment) and how (risk response) questions that hold the logic chain together. PLM, supported by the ABC/M calculated costs, can be used to hone risk-based budget and operational decisions and pinpoint areas requiring deeper analysis.

ABC/M provides the most useful management construct for enabling integrated risk management measurement and reporting. Traditional ABC/M models are relational tools that codify the causal linkages between resources, activities, and cost objects. They show how resource costs are consumed by an organization's activities, and how activity costs are, in turn, consumed by cost objects. ABC/M models display costs in monetary terms, providing managers with a recognizable metric for interpreting results and analyzing tradeoffs. Organizations are constantly faced with tradeoffs. This is no less true in the area of risk management. Investing in building a capacity, or risk resiliency, is a long-term process designed to prepare an organization for events that may never transpire.

Cost objects are normally products, services, channels, and/or customers, but for government agencies they are also programs, objectives, and/or even risk categories. Since risk responses are synonymous with activities, an organization can readily associate the actions taken to mitigate a risk, transfer it, or otherwise control it to risk categories, creating a risk-informed, cost-based decision support network.

Most ABC/M systems today also support *attributing*, or tagging model elements with additional data. For example, suppose an organization conducts an operational risk assessment and determines that a credible threat to its building exists—someone may want to damage or destroy the building. The organization can create an attribute called "likelihood" with a possible range of values of "low," "medium," and "high," and assign an attribute value to this and every threat in the model. Suppose the organization believes the likelihood of someone damaging or destroying the building is low. It now has an additional way of viewing the risk and cost data—that is, instead of just being able to see how much it spent to protect the building or how much was spent overall to mitigate operational risk, it can also see how much was spent on all items that had low, medium, or high likelihood of occurring. More attributes would add to the dimensional richness of the model. The benefit of this approach is that it shows the cost impact of various resource deployment scenarios and risk-based decisions, and could be used to support regular cost-benefit and portfolio analyses.

Although issues remain, such as how to assign and distribute activity costs that have more than one benefiting risk category, these are largely procedural and could be addressed in implementation. In contrast, the potential benefits to using an activity-based risk management approach are compelling. It could serve to highlight the type and magnitude of risk exposures, identify the cost impacts of risk responses, and surface unacceptable risks and costs for further deliberation. Ultimately, it could challenge how control is actually performed, and become the catalyst for embedding risk management in the organization's processes and culture.

THE INTEGRATION OF ABC/M AND PERFORMANCE MEASURES IN RISK MANAGEMENT

Risk is ever present. Knowing how to successfully address risk requires great judgment and skill. To help contend with constantly mutating and dangerous threats in both the corporate and national security realms, organizations have developed and implemented risk management frameworks such as the COSO and DoD (*QDR*) models. However, these methods are not sufficient for genuinely managing risk. While they do bring risk thinking to planning and assessment processes, they fail to produce transparent, timely, and useful information that leaders can use to assure reasonable control and make decisions.

An integrated cost and risk management framework provides a perspective that will allow managers to make more informed decisions and improve resource management practices, process designs, organizational structures, and strategic planning. It will:

- Encourage a more strategic view of the cost function and ABC/M information.
- Enable rationalization of enterprise-wide risk expenditures.
- Bring visibility to the "cost of control" and enhance earned value management (EVM) concepts.
- Support a more comprehensive view of balanced scorecard key performance indicators.
- Facilitate transparency and reporting to all stakeholders, especially boards of directors, shareholders, and regulatory bodies.
- Leverage any earlier investment in ABC/M knowledge and infrastructure.

Integrating modern organizational control and performance measurement capabilities, like balanced scorecards, performance logic models, and especially activity-based cost management models, with risk management frameworks is a way to overcome many obstacles to routine risk-based measurement, reporting, and decision-making. This approach will help to ensure that our essential decisions are grounded in both the art and science of risk management.

> **"Liberty cannot be preserved without a general knowledge among the people. ... The preservation of the means of knowledge among the lowest ranks is of more importance to the public than all the property of all the rich men in the country."**
> —John Adams, Second President of the United States, *Dissertation on the Canon and the Feudal Law* (1765)

> **"When you come to a fork in the road, just take it."**
> —Driving directions from Yogi Berra, U.S. Baseball Hall of Fame athlete, quoted by New York Yankees teammate Joe Garagiola

Chapter 9

Implementing ABC/M through Rapid Prototyping

"It is piously spoken that the Scriptures cannot lie. But none will deny that they are frequently abstruse and their true meaning difficult to discover. … I think that in the discussion of natural problems we ought to begin not with the Scriptures, but with experiments and demonstrations."

—Galileo Galilei, Italian astronomer, *The Authority of Scripture in Philosophical Controversies* (1632)

"Failing to prepare is preparing to fail."

—Vince Lombardi, famous coach of the Green Bay Packers, U.S. National Football League

ABC/M rapid prototyping followed by iterative remodeling of each of ABC/M's prior results has been proven as a superior approach to implementing ABC/M systems. It is a way to overcome the temptation to construct an ABC/M system that is too detailed prior to the organization's ability to absorb what ABC/M is all about and how it can work for the organization. Prototyping is accomplished in just a few days. ABC/M rapid prototyping is also an effective way to drive out the natural fear and resistance to ABC/M through training and participation.

ABC/M rapid prototyping accelerates the organization's use of ABC/M data by relying on only a few key employees to first rapidly construct a high-level ABC/M model for their entire organization (or, alternatively, for key processes or portions of their organization—"local ABC/M," as described in Chapter 4).

Once the initial ABC/M has been modeled and the participants have a good grasp of what ABC/M is and does, then with the help of co-workers they all can selectively adjust the model to lower levels of detail and higher accuracy. With the subsequent models, additional employees from the local areas highlighted in the initial ABC/M model can revise and modify the initial effort. These employees are in a much better position to improve the prior version of the ABC/M model because they are more knowledgeable about the work in their respective areas and their outputs.

The intent of ABC/M rapid prototyping is to make your mistakes quickly, up-front, and early in the process when it is easier to change the ABC/M model, not later when it is far more difficult. Through prototyping, organizations can build a working and useful ABC/M model in days as opposed to trying to build a Rolls-Royce ABC/M model in months. With this speed-up approach, the benefits from improvements gleaned from the ABC/M data can be reaped almost immediately. The initial ABC/M models can then graduate into a repeatable, reliable ABC/M system. This implementation approach is more practical and sensible than ABC/M pilots or one-shot, big bang ABC/M implementations where the implementers cross their fingers and pray that it will all work at the end.

ABC/M IS PERFECTLY OBVIOUS—AFTER THE FACT

At first glance, the idea of ABC/M can be overwhelming, and this perception might prevent an organization from even proceeding with implementing its system. Those unfamiliar with ABC/M share a general misconception that it involves a massive enterprise-wide involvement of people with a mudslide of data that must address activities in great detail from all parts of the organization. Another misconception is that there will be no results until the ABC/M system is completely constructed and operating like a production information system. These people are unaware that ABC/M is an analytical tool that is best designed as a layer of reporting that sits on top of and apart from the transaction-intensive information systems.

An additional misconception about ABC/M is that it will take forever to implement and perhaps may not be worth the effort. With ABC/M rapid prototyping, an ABC/M system can be launched quickly and cheaply. By reducing the administrative effort but still raising awareness of the benefits, ABC/M rapid prototyping shifts the cost-vs.-benefits evaluation from reluctance to higher levels of interest. These include a desire to move ahead with haste and a genuine motivation to finish the ABC/M model iterations so that a permanent and repeatable ABC/M reporting system can be installed.

ABC/M rapid prototyping is an implementation approach where the initial ABC/M model is immediately followed with iterative remodeling of the same costs included in the prior model, but deeper and with more resolution and visibility. Any issues related to data can be quickly flushed out. Figure 9-1 gives a sense for a succession of models plus some key benefits. ABC/M rapid prototyping is a valuable accelerated learning technique for a small but important number of employees and managers. These key participants, referred to as "functional representatives," not only can get a solid vision of

FIGURE 9-1 Iterative Prototyping

Iterative ABC/M prototyping with expanding granularity (but same scope) accelerated learning about model design and cost behavior.

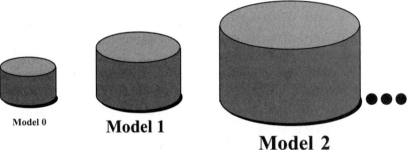

Model 0   **Model 1**

Model 2

Benefits:
- **Answer your questions about ABC/M with experience!**
- **Make your mistakes early on, not when it's harder to change.**
- **Don't overplan and agonize about assumptions ... simply do it, build it, and adjust it.**
- **Each successive model's benefit pays for each effort.**

what their ABC/M system will look like, but they also start thinking about what they will *do* with the more robust ABC/M data when they get them.

One must adjust one's thinking to understand ABC/M. It is not initially modeling a work flow chart. Work flow charts are somewhat easier for people to follow since they are time-sequenced, left-to-right. ABC/M can place the activity costs into flow charts later on after the costs of the many and diverse outputs are known. Once an ABC/M model is designed, it becomes more obvious to the employees who constructed it; and there is agreement that the resulting costs are logical and defensible.

ABC/M rapid prototyping is effective because it starts where people already are—they know what their organization is doing. They also recognize that they do not understand their costs and that they mistrust the cost data. ABC/M rapid prototyping gives them a chance to model their cost structure. The enthusiasm for implementing ABC/M comes more easily after an initial ABC/M model is completed, regardless of its size or scale. After the first ABC/M model is quickly completed, the participants can then see multiple views of their organization's costs—its resources, activities, processes, and outputs. They also realize how ABC/M data can collectively provide answers to questions they just could not fathom with the limited information provided by their existing accounting system.

Rapid Prototyping: Eighteen Holes of Golf on a Polo Horse

ABC/M rapid prototyping is a much faster way to get phased-learning, buy-in, and results compared with the traditional approach to designing an ABC/M system. Traditionally, full-fledged ABC/M system implementations have been accomplished through intensive interviewing of many employees. With ABC/M rapid prototyping, only a few employees who are knowledgeable about the majority of what the organization does are brought together. They construct the first ABC/M model in just a couple of days with a trained facilitator and an ABC/M software specialist. The focus is far less on achieving accuracy or results and much more on learning and getting a vision.

The exercise begins the same way as a traditional proof-of-concept ABC/M pilot, by forming a cross-functional team of functional representatives. After that, however, the similarities to a pilot end. All too often, ABC/M teams improperly build an ABC/M pilot too deep and too detailed—and they don't even realize it. They over-engineer the system design and resulting costing system, and then don't get the results they expected. It is death by details. An ABC/M pilot takes a long time even though it is supposed to be brief. As a result, the organization can develop skepticism or lose interest since they conclude that no payback will be coming any time soon. The ABC/M effort may then go dormant. (ABC/M projects never die. It is inevitable that ABC/M will be installed. It may take a future catastrophe that jars an organization that stopped its earlier ABC/M project to admit that the current accounting system has either mislead them or left them clueless about their costs. When a major decision in hindsight is deemed a big mistake because the traditional costs were misleading, then the ABC/M system implementation gets restarted.)

In contrast to pilots, which often are formally announced to employees with a loudly broadcast "banners-and-bugles" procession, an ABC/M rapid prototype is more stealth-like and non-invasive. When senior management makes a major announcement that an ABC/M system will be installed, some employees only hear the "C" in ABC/M for the costing, and their defensive shields of fear and resistance go up. Employees may interpret the project as a cost-cutting exercise, perhaps cutting their jobs, rather than as a way to provide for better decision-making.

The purpose of the ABC/M rapid prototype is not to be secretive but rather for a select few employees within the organization to quickly gain some understanding. A key lesson learned is how to balance the tradeoff between higher accuracy and a greater effort to maintain the ABC/M system. The functional representatives learn a lot about the properties of ABC/M; they also learn about some of the behavioral implications of how people might react when they see the ABC/M data. With ABC/M data, many employees will see things they have never seen before. It is important early on to learn how to treat the ABC/M data responsibly. ABC/M is not an accounting police tool to punish or embarrass people. It is more like a managerial information database and enabler for organizational improvement.

In contrast to ABC/M pilots that begin with collecting vast amounts of data through extensive interviews and questionnaires from many people, the initial ABC/M rapid prototyping is, as noted, conducted in a burst of a couple of days. The exercise involves as few as four or five knowledgeable employees with a facilitator and a trained ABC/M modeler using commercial ABC/M software. Many adults learn better and more quickly through doing as opposed to listening to lectures about the concepts. So the ABC/M model construction begins almost immediately. A key insight the team learns—and will share with their co-workers—is that incremental improvement is preferable to postponed perfection.

The participants are always intellectually engaged in constructing the ABC/M prototype since they are not modeling some fictitious case study organization; it is their *own* organization. The modeling also deals with and represents the people they know and work with, the things these co-workers do, and the outputs they provide to others. The participants are never bored during this fast-paced exercise. Simple rules are used to speed things up. For example, no one is allowed to bring in any data with them; the model is entirely constructed with what they already know. The only exception to this rule is for the financial data. Total expenses for the period being modeled, usually the current or past year, are a good starting point. Senior managers who will eventually see the ABC/M model will be able to relate to these total costs since they are already familiar with them. This also ensures that the initial ABC/M model will be complete and not mistakenly omit a function. No stones are left unturned.

Building the First ABC/M Model—Tap Dance Now, Waltz Later

The first step in building the initial ABC/M model is quite simple. The organization chart of employees and contractors, if applicable, is divided into groups of people who do similar things. These groups are often (but not always) the functional departments. This may result in 10–15 groups. The key is to count and sum the number of employees from each group to ensure that no portion of the cost structure to be analyzed is inadvertently left out. When the entire organization is initially modeled, validating this completeness is no problem since the total number of employees tends to be a well-known number and can be reconciled to. Each functional representative takes responsibility for the groups of people he is most familiar with. Next, the functional representatives define three significant activities for each group they have selected to represent. Figure 9-2 shows an example of a time-effort worksheet that has been successfully used to collect the ABC/M data.

Within 20 minutes, each form for each group is completed. Simple rules can be applied when defining the activities. As examples, the work activities should follow a "verb-adjective-noun" grammar convention. Assume that people are productive only five hours of an eight-hour day and ignore the other three hours for work breaks and social time. (The three hours will later get baked into the five productive hours. Treatment of those hours is more of a work culture issue.). Instruct the functional representatives that the three activities should account for more than 90 percent of what the group does throughout the year. This rule forces each activity definition to be worded in what may appear to some as being too summarized for each group. But about 40–60 activities will result from all the input forms, which is more than adequate to trace the activity costs to cost objects with higher accuracy than their organization's traditional method can.

Use estimates for the employees' time-effort in increments of 5 percent. Discourage allocation of 80 percent or more to any one of the three activities; if the participant struggles with that, allow only that activity to be subdivided into two components, thus yielding four activities for that group but still summing to 100 percent. Do not allow these two specific activities: "supervise and mentor employees" and "attend meetings" (even though these activities occur). Excluding them will ensure that all the work activities will lend themselves to being traceable to cost objects.

Ignore salary and wage differentials. Simply use an average salary for every employee. In effect, the mail clerk earns the same salary as the president in

FIGURE 9-2 Work Activity Input Form

Work Activity Input Form

Example for sales function with 45 license processors

Natural Work Group Name (e.g., sellers) ___ No. of employees ___

Work Activity Description	%	Ideal Activity Cost Driver	Code	Example
1. process license application	45	no. of license applic	C	
2. resolve customer disputes	35	no. of customer disputes	C	
3. create strategies	20	no. of planning sessions	D	
4.		no. of		
5.		no. of		
	100%			

Codes:
A = Suppliers
B = Products, Services
C = Customer Prospects
D = Business Infrastructure
E = Intermediate Assignments (to other activities)

this first model. In most cases, this assumption won't make a significant difference to the costs of outputs, service lines, and customers for purposes of this first model. ABC/M's property of error dampening will help bring about that result. In future model iterations, salary differentials for different departments can be considered.

Additional rules to speed up the process involve not allowing consensus among the "functional representatives" when it comes to defining the activity dictionary, the drivers, or the driver assignments, nor for estimating the quantities that flow through the drivers. Each functional representative knows his own area sufficiently and does not need any help from the others. Functional representatives "own" their area of coverage. Any estimating error on their part cannot have any grave consequence. The consequence of error is simultaneous over-costing and under-costing, but these minor errors offset and wash out anyway when the costs reassign to the cost objects. Regardless, the intent of this first ABC/M prototype model is not precision costing. It is stimulating for the participants and the ABC/M project team. What they will have at the end is an economical and low-risk technique to get to their eventual ABC/M system.

Cost Object Profiling: A Key to Getting Desired Results

The use of preliminary estimates works well with ABC/M, as just described, because any estimating errors in the activity costs will offset when they are further traced (combined) into the outputs, service lines, customers, and service-recipients. (The concept of offsetting error may be counterintuitive, particularly to accountants who are trained for high precision and perfection, but the properties of an ABC/M assignment network as a "closed" system make offsetting errors possible.) Error dampening works even better when no activity cost is too large relative to the other activity costs. This way any estimating error of any single activity cost cannot materially affect the cost of all the outputs. Error dampening also works better when the cost objects are deliberately pre-defined into look-alike groupings that already reflect the diversity and variation that ABC/M is so good at tracing into. The facilitator can ensure that well-segmented costs are easily accomplished by pre-defining the groupings to achieve this effect.

Like a caricature sketch artist at an amusement park, the facilitator is skilled at selecting just enough activities and cost objects to reasonably represent the organization without choosing so many that the ABC/M model goes too far past diminishing returns in extra accuracy for extra effort. The technique of pre-defining the groupings of final cost objects is accomplished through "profiling." In most cases the organization has already been referring to families of its products and service lines. The functional representatives realize that there may be dozens or hundreds of specific products and service lines within each family. Those subdivisions are already known and likely codified by their organization.

Cost object profiling is much more needed for service-recipients and customers because the standard groupings that organizations use do not usually work well for ABC/M. For example, some organizations may segment their customers or service-recipients by geographic territories. But large differences in how customers consume the workload may have little to do with where these service-recipients are physically located. Segmenting customers by demographic groups or by the levels of special attention required may be a much better segmentation to reflect more dominant ways in which workloads are disproportionately consumed. Some ABC/M teams refer to these customer groups as "clusters" or "centroids."

Figure 9-3 shows a worksheet that the facilitator uses to define multiple and various types of customer or service-recipient groupings. At a minimum, by selecting only three bases of difference, with only two extremes, the eight unique combinations (i.e., 2x2x2=8) are ensured to pre-set the diversity of any costs into these eight cost objects.

With profiled final cost objects and 30 or more work activities, no one activity being too large, the functional representatives are assured that they will trace to and calculate fairly reasonable costs in their first effort.

TEACH THEM TO FISH, AND THEY CAN FISH FOREVER

The construction of the model is fairly straightforward. Each activity is traced to the cost objects that cause the activity levels to fluctuate up or down. This link ensures that a causal relationship exists. Next, measurable activity drivers are identified for each activity, and finally activity driver quantities are estimated in total and for each cost object in relative proportions. Commercial ABC/M software does the rest by reassigning the costs through the linked cost assignment network into the final cost objects.

After the costs related to salary and fringe benefits have been totally assigned to the cost objects, distribution of the remaining resource expenditures goes quickly. The financial controller provides the top ten non-wage expense items in a way that they account for roughly 90 percent of the

FIGURE 9-3 Final Cost Object Profiling

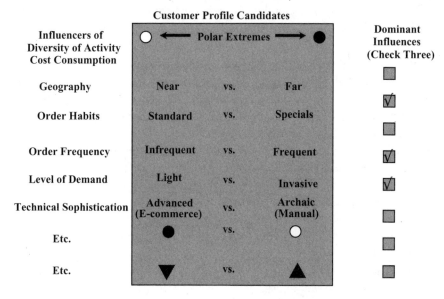

A key to initial ABC Rapid Prototyping to identify major sources of diversity.

non-wage resource expenses. Non-wage expenses almost always follow the work, and each expense item usually traces into less than four of the many defined work activities. Sometimes the expense type is dedicated to only one activity. Since the ABC/M cost assignment network was already completed an hour before this exercise, all that needs to be done after these last resources are connected to activities is to recalculate the model. The non–wage-related costs trace all the way through into the final cost objects. The ABC/M model is then complete and ready for analysis.

The combination of using informed estimates by knowledgeable workers and the error-dampening property of the ABC/M assignment network has very significant implications. Together, these mean that using estimates in place of facts will have a minimal adverse impact on the accuracy of an ABC/M system's final cost objects. This also means that only a few key employees are initially needed to provide the data. Everyone is somewhat surprised that their organization can achieve ABC/M results without having to have all the data available from a sub-system to get started and see reasonable results. This revelation also ensures that ABC/M will get some traction as a way to improve the organization's performance rather than potentially stall out as a complicated information technology (IT) and systems project. The IT aspects of ABC/M come much later and well after a few users are already relying on the ABC/M data for making better decisions.

The ABC/M rapid prototyping experience is like a practice round in a sport without keeping score. By having a few key employees construct the initial model from scratch, they much better understand what they have created. There is ownership. The results are sufficiently credible to them, despite the resulting calculated costs usually being quite different from their beliefs and from the standard costs provided by their existing accounting system. These traditional accounting costs will likely have been calculated based on flawed allocations and misguided thinking. ABC/M is very logical. Allocating costs using factors without any causal relationships is not.

Constructing and Populating ABC/M Model #0—The Starting Point

The initial ABC/M rapid prototype is nicknamed Model #0 to reinforce an understanding that Models #1, #2, and so on will be used as further refinements. An ABC/M cost assignment network is scalable. Revisit Figure 4-14. It illustrates how the ABC/M cross has scaleable depth and can always be further disaggregated into lower levels of detail.

Groupings of resource expenses, work activities, types of outputs, and types of customers or service-recipients should be subdivided (i.e., disaggregated) only if more segmentation achieves needed visibility or additional accuracy. The participants learn the ABC/M rule to always ask, "Is the climb worth the view?" After Model #0, the ABC/M project team can gather additional specific data when it becomes apparent that the accuracy of outputs is more sensitive to those specific data. They can then substitute the higher-grade data for the estimates. The project teams can also substitute a few different activity drivers as better drivers than the ones they initially and spontaneously selected and used.

Instead of presuming that detail is needed everywhere, ABC/M rapid prototyping deliberately starts at high levels and adds more detail selectively and only where it is justified. Sensitivity to error can always be tested by adding more detail to the existing ABC/M model. The team learns the properties of estimating error in an ABC/M cost assignment network. To some, particularly to accountants, the result is counterintuitive. The impact of estimating error for the activity costs means some are slightly over-costed while the others must be under-costed; there must be zero-sum error. But as the activity costs combine further down the network into the final cost objects, any error begins to offset. In ABC/M, error does not compound, it dampens out. Revisit Figure 3-9. It reveals how high levels of accuracy can be quickly achieved with minimal effort. Then much less additional accuracy comes from more effort.

In a short time, the epoch of ABC/M models graduates into the ABC/M system that can be repeatedly and reliably refreshed. With iterative remodeling, the ABC/M team learns to identify and include activity drivers as they are needed rather than assume they are required. Figure 9-4 expands Figure 9-1 and illustrates how the ABC/M models eventually become the ABC/M system. It also illustrates that as model iterations become more detailed, the uses of the data can be more operational.

Refreshing the ABC/M rapid prototype models or the ABC/M production system is done with a blend of updated measured data and estimates for the remaining and less vital areas of the ABC/M model. Of course, the financial ledger expenditure data, with its 100 percent resource data, should be a source. (Some organizations, however, have simply begun with the total expenses from their most recent run of their payroll.) The purpose of the initial rapidly prototyped models is not to pin down all the details right away, but rather to stimulate the participants. It gets them thinking, exchanging ideas, realizing how their current data are limiting or misleading, and most importantly envisioning how their organization may use the output data to address problems and make decisions.

ABC/M is basically a self-discovery experience. Even when a much larger ABC/M system is up and running, the ABC/M data do not necessarily provide final answers. It tells people where to look and what additional questions to ask. These early participants begin experiencing what ABC/M is and what it is not. They will likely become a much more effective means of informing their organization about ABC/M's benefits than the designated ABC/M project team or hired consultants (whom other employees may suspect have self-serving motives).

ABC/M rapid prototyping helps prevent "death by details." ABC/M project teams often have a problem determining the right level of detail, work activities, products, channels, and customers to focus on. There are pitfalls if an ABC/M system is designed using traditional IT development methodologies

FIGURE 9-4 ABC/M Prototyping with Iterative Remodeling

Each iteration enhances the use of the ABC/M system.

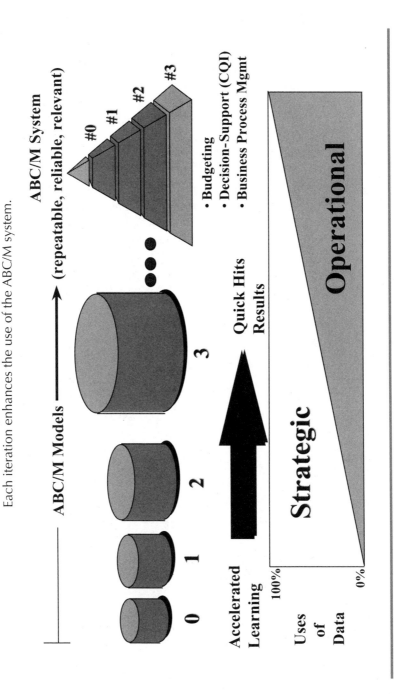

to solve this problem—the "ABC/M leveling problem." With IT methodologies, one of the worksteps in the traditional schedule for the first few weeks is usually to perform the "data requirements definition." But this step is not appropriate for designing the ABC architecture. This is because there are too many interdependencies among ABC/M's resources, activities, and cost objects. There is interplay among the levels of detail, each affecting the ultimate accuracy of outputs to be costed.

The intent of the ABC/M rapid prototype is to get reasonably right results in a workable and timely fashion. Drilling too deep too soon is a trap that should be avoided. The extra benefits of a little more accuracy aren't worth the extra effort. Ironically, after Model #2 or so, the data requirements are a derivative of the ABC/M rapid prototyping exercise. Ideally Model #0 should be completed in two days so that the third and last day of the experience can be dedicated to playing with the model, analyzing the ABC/M data, and learning the principles and properties of ABC/M.

Perhaps the most important thing the ABC/M team can do on the last day of their exercise is to add a few attributes to the model. Two effective attributes are the level of importance and the level of performance. This lets the participants appreciate that their ABC/M system delivers much more visibility than just calculated cost amounts. They realize that attributes begin to suggest what general directions they should investigate. Where should they scale back on spending? Where should they invest more energy? What processes might they consider outsourcing? What activities, products, or customers should be promoted more?

Analyzing Model #0 to Get Buy-In

Finally, the ABC/M team can begin analyzing their model with the intent of evaluating the impact of specific changes. By adding volume and quantity data, the model quickly computes the unit costs for each product, service-line, and any intermediate output such as the cost per equipment hour if that is relevant. As part of the unit cost calculation, ABC/M also reveals the unit cost of each contributing element, such as for each activity cost. Since unit-of-work output costs can substantially vary even for outputs with comparable *total* unit costs, the team can begin their own form of internal benchmarking to explore best practices.

Through this mock analysis, the team inevitably begins to test the feasibility of using the ABC/M data for some of the pressing issues their organization may be struggling with, such as estimating the costs of taking on certain types of orders from specific types of customers or service-recipients. They can learn what options are available by examining the assumptions they initially made related to fixed and variable costs that they now have displayed. They can play with alternative ways to assign depreciation costs to equipment other than the traditional way the existing accounting system is assigning depreciation. And they can see costs without any depreciation, since depreciation is a sunk cost (not just a fixed cost), if they want to consider using a marginal cost rather than a fully absorbed cost in their analysis.

The functional representatives and the ABC/M team can get a glimpse of how much of their cost structure is organizationally sustaining relative to costs that make and deliver products or serve their customers and service-recipients. That ratio may be shocking. The total sustaining costs may be greater than 30 percent of their cost structure, excluding purchased material costs. Is that good or bad? It probably depends on other factors. But at least they can see the amount and consider whether they want to maintain those same levels of spending on non-product, non-service, and non-customer-related costs. The functional representatives can also discuss the concept of unused capacity management now that the cost data are structured in a format that makes more sense to them.

The point here is not to over-analyze anything. It is to get the participants to connect the data to uses of the data—and to connect some of those uses to some of the burning high-priority issues of the organization. This creates the needed buy-in to proceed with building the next ABC/M Model #1 and ABC/M in general.

Securing and Propagating the Learning: A Communication Plan

A useful way to expand learning and simultaneously gain further buy-in is to immediately have the Model #0 participants make a brief unrehearsed presentation to specially selected peers, and perhaps an executive or two, covering the following points about their few days building Model #0:

- What did we do?
- What did we learn?
  - About our organization's cost structure?
  - About the ABC/M methodology and ABC/M model properties?
- What are our options for next steps?

It is important that these invited guests also have their expectations well managed, just as the functional representatives' expectations were. The peer group needs to know that the ABC/M model structure they are witnessing is a miniature-scale model and that the calculated costs were derived entirely from estimates (except for the starting financial expenditure totals). Fortunately, even in first ABC/M rapid prototype Model #0, the ABC/M properties begin to pile up the output costs in roughly the same relative amounts as will the subsequent larger-scale ABC/M models #1, #2, etc.

An important reason to conclude the first ABC/M rapid prototyping session by presenting to peers is for the ABC/M project team to much better appreciate that they really need two ABC/M plans: (1) an implementation plan, and (2) a communication plan. The second plan may well be more important than the first. ABC/M is about behavioral change management. Who is initially exposed to ABC/M and subsequently the sequence of who else is exposed really matters. If naysayers or threatened managers who have clout are introduced too soon into the process, they can poison the project before ABC/M has a chance to take hold.

By generating some visible benefits with an initial group of positive-attitude employees, enthusiasm builds. Invariably, everyone will learn that costs are abstract and intangible. Costs measure the effects of the things that are placing demands on work. So measuring and calculating costs is actually modeling to get a representation of how resource expenditures are used. Resources are where the capacity to do work resides. Capacity is what expenditures pay for. By working with and refining ABC/M models, workers find their knowledge growing, and they begin to appreciate the ABC/M adage that "it is better to be approximately correct than precisely inaccurate!"

ABC/M MODEL DESIGN AND ARCHITECTURE FOR SPECIAL CASES

An effective starting point for the ABC/M rapid prototype model is to be as broad as possible. This means that one should try to include all the headcount that fully or partly is involved in supporting and directly serving all the customers and service-recipients. But for certain kinds of problems, the focus may be on only a specific process with a more narrow interest in simply needing the costs of standard services (excluding non-standard services). Or the interest may be in knowing only the costs of certain outputs that are components of a standard service, such as the workstep to check a customer's credit when processing different types of sales orders.

In some cases, broad-scope ABC/M models begin by being divided into multiple "children" ABC/M models that are later consolidated into a single "parent" ABC/M model. Commercial ABC/M software accommodates consolidations. In the opposite cases, organizations start with the enterprise-wide ABC/M model and then later divide portions of it into dedicated "children" models. Both of these cases are visualized in Figure 9-5.

BUILDING THE ABC/M SYSTEM: BASIC FACTORS

As the reader has undoubtedly gathered by now, several factors are critical to building an ABC/M system and getting it right. Three key factors are size, staffing, and time-phasing.

FIGURE 9-5 ABC/M Consolidations—"Children" Models into a "Parent" Model (or Vice Versa)

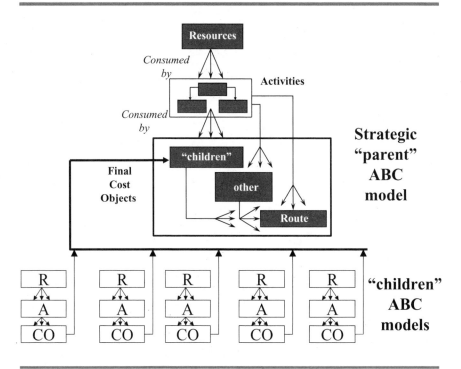

Right-Sizing the System

In the field of photography, you cannot presume that handing a camera to person means that he knows how to take pictures. ABC/M rapid prototyping is similar to giving an organization a chance to snap some photos to see how they turn out.

The key to ABC rapid prototyping is right-sizing the initial ABC/M models to a proper level of detail that meets the organization's needs and allows for accelerated learning of the ABC/M concepts and implementation practices. This will facilitate the ultimate construction of a repeatable, reliable, and relevant ABC/M production system. The prototype quickly provides the new types of cost information that organizations are very interested in. Speed-to-results is becoming increasingly important for senior managers who are exhibiting less tolerance for lengthy projects with potentially shallow results.

With ABC/M rapid prototyping, after ABC/M data have been analyzed, the functional representatives can consider how much deeper to dive into the cost structure in their next iteration of the model. Unfortunately, once an ABC/M team gains some competence in increasing the resolution and granularity of the costs through iterative remodeling, the appetite for more data may grow. (Remember that the scope and amount of costs remain constant among the successive ABC/M models.) There is some risk that the team will soon try to build a massive model intended to answer everything. This can be a recipe for failure. Instead, the team should consider limiting the intended use of the ABC/M model to target one or two areas or problems relevant to the organization. An example is to isolate which customers or service-recipients consume both the more costly services and also extraordinary time from the organization. Altering the behavior of these types of customers can lighten the organization's workload and ultimately reduce costs and free up capacity for more profitable use.

Time-Phasing ABC into ABM

With ABC/M rapid prototyping, after an organization understands how the diversity and variation of its outputs create its cost structure, it can much better understand how the *same* activity costs can be oriented to the time-based horizontal process view. This facilitates "process analysis."

Figure 9-6 indicates that organizations should first perform cost assignments vertically to discover how diversity and variation in outputs, products,

FIGURE 9-6 Time-Phasing ABC into ABM

Some organizations initially design highly disaggregated activity models with intent to reduce cost. By first reporting on the costs of outputs, senior management will be engaged and know where to focus.

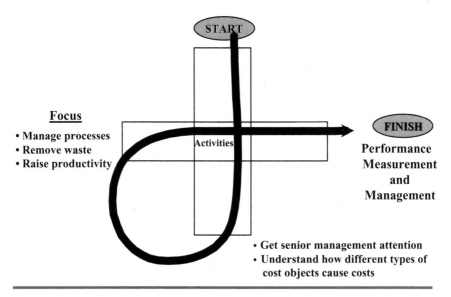

service lines, and customers relate to complexity and thus to higher support costs. ABC/M rapid prototyping reinforces this lesson.

With ABC/M's cost assignment view, the functional representatives can first examine the work activity costs on a *per-unit cost* of output basis. Comparisons can be made between and amongst identical work activities and their costs, on a per-unit-of-work basis, as well as for different kinds of outputs.

Some costing approaches, practiced when the business process reengineering (BPR) movement was at its high point, simply calculated a one-step allocation of the general ledger into activity costs—and stopped there. The activity costs were immediately applied as costs across the processes. They lacked the emotional charge from also seeing the unit costs of the variety and mix of the outputs from those same business processes.

Some organizations have business process flow charts on their conference room walls but have not committed to significantly changing their processes. When ABC/M data reveal the true per-unit-cost of each output, including intermediate outputs, "organizational shock" often sets in. Then genuine "root-cause analysis" problem-solving begins. Fortunately, ABC/M provides reliable and fact-based data at an early point to assist the ABC/M project team and functional representatives. In short, the lesson is do ABC vertical assignment first, and perform process analysis afterwards.

"You can observe a lot by watching."
—Yogi Berra, U.S. Baseball Hall of Fame athlete (Yelled at teammates who were not paying attention to the game)

"It's not the time it takes to take the takes that takes the time; it's the time it takes between the takes that takes the time."
—Steven Spielberg, Academy Award Oscar-winning cinema director

Chapter 10

Examples of ABC/M in the Public Sector

"There are three classes of people: Those who see. Those who see when they are shown. Those who do not see."
— Leonardo da Vinci, Florentine painter and inventor, Note Books (c. 1500)

THE CENTRAL MESSAGE in this book is that public sector organizations are facing intense pressure to do more with less. This challenge is requiring government agencies to:

- Recognize the importance of satisfying their service-recipients and customers
- Determine the true costs of their services and rates
- Implement process improvements more aggressively than ever before
- Evaluate make-vs.-buy outsourcing and privatization decisions
- Align their work activities to mission and strategic planning.

In the federal, state, and local government environments, activity-based cost management (ABC/M) has become one of the most effective enablers to meet this challenge. In this chapter, we will read about several public sector organizations that have implemented and continue to improve their ABC/M systems. Some used pilot projects rather than rapid prototyping in the development phase but are nonetheless pleased with the benefits evolving from their implemented systems. I would like to thank the authors who contributed these anecdotes on their positive experiences with ABC/M.

Several of the case studies that appear in this chapter originally appeared in *Bettermanagement Quarterly* (formerly *As Easy As ABC*), published quarterly by ABC Technologies, Beaverton, Oregon (acquired by SAS Institute Inc. in 2003). Reprinted with permission.

AN INTRODUCTION TO PUBLIC SECTOR CASE STUDIES

by Alan Fabian

Alan Fabian is CEO, The Centre for Management and Technology (www.cmat.org). Alan wrote several of the case studies appearing in this chapter.

ABC/M is the best solution to address the challenges mentioned on the previous page. A common mistake is to view ABC/M as a trend with no real impact on operations and no meaningful measures of results. The good news is that, trendy or not, ABC/M actually works. Furthermore, it is the most cost-effective method of enabling operational managers and day-to-day workers to effect change in a government environment.

The current emphasis on the Chief Financial Officers Act and the Government Performance and Results Act, as well as the FASAB 4 requirement to have an operational cost management system, has focused CFOs and accountants on the potential afforded by ABC/M to meet these new standards. Although these needs are real and must be met, they only begin to scratch the surface of the benefits of ABC/M.

The starting point for any government organization is to develop an activity-based cost management (ABC/M) model. This provides a top-down look at the organization's resources and activities and the relationship between the activities and the resources they consume. Why is this so important, you may ask? The answer is quite simple . . . a cost, any cost, can only be incurred if someone does something. In other words, if you want to understand your costs, you must clearly understand which activities your organization performs and which departments and services these activities support. The ABC model will address many of the reporting requirements required by various new cost standards.

The real benefit, however, is in providing data of varying detail to managers, supervisors, and regular employees in a distributed fashion that allows each person to see, analyze, and manage the costs and activities that are within their control. It is at this level that real and meaningful changes in cost structure, performance measurement, and service delivery will occur. Today, this type of management data can be provided with commercially available software products that link to existing cost and metric systems and can deliver meaningful reports at the individual PC user level. There is absolutely no more cost-effective way of achieving performance improvement.

The output of an ABC/M calculation includes:

- Resource allocations
- Cost reporting compliance
- Operational management data
- Accurate service pricing
- Activity-based budgeting and planning (ABB/P)

A wide variety of needs have been met by implementing an ABC/M system. In some cases the system required certain manual updates, and in other cases the system has been fully automated. These solutions were designed not from some cookie-cutter approach, but individually to meet the needs of the specific government agency involved. Typical implementation periods ranged from three months to nine months.

CASE STUDIES

The following case studies demonstrate the variety of management needs and complex problems that can be met with ABC/M in actual government agencies, whether Federal, state, or local.

Parks Canada

Contributors: John Bottriell and Nabil Aboutanos, who were senior cost analysts with the Canadian government's Canadian Heritage Ministry at the time this was written.

Parks Canada, the government organization responsible for managing Canada's National Parks and Historic Sites, undertook implementation of activity-based cost modeling at its facilities across the country. The goal was to create standard ABC/M models for each of 32 sites, a process expedited by developing a national template model and rolling out the product through a "train the trainers" approach.

Background

Covering 224,466 square kilometers (2 percent of Canada's land mass), the national parks system includes more than 40 national parks and reserves. In addition, 131 historic sites and several active and historic canals are administered under the Parks Canada mandate. Managing these resources in the context of government funding pressures and increased revenue targets provided the impetus for improving costing information. Existing cost accounting information, derived from legacy accounting and operating systems, proved to be inadequate for the demands of fully costed activities and services.

The ABC/M Pilot

In researching alternatives to meet our costing needs a pilot development was undertaken in our Rocky Mountain District, home of such well-known National Parks as Banff, Jasper, Yoho, and Kootenay. ABC Technologies' Oros ABCPlus was selected as the software tool of choice. (ABC Technologies was acquired by SAS Institute Inc. and Oros renamed SAS ABM.) The pilot proved our ability to develop full cost assignments to activities and cost objects. Based on the success of this pilot, senior management endorsed national implementation of activity-based costing.

The ABC/M System Implementation

To ensure local ownership of the data and analysis, models were developed for each of the 32 business units organized to manage Parks Canada sites.

We (John Bottriell and Nabil Aboutanos) formed the national implementation team to select the appropriate ABC/M software tools, develop national model standards, and develop training tools. Each of five regions established local implementation teams of two officers to complete regional implementation at the business unit level. Our approach was to combine the training of the regional team and business unit operator with the installation of the software and the construction of a business unit model. Once completed, the regional team proceeded with implementing the models through the business units in their region.

Our very aggressive implementation plans called for training users, installing software, and implementing a business unit ABC/M model in each region—within three months. Regional teams would then continue with the balance of ABC/M model implementations for their region. The ABC/M software was selected, and within months we had at least one working ABC/M model in each region.

To meet this schedule, a two-week cycle was established for each model. A business unit implementation consisted of an introduction to activity-based costing for the management team, followed by a question-and-answer session and then the setting up of interviews with managers. Software was installed and interviews were conducted over the first week. During this data gathering stage, users also were being trained, and the resource and activity modules were being built.

A validation of the activity module was conducted with responsible managers. The second week consisted of development/validation of cost objects and the development and building of activity drivers. By day nine, a complete site model was ready for presentation. The exit process included a review of the concepts of activity-based costing, a presentation of the business unit ABC/M model, and an opportunity for managers to work with the resulting model information.

ABC/M Model Development

Preliminary experience gained from the development at our pilot sites allowed us to create a conceptual ABC/M model prior to our national implementation. We chose to define our resource centers as either overhead or program delivery, based on the premise that a center provided services to either an internal client or external client. We chose to make intra-module (i.e., intermediate) assignments of resources between overhead and program delivery accounts. This allowed for a more intuitive development of resource drivers.

Once overhead costs were assigned to program delivery resource centers, operational measurements were applied as resource-to-activity drivers. In our case, the driver data that related to our maintenance and fleet management functions were imported. We relied on the flexible bi-directional exchange of data between the commercial ABC/M software and our external systems. We also imported data into our models using Microsoft Access and Microsoft Excel.

We chose to build intramodule assignments in the cost object module to allow costing of infrastructures (such as buildings) as well as final products and services. This served the generation of activity drivers, which could often be attributed directly to these facilities. Internal cost object drivers also were derived to assign these costs to final cost objects.

Success with ABC/M

Success was measured by the positive reaction of managers at the business unit level to a complete ABC/M model within a two-week time frame. We also were able to capitalize on our pilot models by ensuring adherence to a national standard for model construction, consistent definitions for overhead, program delivery, our dictionary of activities, and groupings of cost objects.

We were able to download financial data electronically from our legacy financial system and manipulate the data easily for import into our ABC/M software models. We look at the modeling capability of our ABC/M software as a plus while we encourage our users to develop alternative models for specific purposes. In a government environment, we initially report and model cash expenditures. ABC/M modeling allows us to retain the integrity of the base data but to add additional "costs" such as depreciation, external support services, and grants in lieu of taxes.

Parks Canada is beginning to use ABC/M models to support pricing strategies, assist in assessing employee takeover proposals, and consider alternative service delivery options. We, as implementers, are cognizant of the ongoing need to nurture the concept of activity-based costing in the organization as a viable tool for effective decision-making. We look forward to a further validation of the ongoing viability of our ABC/M models.

U.S. Office of Rural Economic and Community Development
Contributor: Alan Fabian, CEO, The Centre for Management and Technology (www.cmat.org)

This case study is about applying ABC/M for improvement in operational management and efficiency. The U.S. Office of Rural Economic and Community Development (RECD), formerly the Farmers Home Administration, volunteered to participate in an ABC/M pilot to analyze their Management Control Process (MCP). At the time the RECD was involved in reviewing and improving its MCP. The goal was to identify the true cost of performing management control, to identify areas of improvement in management control, and to realize cost savings from improving key areas.

The activity model was developed through the use of interviews with field offices, as well as organization charts, payroll and expense records, management performance reports, and volume analysis. Costs were assigned to each activity based on labor hours incurred for each task, specifically identified costs, or allocations based on the sum of direct costs. The RECD also developed a set of value criteria to apply to the activities identified. The purpose of the value criteria was to identify those activities that enhance the process by contributing to the provision of services or satisfying the goals and objectives of the organization. Opportunities for streamlining and cost reduction became focused on those activities that were judged low in value-added.

The value-added criteria used included:

- Can the activity be incorporated into day-to-day operations?
- Does the benefit of duplicated activities exceed related costs?
- Is the activity in line with strategies and performance measures?
- Does the activity favorably affect the delivery of services?
- Does the activity generate empowerment and accountability at the most practical level closest to the point of delivery?
- Does the activity test key controls based on risk?
- Does the activity provide timely identification of problems and allow for timely correction?
- Does the activity facilitate ongoing monitoring and early warning?

Finally, a new Management Control Process was developed. The new MCP was based on the following guiding principals: duplicative activities were eliminated wherever possible; decisions should be made at the lowest point in the process capable of making the decision and affected by it; risk assessment was utilized to focus resources more effectively; and management control was more fully integrated into operations to identify and correct problems at the earliest feasible point in time. The new MCP eliminated five review processes and replaced them with one consolidated process.

The overall results from this effort were dramatic. Over 55 percent of the old management control costs were expended on non–value added activities as defined by the RECD. The expenditure of so much on non–value added activities was causing field auditors to spend 52 weeks out of the year conducting audits and no time following up to ensure that audit findings were being corrected. As a result, the same audit findings were reported year after year. Further, the new Management Control Process lowered operational costs by 37 percent per year.

U.S. Army, Fort Riley
Contributor: Gary LaGrange; Director of Logistics; Colonel, U.S. Army, Retired

An activity-based cost management (ABC/M) and activity-based budgeting and planning (ABB/P) program at the U.S. Army's Directorate of Logistics, Fort Riley, Kansas, produced remarkable results—a 34 percent reduction in manpower and $6 million in annual savings.

Every employee in every activity center participated in defining step-by-step activities to accomplish every task in the directorate. By measuring the accomplishment time and applying skills and grade and workload data, we were able to define the true manpower requirements for each activity, which were almost always less than we had expected. Using this methodology, we refined our processes and restructured our organization to focus on the customer. The result was a dramatic improvement in operating efficiencies.

Background

Facing the inevitable pressures that come when a nation begins to place a higher proportion of its national treasures into programs other than defense, the Directorate of Logistics at Fort Riley, Kansas, sought a method to change itself. It had to contend systematically with fiscal reductions, an upcoming A76 Commercial Activities Study, and the need to realign its cost structure because of obvious inefficiency. To continue the usual "salami slice" approach to reducing resources simply breeds greater inefficiency, and it was clear that a measured approach to realigning the logistics work effort was in order.

Furthermore, the Commanding General had given the new Director of Logistics, a former CEO and president of a mid-size corporation, the mandate to examine the organization very closely to determine its efficiency and effectiveness. Change would occur, if required, to bring the organization into line with customer need and at the right cost.

The installation's Directorate of Logistics is a 650-employee organization with a $34 million annual operating budget and a $130 million stock fund (supplies). It is responsible for all transportation (unit movements, air, rail, freight, household goods); supply (rations, general supplies, fuel, ammunition, major end items); maintenance (tactical equipment repair and component re-manufacturing); services (dining facilities, laundry, commercial vehicles); automated systems support; tactical equipment readiness; and logistics policy and procedure. The Directorate was a conventional model of bureaucracy, and the challenge was to superimpose best business practices on that bureaucracy so that service to our customer—the soldier—could be efficient, effective, and at least cost.

To do so required a paradigm shift from "It's the way we've always done it" to "An enthusiastic, innovative environment with a customer-focused, process-oriented management scheme geared toward continuous improvement."

We felt that we owed that shift to our soldiers and to the nation's taxpayers.

Our approach was to conduct an in-depth, process-oriented management study. We would build a team to do so and give it a charter undergirded with a set of business rules. We would ask the team to start by examining our reason for existing, then lay out the step-by-step requirements to accomplish our goals, and then let a lean, minimum-overhead organization with attendant resource requirements fall out. The study would also have to provide for continuous improvement opportunities.

It was clear that one best approach existed: activity-based cost management (ABC/M), the natural and common-sense approach to accomplishing the task at hand. We determined that we would phase our efforts:

- Phase I would consist of reengineering our processes.
- Phase II would fully institutionalize activity-based cost management and budgeting (ABC/M/B) and sustain the management methodology for the long haul (into the 21st century).

We built an "Eagle" team of five bright, dedicated specialists to manage the project, and, most importantly, we involved every employee in the organization. The team was given a resolute set of business rules to guide its activities. All communication channels were opened widely, and everyone was encouraged to participate enthusiastically and innovatively. The upcoming A76 study caused the workforce to gel around the strategy to retain or bring all of our activities "in-house" so that these important and valuable people could retain their earned civil service benefits. We trained our workforce and selected the ABC Technologies' commercial ABC/M software, Oros. (ABC Technologies was acquired in 2003 by SAS Institute Inc. and Oros renamed SAS ABM.)

We adopted an academic principal that Southwest Airlines has enjoyed success with—that of turning our organization "upside down." To better focus our efforts on the essence of this project—improved service to our customers—the soldier was placed at the top of our organization chart. The top organizational line became those activity centers that touched the customer on a day-to-day basis, the most important elements in our organization. This empowerment of employees would prove to be extremely valuable. Overhead, including the Director, became the lower element of our organization, with the primary mission of providing resources to the first line to enable first-class customer support. We began to learn from other businesses and to adopt applicable best practices from them.

Because the Commercial Activities Study requirements loomed, we sought assistance from a consulting agency that could provide us with an experience base to accomplish A76 requirements as we proceeded with our ABC/M based study.

We began with an examination of our strategic plan by looking very closely at our "reason for being." Our key processes fell out of that examination, and they became our cost objects. Then, every employee of each activity center (generally aligned with organizational elements) attended iterative workshops to lay out the step-by-step activities, the heart of ABC/M, required to accomplish our reason for being (cost objects).

As a note, we considered it very important to bring in ABC/M experts who had experienced multiple full deployments. Because we viewed this adoption of ABC/M as an overarching change in management methodology, metaphorically akin to open chest surgery, we sought out experienced ABC surgeons from whom we interns could watch and learn. ABC/M/B is too often viewed as a financial technique or a financial management system. It is instead, if properly applied, a revolutionary means for the Army, and perhaps the Defense Department, to manage as it has not ever been able to do before. Using this methodology, tremendous efficiencies can be attained, and the costs associated with maintaining trained and ready soldiers, ready equipment, and a satisfactory quality of life can be seen much more clearly. Further, ABC/M may very well unveil from within the resources required to underwrite necessary Army reshaping initiatives.

The results of our efforts have been significant. Most importantly, our organization is now focused on the customer. Our "upside-down" organization has two layers rather than seven, with the customer at the top. Employees feel empowered and important. We have eliminated deputies, division chiefs, branch chiefs, section chiefs, and sub-section chiefs. Communication channels are open, short, and quick. Administrative help has been pooled. Co-locations and consolidations have eliminated redundancies. We have reduced our non-contracted manpower by 34 percent and reduced our annual operating costs by $6,000,000 … and we are only beginning. Future iterations will result in exponentially larger increases in efficiency at much less cost.

City of Philadelphia Department of Streets

Contributor: Alan Fabian, CEO, The Centre for Management and Technology (www.cmat.org)

This case study describes applying ABC/M in operational management for local government.

Mounting pressure to maximize taxpayer value by providing the most effective and efficient service delivery created a need for the City of Philadelphia Department of Streets to better understand and manage its costs. To address this challenge, the department engaged in the development and implementation of an activity-based cost management (ABC/M) system. The goal was to improve its cost visibility and provide more effective cost management to line managers and employees.

The department performed one of the most thorough process-mapping and activity-analysis efforts ever undertaken by a local government. The effort to develop the ABC/M system effort took place over a span of a couple of months. The department began this effort in the Traffic Engineering and Streetlighting Divisions. In defining key activities and performance metrics related to those activities, individuals at all levels of the organization from field crews to senior management engaged in multiple focus groups. This broad-based staff involvement is critical to the development of a meaningful ABM system.

In developing the ABC/M model, the department was able to successfully model 84 major processes and numerous sub-processes and activities. In modeling these processes, the department identified key cost drivers and activity drivers, output measures, performance metrics, and activity attributes. The orientation throughout the project was to ensure the development of a system that would provide useful data to field managers. To be useful, the system had to provide controllable cost data at the field level while at the same time providing full cost data at the divisional and departmental level.

The ABC/M model as currently constructed allows for any personnel for whom it makes sense to track time on an activity-by-activity basis. Other employees, such as administrative personnel, track their activities based on percentage of total time worked in a given period, i.e., monthly, semiannually, or annually. Each cost center in the department's budget is mapped to every activity that may consume some of these costs. This broad-based mapping allows sufficient flexibility to accommodate workers who may perform a set of activities in one period and a completely different set of activities in another period.

The department also relies on numerous databases in various formats to track service calls, provide inventory control, provide financial information, and collect key data related to the day-to-day management of each of its divisions. The ABC/M system will provide for the electronic linking of these databases and the importing of the relevant data from each of these systems into the ABC/M model. This provides the single most cost-effective approach to leveraging existing legacy financial and database systems in providing usable ABC/M data.

U.S. Navy, NAVAIR

Contributor: Stu Schaefer, CEO, Spectrum Group Management Consulting (www.spectrumgroupMC.com)

The NAVAIR unit of the United States Navy operates the Atlantic and Pacific Range Complexes, which are comprised of several air and land testing and training facilities located along the Eastern seaboard and Pacific Coast. The test ranges provide flight test control, range safety functions, and area frequency coordinator services and coordinate special-use airspaces.

Safe, effective aircraft, weapons, and equipment, essential for military success, require rigorous, comprehensive testing. Before a new or modified weapon or piece of equipment is introduced to the fleet, NAVAIR thoroughly tests it in every conceivable operational environment. Before proceeding with the acquisition process, program managers need high-quality test data on which to base decisions—and that's where the NAVAIR range department excels. NAVAIR range employees at Patuxent River, China Lake, and Point Mugu recognize the value of testing and the need for decision-quality data. In fact, creating the data is their primary mission.

Obtaining this decision-quality data requires highly sophisticated, expensive test instrumentation. Instruments—radar, cameras, communication networks, telemetry—must be capable of monitoring every aspect of an aircraft's or weapon's performance at high speeds and across great distances. Aircraft, weapons, and equipment are monitored on NAVAIR ranges for performance and effectiveness in real-world conditions.

The business of running the ranges is very complex. Scheduling all the various types of tests and training exercises is a real challenge. A large portion of the ranges are run like a service provider, with fee-for-service being charged to the various "customers" that come and want to use all or a portion of the capabilities the range has to offer. The challenge for the leadership is to ensure that the fees charged cover the costs to deliver the services. This is further complicated by two key funding policies that in essence try to cover a portion of the total costs, so that not all costs are passed on to the users.

The first of these policies is designed to fund the existence of the range capabilities that are capital investments in equipment. It pays for the creation of facilities, large-scale test equipment, and other long-term assets. There is no depreciation passed on to the customers.

The second policy is designed to fund the existence of the operating capacity, to ensure the ability to deliver at least one unit of capability to the customers.

The remaining operating costs are what are to be passed on to the range customers through a fee-for-service.

The business issue here is to ensure that the fee charged is sufficient to cover the costs that are to be recovered. Complicating factors in determining the fees were isolating the costs of activities to be excluded from recovery, and properly assigning the shared support activity costs to the direct activity costs to calculate more accurate costs. Management suspected that some of the fees were too low and that some were too high, but was unable to quantify the issues using the existing financial and data collection systems.

The solution was to use a business model that could handle all the detail and all the variables while getting at a good picture of the causes of the costs to deliver the various services. Furthermore, the business model could give management the various views of cost it required to be able to ensure that it responded to changing requirements.

The organization is divided into different ranges, each delivering some unique services and some overlapping services. Each of the ranges is then further divided into various divisions that specialize in what they deliver, either to the customers or in support of the organization. Each of the ranges had around 500 employees, who tended to be organized into functional silos.

This organization works well for getting the test events done, but makes it difficult to understand the cost of any one event at the range because of the variety of the events and the corresponding different requirements that they create on the organization. Understanding the complexity and variety were two of the key elements in building a business model using activity-based costing (ABC) methodologies that would adequately reflect all of the differences.

The ABC project team set off to gather information and ask more and more questions to enable themselves to build the model. The team consisted of a few internal folks dedicated to the effort and a couple of outside consultants.

The effort took a short three months from the kick-off to the results presentation, and the results were impressive.

The primary objective for the project was to determine the true and complete cost versus the fee-per-test produced by the main processes, including the amount of the organization's sustaining support expenses.

The ABC/M model's structure can be described as follows:

- Final cost objects: Tests per the range standard fee schedule
- Activities grouped by:
  - Processes and work centers involved in each type of test
  - Indirect support for the processes/work centers
  - Other development, maintenance, and sustaining processes not to be recovered by fees but to be identified and measured.
- Resource expenses:
  - Organized by department, resources included all of the full time equivalents (FTEs) and non-FTEs, including contract labor, third party contracts, materials, and other non-labor resources purchased and consumed during the fiscal year modeled.

To enable analysis in a wide range of management issues, many measures were included, some of which follow. People had these measures: number of FTEs, total hours worked, gain/loss dates, grade, retirement eligibility, etc. Activities could be reported on by mega-processes. The resulting outputs had these measures: number of events/hours, fee per unit of service, total charged, overhead amount assigned by financial system, write-offs, total collected, output quantity, and the standard unit costs.

A key to the use and acceptance of the results was that the range's existing information was applied whenever possible. Many of the systems of record were used as key inputs into various parts of the overall model.

The first calculated result from the ABC/M model quantified the costs of the various types of outputs. The results were:

Outputs by Various Types	% of Total
Outputs per standard rate schedule	15%
Non-standard-fee services	42%
Organization sustaining services	31%
Capabilities not currently billing for	8%
Other groups supported (non-paid)	4%

The percentages were based on the dollar amounts. The amount of services that were non-standard and the other capabilities that were not being billed for was a real eye-opener for management. The prevailing thought was that most of the services were on the standard fee schedule. One of the first management actions out of this effort was to make a concerted effort to change the non-standard services into standard services. The second management action was to go after the capabilities that could be billed for and get those onto the standard rate sheet as well.

The next key result from the effort was summarized by a graph, which showed the percentage of difference between the standard fee and the unit cost of delivery. Because broad averaging was involved in establishing the standard rate fee, some of the ABC unit costs were above the standard rate fee while the remainder were below. The errors were substantial and ranged between −100% and +300%. You can think of this as the errors that were over and under offset to a sum total error of zero. This graph supported what management suspected—that the true costs were very different than what they believed them to be. The graph provided tangible evidence, identifiable by each service, and quantified how much the unit cost differences were.

The resulting management action in response to this graph was to confirm the results, and then, based on the final results, reset the standard rates to fees that more accurately reflect the cost of the resources required to deliver the activity. Doing so meant that, in subsequent periods, the graph was changed such that the blue line moved much closer to the zero line from both directions. Taking these actions and measuring the change is activity-based management, which is the next step from activity-based costing.

Although the fees charged by the test ranges balanced out in total, compared to their existing fees considerable cross-subsidies were occurring from one standard service to another standard service. That is, some were over-charging while others had to be under-charging. Revealing where the subsidies are and how much they are is one of the key outputs of activity-based costing. As has been shown in many ABC articles, the profit cliff curve also reveals competitive issues. For the underpriced services, there is hardly any competition because an organization cannot sustain cash deficits forever. For the overpriced services, competitors are sure to offer lower prices and therefore take away existing business. Both undesirable outcomes were adversely affecting the cash flow of a test range. The ranges have competition primarily from other ranges in the U.S. Navy but also from the U.S. Army, U.S. Air Force and U.S. Marine Corps. There is also competition from commercial companies. The range services that are overpriced and under-priced reveal that each of them may be in very different competitive price arenas and need to be examined in that light.

These results, especially at the far ends of the graph, were very contro-versial. In fact, during one results review briefing, one individual stood, slammed the table with his fist, and exclaimed loudly, "That cost can't be right!" This is where the cause–and-effect linkages built into an ABC model of a business really come to full advantage! We asked for a chance to go through the details of how we arrived at the cost of that particular service.

After going back through the model and being able to show the linkages of all the activities that it took to deliver the services, then looking at the logic of what the cost driver was that had caused a portion of the activity's cost to be consumed by the delivery of the service, the objector made the comment, "Oh, I hadn't considered that." His comment was in response to the amount of indirect support consumed by the service. He was very much aware of the direct actions, yet had not been aware of all the indirect support it took to deliver that service.

This example shows another wonderful benefit of going through the results, especially the results that seem the most outrageous. If the results are gone through with an atmosphere of exploration, the management of the organization can learn many things about what is really going on in all parts of the organization concerning how different parts of the organization sup-port each other. Many discoveries can be made, and as a result many deci-sions will be affected for the better because the management now has a more accurate view of what is really going on. No one prior to this effort would have guessed the degree that this cross-functional support was going on. I know this because at the very beginning of the effort, I had the leadership take their best shot at certain values that I knew we were going to present in the results. It was very revealing to them to see how much the results varied from their hunches.

I will conclude with the remark that has stuck with me and has lead me to say that not all ABC efforts are created equal. On review of the results, one leader made the comment, "I've seen a lot of ABC systems in my day, but this is the first one I could use!" Our team took that as one of the best things that could have been said about the results of the model and the following management actions.

U.S. Veterans Benefits Administration

Contributor: Richard F. Norwood, who was the VBA's ABC Project Manager at the time this was written

Unlike the private sector, the public sector is not motivated to review costs to shore up the profit line. The public sector, specifically in the Veterans Benefits Administration (VBA) of the U.S. Department of Veterans Affairs, is motivated to meet requirements established by the executive branch and legislative branch of the government. Compliance with those requirements becomes the responsibility of the department through issuance of guidelines to its administrations. The Department of Veterans Affairs consist of three administrations: Veterans Benefits Administration, Veterans Health Administration (VHA), and the National Cemetery Administration (NCA).

Organizational Structure

A quick look at the organizational structure of VBA will provide a picture of the complexities that must be solved to successfully build a cost accounting system using the activity-based costing methodology. VBA's mission is to "Provide benefits and services to veterans and their families in a responsive, timely, and compassionate manner in recognition of their service to our nation." There are six Lines of Business (LOB) and several support staff offices responsible for carrying out that mission. The six LOBs are: (1) Compensation, (2) Pension, (3) Education, (4) Loan Guaranty, (5) Vocational Rehabilitation and Counseling, and (6) Insurance. There are 65 field sites and a central office that are staffed by approximately 11,000 full-time employees. Annually, approximately 700,000 Compensation and Pension claims are processed; 440,000 veterans trained; 360,000 loans guaranteed; 5,000 veterans rehabilitated; and 470,000 insurance award actions completed.

Historical Perspective

In the late 1990s, the Department of Veterans Affairs drafted general guidelines for establishing a full-cost accounting system. These guidelines were issued because of requirements in Financial Accounting Standards Advisory Board (FASAB) Statement No. 4, Managerial Cost Accounting, the Chief Financial Officer Act of 1990, Government Performance and Results Act, and recommendations from the National Performance Review. The Office of the Chief Financial Officer (CFO) within VBA was tasked with developing a nationwide full-cost accounting system for VBA. The system would identify the true costs of providing a service or producing a product and would be based on sound cost accounting principles that would support VBA's performance-based strategic plans.

The CFO's office took an aggressive approach toward achieving this task since VBA was constantly bombarded with questions from our stake holders about how we accounted for our costs. Questions that begged to be answered include, "Did we really know what our employees were doing for us?" "Did we know how much time and resources it took to provide a service?" "Did we know what it took to generate an output or an end product?"

All of these questions pointed to the one big question—"Did we really know the cost of VBA doing business?" The answer was no. We did not have a system in place that could tell us how, why, where, and on what we were using the funds that had been entrusted to us as VBA managers.

We needed a system in place that would allow VBA to answer that one big question. We needed a system that would allow VBA to develop full-cost accountability and allow our managers to better manage their resources. The decision as to how we would proceed, what we would use, and where we would use such a system was subject to much discussion. The system in place did not accurately reflect the cost of VBA's business. The solution was to develop a mechanism for capturing the cost of doing business in VBA.

We knew from the beginning that attempting to implement such a system would require change in VBA. Consequently, we in the CFO's office needed to think of ourselves as change masters and change agents. We also needed to think in terms of providing people with all of the tools necessary to implement change. It would not be an easy task since the environment in which we worked did not easily lend itself to change. Change had to be sold, taught, learned, practiced, and, above all, it had to evolve.

After researching several costing methodologies, it was determined that the activity-based cost management (ABC/M) methodology satisfied the VBA's way of doing business. Once that decision was made, some of the CFO's staff attended informational seminars. We selected the SAS Institute Inc., SAS ABM software and completed training on the use of ABC/M software applications. Other government organizations involved with costing were interviewed to get their perspective on implementing a costing system using ABC/M. Armed with this information, the CFO's staff was ready to proceed.

As we consulted with other federal entities involved with ABC/M, we noticed that several were using ABC/M only in "pockets" of their organizations. We determined that VBA would implement its costing system enterprise-wide, rather than piecemeal, and that all costs would be allocated to the six lines of business. This would provide consistency in the production of cost data that would meet one of the requirements in the Chief Financial Officer Act of 1990 and promote the standardization of procedures and guidelines used to manage cost data.

ABC/M Pilots

One of the requirements in the Joint Financial Management Improvement Program's Guidelines for Implementing a Cost Accounting System is the need to do pilots to validate the methodology you are going to use to develop a costing system. The VBA began with two ABC pilots. The first pilot, which was a four-week effort, validated the cost of the Education Line of Business at the St. Louis, Missouri, Regional Office (RO). During this pilot the following actions were accomplished:

- An activity dictionary was developed and measurable outputs were defined.
- Costs were assigned to activities and their associated output measures.
- Unit costs were developed from the quantity of outputs associated with the activities.

The second ABC/M pilot determined the cost of managing the Insurance Line of Business, including associated support costs, at the Philadelphia Regional Office and Insurance Center (RO&IC). This was a full-blown ABC/M pilot consisting of an 11-week effort that included a cross-functional process analysis of the insurance LOB and support areas. Four core processes were defined; 15 outputs were associated with these core processes; and approximately 60 activities were associated with the outputs. The use of ABC/M to allocate administrative costs to the Insurance LOB was validated by the Department of Veterans Affairs Inspector General.

Four additional ABC/M pilots were conducted. These were at the Debt Management Center, Hines Finance Center, Hines Benefits Delivery and Systems Development Center, and VBA Central Office. The pilots' results supported VBA's decision to continue to implement a nationwide full-cost accounting system using ABC/M.

From the results of the ABC/M pilots, VBA knew it could determine cost by activity, process, and output, and allocate that cost to the applicable lines of business. Additionally, we found the pilot participants at the field sites wanted to have the capability to continue to implement ABC/M at their individual sites.

The ABC/M pilot participants received a copy of ABC Technologies' ABC/M Oros software (subsequently renamed SAS ABM following SAS Institute Inc.'s acquisition of ABC Technologies) that included the enterprise-wide package. Everyone involved was provided technical training on the software. We expected that these pilot participants would in effect become our ABC/M subject matter experts.

Implementation Plan/Effort

To ensure continuity of development and consistency of approach, a detailed implementation plan was developed that we used as a roadmap guiding VBA toward the full implementation of ABC/M.

We implemented ABC/M in two phases. Phase one satisfied the Executive Management's needs to meet the new administration's goal to provide unit cost at the Activity, Process, Line of Business, Regional Office and Service Delivery Network level. Completion of phase two put us into a full costing environment. These results allowed the VBA to meet the requirements of our internal and external stakeholders.

ABC/M is not only about costs but about how we manage those costs. It is about defining relationships among resources, activities, and outputs. What was spent? How was it spent? What was produced? By defining those relationships and answering those questions, managers can move from ABC to ABM (activity-based management) because they then have information necessary to determine the costs of activities associated with delivering a service and the cost of the service itself.

The value of ABC/M data is best summed by text included in the National Performance Review: "...Management is not about guessing, it is about knowing. Those in positions of responsibility must have the information they need to make good decisions. Good managers have the right information at their fingertips. Poor mangers don't. Good information comes from good information systems."

Moving to phase II of implementing ABC/M in VBA brought with it a number of challenges. Changing our management philosophy was of paramount importance. To move to the next level of "full implementation of ABC/M" required use of more of the "M" of ABC/M in our decision-making processes. The VBA needed to move from a philosophy of managing resources (people) to managing those things (activities) that consume our resources.

Conclusion

The imminent completion of the above objectives will put VBA in a full costing environment with a fully functional integrated cost accounting system that will be referred to as VBA's Cost Information Management System (CMIS). CMIS will provide consistent cost and workload data at regular intervals, as well as meet the cost accounting guidelines of the department and standards set by governing bodies inside and outside of government.

U.S. Forest Service

Contributor: Alan Fabian, CEO, The Centre for Management and Technology (www.cmat.org)

This case study describes development of service pricing and activity-based budgeting in the public sector.

The Rocky Mountain Research Station (RMS) of the United States Forest Service located in Fort Collins, Colorado, undertook one of the most ambitious activity-based cost management (ABC/M) initiatives in the United States government. The purpose of the project was to analyze the finance, personnel, and procurement functions, identify areas for cost improvement, and most importantly develop a price list for the support services provided to the national forests supported by RMS.

The RMS provides contracting, personnel, and financial support to numerous national forests in their region. Prior to this study, a portion of the funding for RMS was taken from the national forest budgets and the balance was appropriated in the Forest Service annual budget. As a result of budget cuts, the amount of funding provided to RMS was decreasing. At the same time, the workload was increasing rapidly and staffing was being reduced. Senior management at RMS decided to improve the cost efficiencies of its administrative functions and to provide the national forests with accurate costing for the services they used. In other words, RMS created a price list for its services in the same way that any private business would.

In a three-month period, each administrative employee was interviewed individually to identify the activities he performed, the duration for each activity, and the monthly production volumes for each activity and each service delivered. Additionally, numerous focus groups were held to balance the individual interview results with the results of the group as a whole. Data were collected from the National Finance Center (NFC) in New Orleans, Louisiana, to provide independent validation of transaction data. Upon completion of the interviews and focus groups, a process model was developed that detailed each process, activity, and sub-activity in the finance, procurement, and personnel areas. The process model was leveraged in developing an integrated cost management model.

The results of this effort were outstanding. The Rocky Mountain Station identified process changes that resulted in a 32 percent improvement in cost efficiency. It also was able to develop a detailed price list for each service delivered to its clients (the national forests). These included prices for a contract amendment, personnel action, purchase order, third-party draft, credit card payment, etc. These prices were published for the forests and used as guides to set the fee that each forest would pay to RMS each fiscal year. The national forests now had solid cost management data from which they could make decisions, and they did change their behavior based on these data. Now that they knew how much a purchase order cost to process, for example, they decided to perform some tasks at the forest level. In other instances, they had the RMS do more of the work, notably in areas where RMS was extremely cost effective.

The ABC/M model is adjusted each year to reflect new activities and changes in performance, and a new price list is published each year. It is a fine example of an effective ABC/M system in the United States government.

Department of Interior, U.S. Fish & Wildlife Service
Contributor: Kathryn East, Grant Thornton (www.gt.com)

The U.S. Fish and Wildlife Service (FWS) is the Department of the Interior's (DOI) key bureau charged with the responsibility to conserve, protect, and enhance fish, wildlife, and plants and their habitats. The agency is in charge of 500 national wildlife refuges, 78 ecological field stations, and 69 national fish hatcheries and waterfowl production areas, encompassing more than 95 million acres, and overseen by 9,000 employees.

In 2003, DOI released its "Plan for Citizen-Centered Governance," outlining a vision for effective program management among its nine bureaus. It included a departmental strategic planning effort as well as mandates for bureau implementation of ABC as a means to support improvement of products and services as well as to help federal agencies make better decisions about how to spend taxpayers' dollars. FWS understood that, to be truly successful, ABC cannot stand alone; it must be framed within the context of an overarching cost and performance management framework.

The mandate stems from the President's Management Agenda, which is designed to help government agencies become more citizen centered, results oriented, and market based. The agency deployed commercial ABC/M software, SAS ABM from SAS Institute Inc., in June 2004 on a dual-processor Dell server through a partnership with Grant Thornton's Global Public Service business advisers. "The Web capabilities of the ABC/M software makes it possible for the agency to provide up-to-date, online reports to eight regional Fish & Wildlife Service offices and more than 850 field offices across the United States" said Kathy Tynan, chief of planning and evaluation for the Fish & Wildlife Service.

By using the system's ABC information, FWS was able to focus on specific areas of inefficiency and identify potential improvement opportunities.[1] The ABC information also enabled FWS to examine the link between cost and performance of administrative functions and activities in each of its regional offices and compare the results across all regions. With this information, FWS could discuss improving administrative services using a common language and measures, better measure performance across regions, match costs to administrative requirements, use performance-based information to allocate funding to regions, and migrate best practices of high performing regions to the low performers.[2] According to FWS, "It is expected that ABC/M data will be used extensively across the FWS and DOI for process improvement, budget formulation and justification, and performance measurement in upcoming fiscal years."[3]

Measuring Acceptable Costs

The Fish & Wildlife Service has a $2 billion budget and a mission to conserve, protect, and enhance fish, wildlife, plants, and their habitats for the continuing benefit of the American people. FWS delivers this mission at each regional office through five core programs:

- Operation of the National Wildlife Refuge system
- Restoration of fisheries and conservation of habitat
- Recovery of threatened or endangered species

---

[1]*Fish & Wildlife Service web site*, http://www.fws.gov/planning/abc/
[2]www.whitehouse.gov/results/agenda/ report7-05/department_of_interior.pdf -
[3]*Fish & Wildlife Service web site*, http://www.fws.gov/planning/abc/

- Conservation of migratory birds and support of state fish and wildlife programs
- Conservation of international fish and wildlife species

In the past, Tynan says, budgetary data was viewed only to determine how much money was budgeted for specific program expenses and in specific categories, such as equipment, human resources, and improvements in each area. "Federal agencies normally budget by functions, so we're budgeting for set expenses within these five programs," she says.

Unfortunately, this traditional budget perspective does not reveal the relationships or strategies that are shared between programs or offices, or the similar types of work that each program completes in conjunction with sister programs. Nor does a traditional budget compare the costs of similar tasks carried out in different groups or regions.

Using ABC/M, the agency can track every expense and every hour of work back to those individual programs and to hundreds of activities carried out in the various subcategories within each program. Now, the Fish & Wildlife Service also can integrate those program costs as multiple contributions to products or services delivered to the public. As a result, agency leaders can better understand the full cost of business operations and make better assessments about acceptable levels of cost for each activity.

"The opportunity that we have to look at cost and performance with ABC/M allows us to aggregate the programs into a performance view," says Tynan. "ABC/M gives us clear visibility into our performance, and it gives clear visibility of the costs for product delivery, so we have a clear line of sight between costs and results."

Traditional budgeting, on the other hand, doesn't give insight into the cost of agencywide products or performance goals, such as the restoration of wetlands or the enhancement of upland areas. With ABC/M, agency managers can see every activity and every expense that goes into achieving those goals, including the percentage of administrative and overhead costs required to support each goal.

National and Regional Benefits

The ABC/M software technology combines and analyzes data from the federal financial system, the federal payroll and personnel system, and many other local data sources. Using the system, Fish & Wildlife has mapped each of its performance metrics for every program up to agency goals and to Department of the Interior performance goals.

At the national level, Fish & Wildlife Service leaders are already using the results to help develop performance-based and activity-based budgets for upcoming years. "It's really been a team effort between the planning and evaluation staff and Grant Thornton to pull together the information and provide it in such a way that senior managers can begin to incorporate cost data and performance into their budgeting decision process for FY 2007," explains Tynan. "In addition, the Fish & Wildlife Service has used the cost and performance data in an initial administrative study."

The administrative study is a hands-on cost analysis that examines the costs of administrative tasks across the entire Fish & Wildlife Service. Using activity-based cost data, the agency was able to compare relative performance levels across regions to determine which regions appeared to be the most cost-effective from a cost-of-performance perspective.

This data was then used to target surveys of the cost-effective operations and identify internal best practices that are being recommended for adoption across the bureau to improve efficiency and productivity in all the regions. To measure progress toward strategic goals, the White House and the Office of Management and Budget use the Executive Branch Management Scorecard—a traffic-lighting system of red, yellow, and green to indicate whether projects are falling short of, meeting, or exceeding expectations. Using ABC/M, Tynan says, Fish & Wildlife will be one of the first Interior bureaus to exceed expectations in the area of cost performance integration. "ABC/M is the cornerstone piece of us 'getting to green' in this effort," says Tynan.

U.S. Department of Defense, Military Family Housing
Contributor: Joe Clark, Director, Vision Technologies (www.visntec.com)

The Pressure to Act

Since the end of the Cold War, the Department of Defense (DoD) has been pressured to reduce the cost of providing national defense. Changing national priorities and threats have forced DoD to reassess how it organizes, trains, and supports its operational forces. Current downsizing and base realignment and closure initiatives are not only a reaction to government-mandated reductions in spending, but are also a reflection of the way that the role of national defense is changing in response to the new world order.

Over the years, DoD has faced many budget cutting or downsizing initiatives and met these challenges by tightening its belt, sometimes with arbitrary or politically influenced job layoffs, rather than making genuine improvements in the way it does business. However, the pressure to reduce operating costs will not just go away. In response to these pressures, organizations throughout DoD are reexamining their missions and the functions performed in support of these missions. Moreover, DoD is also taking the time to examine the way private companies have streamlined their business processes and has adopted best business practices in developing a process improvement approach for DoD functional managers. This approach includes the activity-based cost management (ABC/M) analytical methodology and business process improvement (BPI) analysis techniques. Together, these methodologies examine and evaluate current business practices and analyze the possibilities for change.

Integrating ABC/M and Business Process Improvement (BPI)

ABC provides insights into the costs that go into the products and services that are provided to our operational forces. ABC provides a baseline assessment required to initiate a successful BPI program. ABC enables the functional area manager to quickly identify opportunities for improving a business process that, when reengineered, will have a high payback potential in the form of actual dollar cost savings, increased productivity, or higher output yield.

One goal of an ABC analysis in the DoD is to quickly identify resource-consuming work activities that are inefficient or redundant, and identify opportunities for reengineering that will produce real dollar cost savings, future cost avoidance, or higher output yield and/or quality. ABC provides managers with a road map that helps them streamline processes and improve customer service. It will also provide them with the necessary information needed to establish prices and rate structures, if applicable, for their products and services.

Business process improvement (BPI) is a systematic approach for improving the way business processes perform to better meet strategic objectives. Activity-based cost management (ABC/M) is one of the primary management tools BPI utilizes to precisely pinpoint the areas and causes of poor performance within an organization and target these areas for improvement opportunities.

By using an ABC/M analysis, one can better understand the reasons that an organization consumes resources, how the resources are distributed and consumed by each activity, and the effects of one activity's performance on other activities within an organization. ABC/M provides the functional area manager with improved business performance. Combined with BPI, ABC/M provides both financial and nonfinancial information in the form of business activity costs, product costs, and business performance measures. This information serves as a baseline for comparing current process performance against expected results. Such comparisons help managers to set business improvement targets and justify technology/process efficiency investments.

In summary , ABC/M analysis is based on the premise that business activities cause costs through the consumption of resources (e.g., people, equipment, supplies), and that customer demands for products and services causes these work activities to be performed. Knowing the cost of business activities, the resource expense they draw on, and the cost driver causing the work allows managers to assess how effectively and efficiently an organization is performing to provide the operational forces with a valued service.

ABC/M as Applied to Military Family Housing

ABC/M data can be constructed to provide information in a variety of ways and can be tailored to meet the specific needs of Family Housing. The drivers of the data become the significant element when tailoring a model to a region-specific need.

Activity-based costing models are generally constructed with five primary elements:

Resources:

> Those items required to do an activity. Resources include labor (personnel) and non-labor (materials, supplies, utilities, contracts etc). Resources include direct and indirect functions and, most importantly, funding.

Resource drivers:

> The measure of the demands placed on a resource (number of personnel, amount or cost of supplies, cost of utilities, etc.) to perform a specific activity.

Activity:

> A verb-noun description of what an organization actually does—work performed. It describes how time is spent producing a deliverable product or service to the customer.

Activity driver:
> A measure of the frequency of demand placed on an activity by the product or service produced for the customer.

Cost object:
> The final product or service produced.

For example:

Resource	Driver	Activity	Driver	Cost object
3- GS-7's	1FTE	Provide Housing Referral	# of referrals	Housing Referral Services

Resources, activities, and cost objects are directly affected by the assignment of the drivers associated with each. Utilizing the drivers correctly is the key to developing a successful model that provides the Family Housing managers the information they require to make sound business decisions. Understanding this allows both the modeler and the client to precisely define the costs associated with a given service or product. For example:

Assume Military Base Southeast has four housing complexes with 100 units each and wants to determine if it is more cost effective to continually repair the older units, perform whole house renovations, or replace them with new construction. Complex A was built in 1998, Complex B 1990, Complex C 1967, and Complex D 1961. Assume the number of rooms, square footage, etc. to be identical, and the only significant difference is age of the complex. In determining the costs associated with maintaining homes in each complex, a variety of activity drivers must be used. Some activity drivers must be weighted to control for or adjust for the difference between the age of the complexes; others must be shared among identical operations that are not affected by age. Some activity driver assignments were dedicated and specific to specific complexes. Labor activity drivers may be applied as a direct contract cost, direct manhour cost, or a percentage of manhours applied to a specific maintenance function.

Once the ABC/M model is complete, actual costs for each complex can be computed for specific activities. This allows the comparison of a specific application between complexes (roof repair, appliance replacement, painting, turnover maintenance, etc.), general comparisons such as cost per square foot for utility consumption within a complex, projected life cycle for utility systems (water, sewer, electrical), grounds maintenance, etc. With a proper model, the Family Housing manager can determine reasonably accurate operating cost for each complex and his projected costs for the next year, and then determine his best course of action: continued annual maintenance, whole-house renovation, or new construction.

Virtually any cost associated with the operation of Family Housing can be modeled and broken down in ways that are meaningful and useful to the Family Housing management. ABC/M data is logical and can be clearly understood. The development of each cost can be tracked forward and backward through the ABC/M cost assignment network. Each resource, activity, and cost object can be broken down to every element derived from the resource spending through the work activities into the final cost objects. The Family Housing manager can, in a matter of minutes, model the what-if scenario of a proposed change by simply manipulating the resource or activity modules to reflect a reduction, realignment, reallocation, or elimination in manpower, funding, supplies, materials, etc. Further, the ABC/M model can be continually refreshed as resource allocations change. ABC/M is obviously an extremely useful tool for determining the effect a proposed reduction in resources will have on the Family Housing operation.

Military Family Housing

The activity-based cost management study for Military Family Housing centered on two basic functional areas within Family Housing: the activities that supported the actual Family Housing units and the activities that support the administration of the Family Housing Office. Its ABC/M model was created with the direct input of the employees who perform the work and provide services. All four Family Housing managers actively participated in the creation of the model, the definition of resources, activities, and cost objects, and the application of resource and activity drivers. The managers have taken ownership of the model and fully understand its contents. The information contained in their ABC/M model has provided the managers and their employee teams with data they need to effectively use business performance improvement (BPI) methodologies to significantly improve the way they manage their assets, regionalize their administrative functions, and staff their storefront operations at each site.

Military Family Housing Business Process Improvement

The Level I ABC/M model created for Military Family Housing managers is the baseline for their BPI effort and the important first step in implementing an activity-based management system for Family Housing.

The Family Housing managers conducted a seven-step BPI program. Their BPI program contained the following:

ABC/M baseline:
  Creating the ABC/M Level I model to establish a baseline cost analysis reference.
Target opportunities:
  Identifying projects, initiatives, or actions that can result in relatively quick short-term changes to realize a cost efficiency. Identifying those areas that require BPI.
As-is analysis:
  Analyzing current operations, process-mapping functions identified for BPI, analyzing allocation of resources.
Benchmarking:
  Internal comparison of cost between sites within the Pacific Northwest as well as cost compared with the private sector commercial housing providers to identify performance gaps and then promote communication of best practices to close the gaps.
Metrics:
  Identifying key performance indicators (KPI) and the method to measure critical performance indicators (CPI) and incorporate them into a Balanced Scorecard which will measure customer satisfaction, financial efficiency, continued process improvement, and organizational learning to meet a predetermined strategic objective as defined by the Family Housing managers.
To-be analysis:
  Developing to-be organization charts and process maps, addressing HRO issues, identifying technology issues and requirements.
Implementation plan:
  Evaluating reorganization and reengineering plans and developing a plan of action and milestones to implement the new organization.

Business performance improvement was not designed to create an illusion of progress under the guise of reorganization for reorganization's sake. Done effectively, BPI will enhance the capability of a functional area to better meet the needs of the customer, attain the strategic objectives of the organization, improve the fiscal performance of the team, and produce a foundation that will be readily adaptable to future changes.

ABC/M Is a Management Tool

An activity-based cost management model is not a silver bullet. It is not designed to replace the current financial accounting system that complies with rules for regulatory agencies. It is a parallel system that reflects the true economics to be applied for decision-making. It does not automatically make an organization more efficient or reduce its cost. It is a management tool. It is designed to translate raw transactional data from the ledger-based accounting system and from other data information systems into information and ultimately business intelligence that is clearly understood by management and will be useful in improving a business process and making better decisions. It allows managers to work smarter, fully understand the cost of doing business, and have a direct impact to manage how their resources are deployed within their area of responsibility. It gives managers and employee teams the information they need to understand exactly what is driving a process cost. It will guide them to a business decision that will allow them to become more productive and efficient in an increasingly budget-constrained environment.

U.S. Small Business Administration

Contributor: Alan Fabian, CEO, The Centre for Management and Technology (www.cmat.org)

This case study describes applying ABC/M to meet federal cost management requirements.

The Chief Financial Officers (CFO) Act of 1990 contains several provisions related to managerial cost accounting. One of these provisions states that an agency's CFO should develop and maintain an integrated accounting and financial management system that provides for the development and reporting of cost information.

The U.S. Small Business Administration (SBA) undertook the development of an ABC model to assist in meeting the new cost management requirements.

Guidance regarding cost accounting is provided to Federal agencies in:

- Office of Management and Budget (OMB) Circular A-11
- OMB Circular A-34
- Statement of Federal Accounting Standards (SFAS)
- Federal Accounting Standards Advisory Board (FASAB)
- Government Performance and Results Act (GPRA)

The Federal Financial Accounting Standards (Managerial Cost Accounting Concepts and Standards for the Federal Government) provide the requirements for cost accounting, as follows:

- The costs of activities are to be accumulated and reported on a regular basis. Procedures are to be established to accumulate and report costs continuously, routinely, and consistently. Standard procedures and practices are to be established for collection, measurement, accumulation, analysis, interpretation, and communication of information. This can be accomplished through a cost accounting system or the use of cost finding techniques.
- Costs are to be defined for each responsibility segment, and the costs are to be measured for each segment's outputs.
- Full costing of outputs should capture direct costs and indirect costs.

The Government Performance and Results Act (GPRA) requires that Federal agencies identify measures of performance to determine the effectiveness of programs. In order to fully comply with GPRA, cost data are needed to link to the measures of program input. Reporting on GPRA began in January 1999 and full reporting began in fiscal year 2000.

The SBA developed an ABC/M model for key program areas, such as loan making, loan servicing, loan liquidation, and economic development. This model allowed the SBA to accurately collect and report on the level of assistance in administrative and management support that each of the major program areas consumes in the course of a year. This, in turn, allowed for a more accurate charging of these administrative services to each of the program areas and promoted better communication of costs and cost drivers to the directors of each of the program areas.

In addition, the SBA is utilizing this ABC/M model to meet certain cost accounting reporting requirements (e.g., the Statement of Net Costs pronounced by Congress and the OMB). The normal financial management system does not provide the flexibility required to produce reports, but that flexibility has been built into the ABC/M model.

Uruguay—Municipal Development and Management Program[4]
Contributors: Clifton Williams, Partner, Srikant Sastry, Partner, Grant Thornton (www.gt.com)

Uruguay may be the first country in the world to implement ABC in all its semiautonomous regional departments, which are roughly equivalent to a state or province and are each an extension of a large municipal center that provides services throughout a region. Almost 90 percent of Uruguay's population of 3.5 million lives in urban areas, which means this ABC initiative is a truly nationwide undertaking.

Emerging from a 2002 financial crisis, Uruguay sought financial assistance from the Inter-American Development Bank (IDB) to help get back on track as one of the more prosperous countries in the Americas. The IDB, which is underwriting the Uruguayan ABC effort and a series of associated projects, provides multilateral financing for development projects and for trade and regional integration programs in Latin America and the Caribbean. In 2003, IDB loaned the Uruguayan Municipal Development and Management Program $60 million to finance economic and social projects to improve the quality and efficiency of local services in the 16 departments outside of Montevideo. Included are neighborhood improvements, upgrades to roads, utilities and sanitation services, environmental recovery operations, and local economic development.

A key part of Uruguay's program is giving local governments financial incentives, technical support, and training to improve fiscal and tax management. In addition, the Uruguay central government was looking for a way to provide more equitable distribution of funds to local jurisdictions. As a result of the ABC project, virtually all municipal governments are better able to relate cost and performance, compare among themselves, and demonstrate resource needs (budget requests). In addition, international donor organizations will have a better idea of how Uruguay uses funds they provide.

ABC/M IS GETTING INSTITUTIONALIZED IN THE PUBLIC SECTOR

As these case studies have demonstrated, ABC/M can be applied in different ways to achieve different outcomes. It is a flexible and powerful methodology that has a unique ability to deliver true cost information, from which critical decisions can be confidently made. As the pressure mounts

---

[4]Grant Thornton, "Grant Thornton member firms team up for Uruguay project," *International Development Advisor*, April 2005.

and budgets are reduced, the public sector needs this kind of information to achieve effective results.

In the next chapter we will discuss some common mistakes that can adversely affect the level of success and speed of an ABC/M implementation.

Chapter 11

Seven Mistakes that Prevent Employee Buy-in

"I discovered in the earliest stages that pursuit of Truth did not admit of violence being inflicted on one's opponent, but that he must be weaned from error by patience and sympathy. For what appears to be Truth to one, may appear to be error to the other."

—Mahatma Gandhi, Hindu national leader, *Young India*
(a weekly journal), September 6, 1922

WHEN ABC/M IMPLEMENTATION PROJECTS fall short of an organization's expectations, it rarely has anything to do with the ABC/M methodology or the technology that supports ABC/M. They are both proven with ample evidence of successes. When ABC/M implementation failures occur, it is usually a result of misconceptions by the ABC/M project team and by other members of the organization as a whole. Regardless of the source of the problem, the potential pitfalls must be considered and addressed to achieve the minimal threshold level for success wherein users can learn to exploit the data beneficially and obtain repeated updates. The key area exposing the project to risk is failure to secure support and buy-in from both senior managers and employees.

Ninety percent of success in implementing ABC/M is managing organizational behavior, and the remaining ten percent is the math. Unfortunately, most organizations reverse these. They spend an excessive amount of effort agonizing about the construction of their ABC/M model and not enough time thinking about how people might react to the new data or even to the announcement of the ABC/M project.

To repeat, because it is so important, failing to get buy-in is one of the major reasons that ABC/M projects do not live up to their expectations. Communication to managers and employees about the true purpose of ABC/M is often not effectively managed. These issues usually pertain to the "soft" side of managing an organization—the people side. Issues will surface related to the psychology and culture of an organization because ABC/M usually challenges the belief system; this, quite naturally, can result in resistance.

The project can fall into the category of "shoot the messenger." Even if ABC/M provides critically revealing information, managers may choose to continue using their old, flawed information because they are comfortable with it and know how to work around its inadequacies. There is an the old phrase, "Better the devil you know than the devil you don't know."

The following seven problem areas related to ABC/M must be addressed if an organization's ABC/M implementation is to have a fair chance of success.

1: LETTING EMPLOYEES THINK ABC/M IS JUST A FAD

Occasionally, reaction to the announcement of an ABC/M project has been, "ABC/M is just another management improvement program. We've seen them come and seen them go. This too shall pass."

Probably one of the major misconceptions about ABC/M is that it is an improvement program. It is not! The ABC/M data are simply a means to an end. If employees and managers are given the impression that ABC/M will be the next magic pill, then it becomes a candidate for "fad of the month." ABC/M data simply make visible the economics of the organization and the cost consumptions that occur with or without ABC/M present. But ABC/M does also provide a sound database that can be interrogated to understand cause-and-effect relationships. The data gives insight to not only what things cost but also why.

Different management improvement programs will continually evolve, yet the laws of physics remain constant. ABC/M itself is basically modeling properties of the real world. And remember that the output of the ABC/M calculation engine is always the input into someplace else. With regard to true improvement programs, ABC/M data can serve as an enabler to squeeze out greater results.

Here is a list of improvement programs for which the ABC/M data can be used as an enabler:

- Strategic planning (rationalizing service levels and types of service recipients)
- Supply chain management
- Performance measurement (balanced scorecards)

- Total quality management (TQM)
  - Cycle-time reduction
  - Business process reengineering (BPR)
  - Behavioral change management
  - Product and service value-engineering and value-analysis
  - Benchmarking
  - Core competencies
  - Shared-service center negotiated contracts (transfer pricing).

Regardless of which improvement programs are initially being targeted for assistance by ABC/M, definitely select at least one, and start by working backwards with the end in mind. That is, clearly define the objective at the beginning. That will help guide the level of detail required. Ideally, start by attacking a problem that will not require extreme detail so that a higher level ABC/M model can be quickly constructed.

2: OVERRELYING ON EXECUTIVE MANAGEMENT BUY-IN

Many ABC/M implementation project teams presume that senior management sponsorship is the critical factor in achieving ABC/M success. It is true that, as in all new ventures into unfamiliar areas, senior management endorsement is required for ABC/M. But in the long run the real judges of ABC/M will be the end-users of the data, not just the executives.

Because the ultimate end-users of the ABC/M data will determine ABC/M's success, senior management sponsorship is necessary, *but not sufficient*. In other words, while ABC/M needs senior management buy-in to succeed, that buy-in alone will not guarantee sustainable results.

Once you get some buy-in, strike quickly. Credibility is a commodity with a short shelf life. It must be continuously re-earned until the end-users understand what they are getting from their ABC/M data. Build off small wins if that is all you get initially, but keep the momentum going.

3: ASSUMING THAT A GOOD IMPLEMENTATION PLAN IS ENOUGH

Some ABC/M implementation teams believe that the key to a successful ABC/M project is having a *great* implementation work plan. In reality, ABC/M projects need *two* plans: (1) an implementation plan, and (2) a communications plan. The second plan is usually more important than the first. The sequence of who initially gets exposed to the ABC/M data and methodology matters because there is a risk that those who feel threatened might immediately discredit ABC/M and seek termination of the project. Since ABC/M involves a significant element of behavioral change management, it is essential to highlight communications in the front-end planning.

Too often the ABC/M implementation plan focuses mechanically on what data should be collected and from where, but it does not acknowledge how one "won-over" employee could positively influence other employees.

Organizational change management is what ABC/M is all about. ABC/M may well be listed some day as a *social* tool. Although ABC/M can be used to modify behavior, it is important to treat the data responsibly and not like another accounting police control tool. To be clear, ABC/M is an excellent support system for decision-making, and its rigor should be used to build stronger cases for those decisions.

4: HAVING ACCOUNTING PUSH THROUGH ABC/M

Some ABC/M practitioners suggest that if the ABC/M project champion is an accountant, the project is doomed to failure. That is, the ABC/M project being initiated or led by the accounting function is the kiss of death.

Both individual and group leadership are closely connected, so it is best to address them together. The early ABC/M projects were most successful when they were born and initiated from an operational or strategic department, such as from a bank's back office processing center. The ABC/M projects that work best are those that are "pulled through" by operations rather than "pushed through" by the accountants.

Two questions determine organizational readiness for implementing ABC/M: (1) Are the conditions right for ABC/M data? and (2) Is the project leader committed and enthusiastic about ABC/M?

Four Conditions for ABC/M to Thrive

A major reason ABC/M is considered is that the *existing* cost allocation scheme has finally been recognized as flawed because it allocates expenses into costs using a broadly averaged allocation basis without a sufficient cause-and-effect relationship. In this situation, there is a high likelihood that products, standard services, and recipients are being improperly costed, and the results are therefore inaccurate and misleading.

These are the four conditions that strongly influence or force organizations to adopt ABC/M:

1. Increasing heterogeneity and diversity of outputs, products, standard services, channels, service-recipients, and customers, which leads to disproportionate consumption of different elements of the indirect and overhead costs
2. Increasing complexity in the support overhead, core administrative, and business processes, resulting in interorganizational activity-to-activity cost relationships that are a step or more removed from the final cost objects
3. Substantial indirect and overhead costs
4. Increasing need to understand how the promotion, recruiting, distribution, general, and administrative period costs are caused and traced relative to their channels, service-recipients, and customers

An ABC/M Project Champion with Fire-in-the-Belly

Whether the ABC/M project leader is an accountant or an operations person is perhaps less of an issue than whether the individual has a real and burning desire to provide end-users with much better cost and managerial data. If the ABC/M project champion passes the "fire-in-the-belly" test of passion, then there is a strong chance that the ABC/M project will be successful.

Finally, put the right people on the bus. That is, provide the ABC/M champion a team of people who care about the destiny of their organization.

5: DESTROYING ORGANIZATIONAL OWNERSHIP BY USING STANDARD DEFINITIONS

Some people believe that pre-defining *standard* activity dictionaries with standard cost drivers will prevent users from building "bad ABC/M models." This is far from the case.

It is very important to secure the involvement of employees and managers in defining the ABC/M model and providing data for it. If the involvement of the ABC/M project team (or their hired consultant) extends beyond their primary role of facilitation, then ownership by the users is dramatically reduced, as well as their interest.

In the cases where standard dictionaries and cost drivers are dictated to the users, a similarly undesirable result is likely to occur. Standards may be applied to ensure consistency and comprehensiveness, but they are best defined as one level of "summary" above the base level where the activity costs are actually being calculated, flowed, and accumulated. It is best to allow users to self-define in their own words the majority of the work activities, cost drivers, and cost objects.

6: HAVING EARLY AND UPFRONT TRAINING THAT IS POORLY CONCEIVED

Some people believe that everyone in the organization needs to be trained up-front at the beginning. Their logic is that everyone's buy-in can be won quickly, and the employees will immediately know how to use the ABC/M system. This approach can backfire.

Timing is crucial when it comes to ABC/M training. While it is a mistake to train too many of the wrong people too early, not training the right people soon enough is another trap. The key is to determine who should comprise the initial three groups needed to successfully initiate the ABC/M project:

- The ABC/M project implementation team
- The "functional representatives," who contribute significantly to building the model but may not be the initial users of the ABC/M calculated data
- The end-users of the data, who may be senior managers but also may be functional operators, such as the employees processing license renewals

Once these groups are identified, the next step is to develop a communications plan to systematically expose others on an as needed basis. It is important to manage people's expectations throughout the entire ABC/M roll-out process.

7: MISHANDLING THE TRANSITION FROM ABC TO ABC/M

Some people believe that managing costs is easy after one finally knows the costs. They believe that once their ABC system is in place calculating costs, then managing them (i.e., ABC/M) will automatically happen.

One major disappointment for ABC/M project teams comes when the prospective users of the ABC/M data fail to act on the information. Sometimes, just like a deer on a highway that is frozen by the headlights of an oncoming car, the prospective users simply do not do anything even when it is obvious that, for the organization's safety or significant benefit, they should. ABC/M suffers when users fail to move from analysis to action.

Finally, after the real, true, and actual costs become known and accepted as credible, there may very well be winners and losers. It would be inappropriate to punish or reward the parties. No one in the organization ever knew the magnitude of the misleading data reported from the predecessor accounting system. Therefore, as I have stated repeatedly, it is very important to treat the *new* ABC/M data responsibly. ABC/M is an organization-wide tool and should be treated as a form of intelligence, not as a new weapon for management to punish employees.

Also, particularly at the beginning of an ABC/M project, be careful not to get caught in a pattern where the potential users keep sending the project team back to the drawing boards to generate more data. If the users are not demonstrating use of the initial ABC/M data, or at least a high interest, that is a warning. When these types of users ask for more and different ways to spin the data, it may be a stalling tactic because they find the new ABC/M information too alien compared with what they are accustomed to. An effective solution for this problem is to encourage one or more senior executives to begin asking pointed yet open-ended questions that could be answered only with the ABC/M data, such as "What could explain why this cost is so high?" That gets people's attention.

As you progress, don't confuse motion with action. Get people to act on what they see in the data.

"90 percent of the game is half mental."
—Yogi Berra, U.S. Baseball Hall of Fame athlete, quoted
when giving coaching tips

Chapter 12

ABC/M Integrates with Other Software Tools

"The most useful piece of learning for the uses of life is to unlearn what is untrue."
—Antisthenes (c. 445–365 B.C.), Founder of Cynic School of Philosophy,
quoted in Noyes, *View of Religion*

PERPLEXING NUMBER of software tools have been designed to assist managers, teams, and analysts. Some of these software tools became popular during the 1990s when business process reengineering (BPR) began to evolve. Business software tools generally fall into these broad categories:

- **Transaction planning and processing**—order management
- **Project management**—project budget and schedule control
- **Economic analysis**—financial projections
- **Product planning and design**—from idea to production
- **Process improvement**—organizational performance management.

Figure 12-1 illustrates three layers of software. ABC/M software resides in the middle layer called "analytical applications." These tools are fed information from the transaction-intensive production systems. Many business production systems have a short-term planning component embedded in the system. For example, in manufacturing there is an advanced planning system (APS) that assists in short-term material ordering and in production sequencing and dispatching. ABC/M can provide useful data for those modules, including order pricing for quotations. I find it easier to categorize ABC/M as an analytical software application, but I recognize that the output of the ABC/M calculation engine is often the input to many other types of systems.

FIGURE 12-1 The Technology Landscape

The "data mining" analytical tools in the solution space extract data from transaction-intensive systems and deliver them to the reporting and viewing tools.

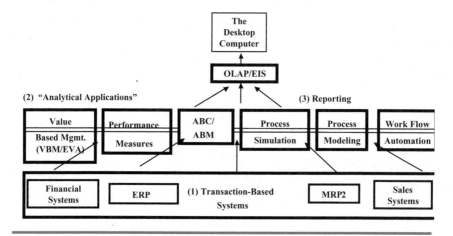

I described how ABC/M supports and integrates with project planning systems, as well as predictive costing, in Chapter 7. ABC/M supports financial projections and investment justification analysis to the extent that cost rates are used. The financial industry, including banks and insurance companies, rely on a multitude of financial projection tools to refine their products.

Regarding product development tools, ABC/M supports target costing, value engineering, and life-cycle costing. However, for this book, I have focused mainly on how ABC/M supports strategic and mission management as well as operational control and learning systems. I lump both of these into the broad category of *process and mission improvement.*

BUSINESS PROCESS AND MISSION IMPROVEMENT TOOLS

The process and mission improvement software tools are designed to address process definition, modeling, analysis, evaluation, and improvement. Figure 12-2 illustrates a framework that categorizes these different

FIGURE 12-2 Taxonomy of Re-engineering Software Tools

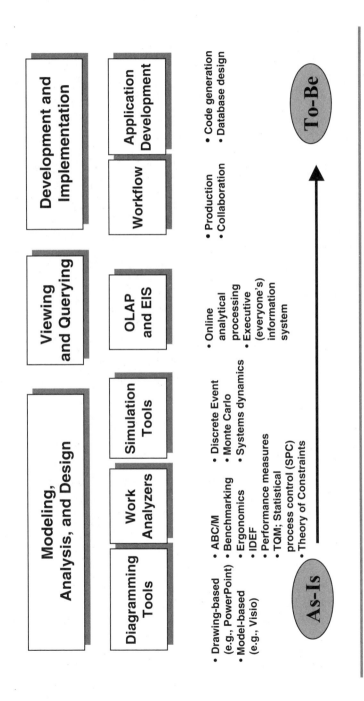

Software allows representing and ultimately controlling.

types of tools exclusive to process management. (I thank Gordon Sellers, an excellent consultant with a big-picture view, for helping me understand this landscape.)

I do not defend this framework as being complete since information technology is not my area of expertise. However, the framework enables me to understand how software tools support the cycle of change. That is, as transformation initiatives take place, there is a logical progression as follows:

- **Diagramming**—In many cases, teams map their existing processes and assumptions.
- **Analysis**—Next comes the analysis of results, capacity, work, policies, forecasts, assumptions, strategy, and all the other elements involved in understanding where you are and where you want to go. ABC/M software resides here. Software tools for economic analysis are also included here (although I also view them as a separate category of tool).
- **Simulation**—In some cases, interdependencies are so complex that simulation tools are used to experiment by using a computer rather than the real world.
- **Viewing**—The output of analytical tools can be overwhelming. Online analytical processing (OLAP) applications permit looking at data from multiple dimensions.
- **Workflow**—The backroom administrative functions, such as customer order entry, are now viewed as an "information factory" that processes and moves data similarly to how physical factories manufacture and assemble parts. Software tools support workflow and document flow.
- **Application Development**—The programming of software continues to evolve as object-oriented thinking introduces unimaginable methods of structure and conservation, allowing for more efficient systems-building and reuse of old code. From this stage, automated systems are deployed.

In short, some improvements begin when managers simply view charts and graphs that reveal a divergence between where they are and where they expected to be. The use of graphics, such as pie-charts and histograms, have long been routine for quickly communicating information. The diagramming tools lead to the work analyzer tools because work activities are the focus of reengineering projects. Outside of process reengineering analytical tools, there are other analyzers, such as customer demographics, that play a role in strategic improvement. Simulation tools are beginning to gain acceptance. The output of these tools often gets exported into the viewing tools (e.g., OLAP).

After modeling and analysis, the software development and implementation software tools kick in to operationalize the new scheme. Some of these include workflow and documentation systems. Of course, the output of the production software systems ultimately gets fed back into the modeling tools to monitor performance and increase understanding.

MULTI-DIMENSIONALITY: PRODUCT/CUSTOMER/CHANNEL/ LOCATION COSTING

The advent of sophisticated ABC/M calculation engines has enabled organizations to look at their activities from a variety of dimensions. Multi-dimensional analysis has been enabled by technical advances in on-line analytical processing (OLAP) tools.

Dimensions are collections of activities and business processes that relate to different cost objects. The obvious common cost objects are product costs, service-line costs, customer costs, distribution channel costs, location costs, and business process costs. In government agencies or the military forces, cost objects can include services, service-recipients, geographic locations, and programs. Although ABC/M's origins in the 1980s emphasized product costing, the emphasis has expanded to other dimensions.

How can you analyze all these diverse data? Figure 12-3 illustrates how advanced software tools can combine data to allow multiple combinations and summaries of the same data. The figure recasts the ABC/M cost assignment network; in place of the "predator food chain" that reflects sequential cost object consumption, multi-dimensionality allows simultaneous views.

Many ABC/M advocates believe that the best way to obtain top management's interest in ABC/M is by asking if they are interested in knowing answers to the questions that they worry about:

- For government officials: Where are we with respect to meeting our mission relative to our resources?
- For private sector executives: Which customers were profitable and which were not? (For example, in the health care industry, patients come from a variety of sources. These sources include physician refer-

FIGURE 12-3 ABC/M and Multi-dimensional Views

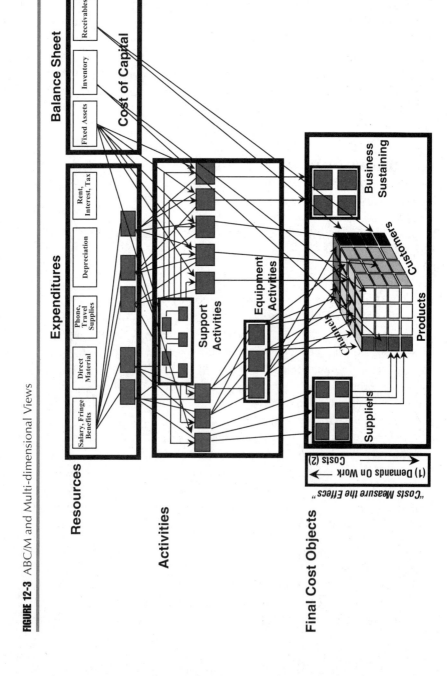

rals, retirement homes, HMOs, PPOs, or indigents. The cost of providing service to patients from these different sources can vary greatly. Unless the provider understands those different costs, the provider could bid incorrectly for additional business.)

As organizations experiment with the Internet and multiple approaches to marketing (e.g., via direct sales, distributors, wholesalers, representatives, telemarketing, direct mail, and joint ventures), it becomes increasingly important to understand the costs of marketing through those different distribution channels.

Geography also may make a difference. Service industries as well as manufacturing can see widely variations in the cost of providing services and products in different parts of the United States and abroad. Competition, pricing, environmental laws, state regulations, work force compensation and productivity, and taxes can vary greatly. Unless organizations understand those costs, they can make incorrect location and marketing decisions. For example, manufacturers often outsource products that have a small amount of direct labor cost to foreign countries with lower wages. They often ignore all the activities and associated costs required to support international operations that can negate any savings from a lower wage rate.

Multi-dimensionality makes it easier to view and understand the differences of one's cost structure. In effect, it adds another tool to the analytical suite of tools.

We now move to our final chapter. We will leave the ABC/M math behind and will ponder what all of this means and where government is headed.

Chapter 13

The Future of Government

"Every scientific truth goes through three states: First, people say it conflicts with the Bible; next they say it has been discovered before; lastly they say they always believed it."
—Louis Agassiz, Swiss-born American naturalist, speech made at Penikese, 1870

"The true lover of learning then must from his earliest youth, as far as in him lies, desire all truth...."
—Plato, Athenian philosopher and disciple of Socrates, *The Republic*, Book VI, 485d

A S I CONCLUDE this book, I am not going to prognosticate about how government should or will behave in the 21st century. However, I will fast-forward the clock and consider a few issues that have implications for government.

KEY ISSUES

Many factors will press government into different behavior patterns in the years ahead, but I would like to leave you with some thoughts on the three I judge to be most critical—or, at the least, the most thought-provoking.

Business Will Spoil Customers—Can Government Keep Up?

Elected officials and government agencies face a slow and subtle change that in a few years may suddenly speed up. This has to do with the rate and impact of changing expectations of people and businesses. In one sense, private enterprise and the public sector both share people as their target for giving service—one can think of them as patrons. By definition, patrons are influential and supportive. Business and government share people in the following way: The customers of one are the voters of the other. But as commercial organizations become increasingly attuned to the importance of customers, they are substantially improving their ability to respond to customers' needs and demands. In this regard, businesses are showing a marked increase in quickness and agility. Those then become the new standard service level for what to expect. As businesses raise standards of service, people are apt to demand better service from government as well.

For example, customers apply for bank loans at automated teller machines, but they still endure slow, one-size-fits-all service at the motor vehicles bureau. Consumers and companies purchase products and materials over the Internet, but they still lose time and possibly money waiting for permits at city hall. People can call 24-hour help lines or travel reservation agents, but government is usually a 9-to-5 operation.

How long will voters maintain their cool as the gap between the levels of commercial and public service widens? Voters are already demanding better value for their tax dollars from those they elect.

Business Will Nudge Government to Understand Costs

In some cases, politics, laws, or regulations prevent governments from pursuing ABC/M methods to reveal their costs. In other cases, public managers are unclear as to what ABC/M really is or they have misconceptions about it. There are also the cases where some public managers with influence simply want to stonewall and not allow anyone to see and know things that were not visible in the past.

In such situations, the private sector will likely open the lid and let everyone see what's inside—the true costs. Accounting and consulting firms are increasingly more effective at selling and economically delivering ABC/M consulting services. Commercial ABC/M software packages make it easy to design and construct ABC/M systems. Local business people will be lobbying their elected officials to practice improved managerial accounting. They may even lend talent to their local governments to launch initiatives such as an ABC/M implementation.

As another resort, the one dreaded by some public managers, businesses will identify new service opportunities on their own or competitively bid on services that are currently delivered by government.

As a caution, however, private sector companies do need to understand that there is one major hurdle when persuading government agencies to consider an outsourcing or privatization arrangement. It deals with the consequences of taking risks. In the private sector, bad decisions can be written off; the company takes a one-time negative hit to its profits and continues. But in government, the newspapers, TV, Internet, and radio can make one bad decision fatal for an elected or appointed official. Understandably, government officials are cautious about transferring any responsibilities to the private sector.

My message here is that if a private company wants to win an opportunity to show that it can do much better than what the citizenry is currently getting, and also make some money, then it must back up its business proposal with guaranteed results. That may be as formal as writing in the contract that money will be paid to the government whether or not the anticipated cost savings or revenue increases are realized. This reduces the risk to the elected officials and creates a no-lose situation for the city, state, or whatever government agency. If the private company truly believes in its plan, it can live with taking a managed risk.

Managerial Accounting Will Support Managerial Economics

As we move into the 21st century, brains clearly are replacing muscle. The knowledge worker has become the intangible asset that all organizations are increasingly valuing. This is leading to a few issues that government may not have fully thought through. Issues often arise because some assumptions must first be exposed as myths to arrive at a solution. Here are two key myths about the requirements and uses of managerial accounting that government should reflect on and consider:

- **Myth #1: All users of cost and other financial information require the same type of information.** In fact, different types of desired information require different levels of detail. The level of detail and accuracy depends on the specific decision being made. Types of decisions vary widely, and each requires assumptions about the planning horizon time frame.

   Some readers may have had difficulty understanding the chapter in this book on predictive costing and activity-based budgeting. As you dig deeper into cost estimating, the more complex you realize it is. My sense is that ABC/M provides an important foundation to pursue reasonable and more logical approaches to the challenge of incorporating financial analysis and other estimative functions into decision-making. And again, different decisions will require not only different types of information but different assumptions as well. Configuring and modeling must mature from a loose art form into a craft.

   ABC/M serves as a powerful translator that receives as input three types of data: financial, empirical (e.g., employee estimates), and operational. The ABC/M calculation engine then deploys these post-calculated data for a multitude of uses. Figure 13-1 illustrates how ABC/M appears on an information systems map.

In Chapter 4, I proposed a fifth stage for cost management systems. This is what I am referring to here.

- **Myth #2: Operational excellence will eventually trump the finance and IT departments.** Some operational managers await the day to get back to basics—like apply common sense in providing good service while living within your means. These managers often view the accountants and geeks from data processing as unnecessary overhead. In contrast, they view their world as the core process for their organization: taking orders and fulfilling those orders. My sense is simply that the 21st century managers and teams will require more, not less, integration of their organization.

If we reflect on ABC/M, we observe that the initial ABC/M projects of the past, led by finance and accounting departments, often did not extend past the desks of the chief financial officer or the president. As a result of the introduction of integrated technologies that now deliver activity-based information direct to any employee's desktop, the pace changes. Organizations can increase their enterprise-wide learning rates. They are able to expand and extend the use of the activity-based information to include operational managers, thereby migrating from an ABC project to an ABM program. Figure 13-2 illustrates the evolution that activity-based thinking organizations pass through.

In this graphic, many organizations are stuck in the bottom left corner by focusing on nothing more than expense recognition and control. Here, the classic confrontation from the accounting police is, "You took two extra plane trips last period. Explain why. Right now." The budgeted amounts become obstacles. Of course, there will always be a place for spending control, but that alone will not advance the organization.

Figure 13-2 reveals how the early ABC pilots of the 1980s, mainly in commercial manufacturing, aimed at simply better understanding product profitability. Then, service organizations like banks and hospitals also began applying ABC to examine their profitability, but they traced their expenses all the way to channels and customers. That use of the data introduced ABC/M. People needed to take new steps and adjust things. Some operational managers cared less about where their organization made or lost money than they did about removing waste,

FIGURE 13-1 ABC/M Production Systems

ABC/M's future is in permanent, repeatable, and reliable production systems.

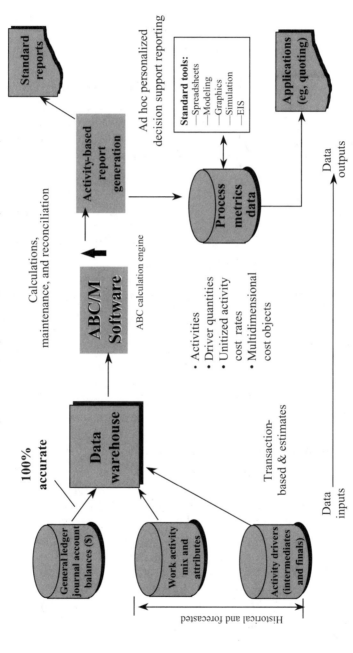

Reprinted by permission of the McGraw-Hill Companies from Gary Cokins, *Activity-Based Cost Management: Making It Work*. © The McGraw-Hill Companies, Inc., 1996.

FIGURE 13-2 The Evolution of ABC

Although ABC for profitability analysis became popular, there was buried treasure in activity data that was useful for improving operational effectiveness.

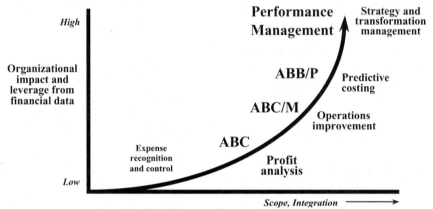

Reprinted by permission of the McGraw-Hill Companies from Gary Cokins, *Activity-Based Cost Management: Making It Work.* © The McGraw-Hill Companies, Inc., 1996.

streamlining, benchmarking, and so on. These operational managers embraced ABC/M.

As you can see, the graphic also extends into ABB/P (activity-based budgeting and planning) and ultimately into ABC/M's integration with the portfolio of multiple methodologies that collectively is referred to as Performance Management. Chapters in this book have addressed these two important topics as well.

As the ABC/M models and system are being constructed, do not omit performing value analysis with ABC/M attributes. Costs are not the be-all and end-all. In addition to understanding what causes costs using driver analysis, it is important to classify the relative value that activities contribute to meeting the organization's goals.

Not all organizations that start an ABC project succeed in deploying it or sustaining it once deployed. The winners are those that recognize the inherent power of integrating activity-based data into their information systems. This integration occurs in three dimensions: financial, operational, and technology. The increasing global acceptance of commercial activity-based information software is proving that executives and operational teams need information that is activity-based, financial data-endorsed, IT-maintained, and routinely used. Activity-based information is obviously a part of organizational decision-making, and overall organizational effectiveness is enhanced by an increase in the number of desktop computers the activity-based information resides in.

The information technology people are critical to the equation. They provide three essential components for the business intelligence (BI) systems their executives and employee teams depend on:

- Business modeling—includes cost assignments, process mapping, discrete-event process simulation
- Server deployment and data storage—collection and distribution of BI to users
- Multidimensional information navigation tools (e.g., OLAP)—includes database interrogation, query systems, multidimensional (e.g., n-cube) analysis

Activity-based information systems have evolved from personal computer-based, stand-alone tools to powerful server-ready and Internet-hosted systems, by complying with industry standards to integrate best-in-class tools in non-proprietary environments.

In short, strategic and operational managers cannot and should not seek isolation from their co-workers in accounting and data processing. They all need one another.

A FINAL THOUGHT: HOW MUCH DO ACADEMICS AND UNIVERSITIES SUPPORT ABC/M?

It is not entirely clear to me why the academic community has been so slow to embrace ABC/M. This does not mean that recently published textbook revisions do not include ABC/M. They do, but the number of pages devoted to ABC/M is minimal. With a few key exceptions, academics have not exhibited much excitement and passion about ABC/M—at least relative to the degree that practitioners demonstrate for ABC/M.

A possible explanation for the lack of interest in ABC/M in most colleges and universities is that academics have concluded that there is little research opportunity for them. That is, there is no ground that has not already been covered and written about absorption accounting (and ABC/M as a refinement of it). In reality, what is apparent is that, in practice, most initial ABC/M cost assignment model structures are poorly designed and reveal a lack of understanding of ABC/M. The ABC/M project is then at risk. A poor ABC/M model design, at best, slows progress in allowing an organization to make better decisions and, at worst, jeopardizes adopting ABC/M altogether.

Managerial accounting previously witnessed a similar "dark age" in the early 20th century, when the responsibility for cost measurement shifted from the mechanical engineers to the accountants. Not much technical progress occurred after Frederick Taylor's scientific management movement introduced the need for standard costing. It is likely that if Frederick Taylor were alive today to examine ABC/M, he would be approving. He would consider the application of cost assignment principles to overhead costs logical and obvious. The fact that ABC/M concentrates on work activities would be an extension to his focus on establishing standards for worksteps.

Perhaps the explanation of slow progress in university educational involvement with ABC/M has more to do with the culture of academic institutions. Some faculty members simplify their instructional materials to the degree that there is little risk that any student will miss any key points. This has perpetuated the perception that ABC/M is restricted to a two-stage allocation scheme. A few academics have quietly proposed to me their pet theory that the faculty authors of the more popular management accounting textbooks are intimidated by the thought of the sizable effort required to revise and enhance their existing money-making textbook.

Anecdotal evidence of problems in academia with managerial accounting can be telling. As an example, in about 1999, the graduate school of business at Dartmouth University reclassified its managerial accounting course from being mandatory to an elective. This implies that the topic has declined in value. Another disappointment that I personally experienced involved seeking research about cost forecasting, specifically on the subjects of predictive costing and activity-based budgeting and planning. It is apparent that one can get different answers for the same problem using alternative cost estimating methods. Despite the incentive of research grant money and the imminent implications of Internet pricing and auction bidding for these topics, there was no interest expressed regarding an appeal for such research by management accounting faculty or their doctoral candidates. One professor suggested as an explanation that faculty from operations management may be better suited than accounting faculty to address this topic.

As managerial accounting evolves into "fifth stage" managerial economics, we may discover that it is the practitioners, and not the academic community, who advance the understanding and applications of managerial accounting. To be certain, this topic is complex. The issue of classifying expenses as being used or idle based on varying assumptions and planning horizons is tricky. To complicate matters, it is even trickier to determine which and when portions of committed in-case capacity, such as employees, can be outsourced to convert those costs to as-needed. And for specific decisions, assumptions must be made about which costs should be included or excluded as relevant or not to the decision.

These are the issues that managerial accounting will increasingly wrestle with as it becomes increasingly relevant to the analytical basis for decision-making.

> **"A man's mind stretched by a new idea can never go back to its original dimensions."**
> —Oliver Wendell Holmes, U.S. Supreme Court Justice, "The Path of Law" (1897)

U.S. Reform Commissions

The United States has a long history of reform commissions appointed to recommend changes in structure and process aimed at improving government efficiency. President Clinton's administration kept the momentum going when it introduced the National Performance Review in 1993. The final document repeatedly called for "performance based management" and emphasized the importance of cost measurements and improved fiscal budgeting methods.

The key 20th-century reform commissions are listed below.

1905–1909: Keep Commission—Personnel management, government contracting, information management.

1910–1913: President's Commission on Economy and Efficiency—The case for a national executive budget.

1921–1924: Joint Committee on Reorganization—Methods of redistributing executive functions among the departments.

1936–1937: President's Committee on Administrative Management—Recommended the creation of the Executive Office of the President.

1947–1949: First Hoover Commission—Comprehensive review of the organization and function of the executive branch.

1953–55: Second Hoover Commission—Follow-on to the prior Hoover commission, focusing more on policy problems than organizational structure.

1953–1968: Numerous study commissions on executive reorganization—A series of low-key reforms that produced subtle, yet important, reforms.

1969–1971: Ash Council—Proposals for a fundamental restructuring of the executive branch, including the creation of four new super-departments to encompass existing departments.

1977–1979: Carter reorganization effort—Bottom-up, process-based effort to reorganize government that mostly ended in failure. New cabinet departments were created independently of this effort.

1982–1984: Grace Commission—Large-scale effort to determine how government could be operated for less money.

1993–1994: National Performance Review—By borrowing from popular principles of business process reengineering, this was an attempt to "reinvent" government to improve its performance and reduce costs.

Source: Ronald C. Moe. *Reorganizing the Executive Branch in the Twentieth Century: Landmark Commissions.* Report 92-293 GOV (Congressional Research Service).

Appendix B

Federal Regulations

In addition to the long history of U.S. reform commissions, including the National Performance Review of 1993, a number of federal regulations have affected financial reporting requirements. Below is a list of federal regulations, mostly since 1990, advocating financial measures that could benefit from the application of ABC/M principles.

The Independent Offices Appropriation Act, 1952

This act contains one of the earlier descriptions of the need for reasonably calculated user fees. The act directs federal agencies to identify services provided to unique segments of the population and to charge fees for those services, rather than supporting and funding such services through general tax revenues.

Cost linkage: This act emphasizes the need to determine cost allocations on a relative and fair basis.

CFO Act (Chief Financial Officers Act), 1990

This act resulted from efforts by advocates of a modernized government financial system. Requirements are defined for the development of methods that would provide more complete, accurate, and timely financial information. The act describes rules for compiling audited financial statements and establishes the role of Chief Financial Officer.

Cost linkage: Organizations must report certain cost information.

GPRA (Government Performance and Results Act), 1993

This was a major event. This act outlines requirements and guiding principles for government organizations in the areas of strategic plans, programs, performance measures, and unit costs. Furthermore, it holds federal agencies accountable for achieving program results as well as high levels of service quality and customer satisfaction. One intent of GPRA is to provide Congress with more factual information on progress in achieving objectives and improving effectiveness and efficiency in programs and spending.

Cost linkage: Unit costs and other forms of cost data serve as inputs to performance measures.

GMRA (Government Management Results Act), 1994

This act reduces the reporting burden on government organizations from a creeping bureaucracy. The act provides guidelines for simplified financial reporting. It also requires government organizations to pay government support elements for full cost recovery of services delivered.

Cost linkage: Cost information assists organizations in providing integrated financial and program information along with an audited financial statement. The full cost recovery requirement spawned widespread debate on how best to allocate expenses into costs.

FASAB (Federal Accounting Standards Advisory Board), 1995

In 1995, this organization released Managerial Cost Accounting Standard #4. Entitled "Managerial Cost Accounting Concepts and Standards for the Federal Government," it provides instructions on what information should be included or excluded in a financial management system. It identifies government managers as the primary users of cost information because they are responsible for carrying out program objectives with resources that are entrusted to them. It explains that reliable and timely cost information helps ensure that managers use their resources efficiently to achieve expected results and outputs. The information also serves as an alert for waste and abuse.

Cost linkage: The standard discusses principles and methods involved in full cost recoveries and allocations. It defines the full cost an output as the sum of: (1) the costs of resources consumed by the segment (i.e., cost object) that directly or indirectly contributes to the output and (2) the costs of identifiable services provided by other segments within the provider entity as well as other entities acting as a supplier or vendor.

ITMRA (Information Technology Management Reform Act), 1996

This act is also known as the Clinger-Cohen Act. It establishes policies and guidelines designed to improve acquisition, use, and disposal of management information technology systems. It directly addresses controls on capital planning.

Cost linkage: Cost accounting techniques provide an analytical method to assess work processes and levels of productivity. The act defines an improved budgeting process for the information technology function of government organizations. For technology investment choices, cost data also assist in studies to determine the best uses of information technology.

FFMIA (Federal Financial Management Improvement Act), 1996

This act was influential in accelerating progress in financial systems development.

Cost linkage: The act defines the requirements to implement cost management as a recognized discipline and practice.

Quadrennial Defense Review, 1997

This review put more teeth into prior regulations.

Cost linkage: The review expressed more commitment for advanced costing systems.

National Defense Panel, 1997

This external mandate improved coordination among the military services.

Cost linkage: The panel expressed a greater need to answer more questions with facts.

OMB (Office of Management & Budget) Circulars, routinely updated

Four significant examples are:

- OMB A-25: This circular establishes guidelines for assessing user charges (e.g., fees) to the general public.

  Cost linkage: Cost allocation methods are needed to fairly reflect chargebacks in accordance with relative consumption by users.
- OMB A-76: This circular describes rules and methods to analyze and evaluate outsourcing and privatization options.

  Cost linkage: This circular describes methods for comparative benchmarking among private and public sectors.
- The President's Management Agenda: In 2004, President George W. Bush restated these five areas for the business focus of the second term of his administration: strategic management of human capital, competitive sourcing, improved financial performance, expanded electronic government, budget and performance integration.

Cost linkage: The first four items are difficult to achieve without excelling at the fifth one.

- The Program Assessment Rating Tool: This initially controversial report card on federal agencies has now been accepted as a motivator to improve performance in part due to peer pressure.

Cost linkage: A reliable and mature cost accounting system is essential to score a high grade.

JFMIP (Joint Financial Management Improvement Program)

Cost Accounting Systems Requirements was published in 1998. It describes applicable government-wide managerial cost accounting system requirements for government software.

Cost linkage: It provides a means to systematize the managerial cost accounting standards that were issued earlier by FASAB.

FAIR Act (Federal Activities Inventory Reform Act), 1998

This act requires identification and performance assessment of an organization's work activities that are non-governmental in nature.

Cost linkage: Similar to OMB A-76, this act describes the need for comparison of expenses and costs between and among private and public sector organizations.

Source: Presentation by James R. Lynch, Comptroller, U.S. Patent and Trademark Office, CAM-I Cost Symposium, Miami Beach, FL, May 12, 1999.

Appendix C

❦

ABC Software

THERE IS SUBSTANTIAL CONFUSION about what ABC/M software is. Vendors of some software products that simply produce flow charts and a one-stage resource cost allocation claim that their software is performing ABC/M. It is a semantics problem. I submit that what those products are doing is activity costing—computing the costs of activities. But from that point on, these tools are incapable of handling the complex arterial network assignment of those costs.

To provide a simple test, I have compiled a list of the top 15 defining characteristics of an ABC/M system. In my mind, any software vendor whose tool lacks these characteristics cannot claim ability to fully support ABC/M.

For each of the characteristics, I have first described what ABC/M software does followed by a paragraph describing the deficiency of impostor ABC/M software regarding that software feature.

Before listing the characteristics, it is useful to review a definition of a *cost object* because it appears numerous times below:

> A *cost object* is a recipient and consumer of expenses. Final cost objects take the form of diverse outputs, products, service lines, channels, customers, and service-recipients.

ABC/M DESIGN AND ARCHITECURE

Stand-Alone Yet Integrated Application

ABC/M systems have sufficient functionality to be fully effective as a stand-alone system, apart from the transaction-intensive subsystems that serve as sources to feed ABC/M. ABC/M systems work effectively as a "data mining" tool serving as an analytical application.

Deficient ABC/M tools are embedded in the traditional general ledger accounting system. In that location, ABC/M costs get commingled with traditional non-ABC/M ledger accounts and ultimately are dismissed by managers as another mysterious blackbox restricted to use by cost accountants.

Minimum Two-Stage Cost Assignment

ABC/M systems reflect how cost objects *use* work activities and how resources *supply* those activities with costs. This requires at a bare minimum two separate cost assignment stages—and usually many stages.

Deficient ABC tools allocate the expenses from the traditional accounting data and usually stop there. In some cases, they may be able to compute the unit cost of an individual activity's output but cannot further relate that cost to each of the many unique cost objects consuming the activity; in contrast, ABC/M does further assign activity costs.

Multi-Stage Cost Assignment Network

ABC/M systems reassign costs through a cost assignment network. A two-stage assignment is the minimum. But most ABC/M designs are multi-stage because of: (1) activity-to-activity assignments and (2) final cost object-to-final cost object assignments (e.g., products into customers).

ABC/M segments the diversity and variation of resources consumed by diverse outputs, products, service lines, channels, customers, and service-recipients. Activity costs may be used *directly* by these cost objects or, alternatively, used by other activities.

Deficient ABC/M tools are restricted by clumsy columns-to-rows cost allocations. They are incapable of linking a source cost to two or more stages of destination costs. Those using spreadsheets, for example, to compute ABC/M often complain how quickly they "hit the wall."

Flexible Modeling

ABC/M systems allow for real-time reconfiguring of the cost assignment path architecture, substitution of alternative driver measures, and immediate drill-down and analytical investigation of the data.

Deficient ABC/M tools require lengthy intervals between when the design changes are requested and when the programmers (who are often unfamiliar with the user's intent) can reconfigure the parameters that will compute the new results.

Consolidation

ABC/M systems allow for multiple children-to-parent roll-up consolidations—with rules to monitor model design consistency. This enables local managers to use ABC/M for managing, while their output data can be combined for enterprise-view purposes.

Deficient ABC/M tools are stand-alone without the capability to combine multiple low-level ABC/M models into a higher-level summarized one.

USING THE DATA FROM THE ABC/M SYSTEM

Contributed and Unitized Cost Elements

ABC/M systems can display for each cost object the entire list of cost elements contributing to the cost object's total cost. In addition, the ABC/M system can accommodate volume or quantity measures to display the unitized cost (e.g., the unit cost per each processed invoice) for both the cost object and each of its constituent cost contributions (frequently from the work activities).

Deficient ABC/M systems often do not even provide for any cost reassignments beyond the activity costs; therefore, they have no cost objects and cannot provide any visibility into the cost elements, total or unitized, that make up a cost object.

Reverse Cost Flowing/What-if Scenario Analysis

An ABC/M system can reverse the flow of costs to reflect incremental changes in the quantity, mix, frequency, and intensity of drivers. These changes can be for planned, budgeted, or hypothetical outlooks and are convenient for users to recalculate with the software. The ABC/M system will convert these changes into the impact on activity and resource costs. This capability is essential for what-if scenario analysis and cost estimating. (This is referred to as activity-based budgeting and planning (ABB/P].)

Deficient ABC/M tools usually cannot even calculate the driver rates, which are a basic prerequisite for attempting to perform what-if scenarios. They do not accommodate convenient user-commanded changes in drivers to forecast future costs.

Balanced Scorecard and Strategy Alignment Integration

An ABC/M system must easily send its calculated output data to become the input for managerial use. (ABC/M systems produce data ... and the "M" in ABC/M results from using that data). Two popular uses for ABC/M data are performance measurements and alignment of the cost structure with the organization's mission and strategy (e.g., how much do the costs support which strategy, and what is the "degree of fit"?)

Deficient ABC/M tools have no automated linkage to (and integration with) performance measurement and strategy definition applications.

Multi-Period Reporting

ABC/M systems recognize that trend analysis across multiple time periods has become a favored way for users to analyze results to draw insights and conclusions. As ABC/M is computed at more frequent intervals, the data serve well as an "actual costing" measurement.

Deficient ABC/M tools, often embedded in the general ledger, do not provide quick and convenient trend analysis.

Attributes (for Scoring or Tagging)

ABC/M systems allow users to conveniently create an unlimited number of unique tags or scores, each one with its own user-defined scale (e.g., high, medium or low value-adding), and to apply them to the ABC/M-derived costs. Then, two or more attributes can be concurrently viewed with any ABC/M cost (see dimensionality below). Advanced ABC/M systems can trace the proportionate attributed costs throughout the cost assignment network *into* cost objects.

Deficient ABC/M tools have no facility to tag or score ABC/M costs with attributes.

Cost Assignment Network Analysis

ABC/M systems allow the user to conveniently and rapidly view the cost assignment path network—from any location in the assignment network. All inward (many-to-one) cost contributions and their source costs can be viewed; similarly, all of a cost's outward reassignments (one-to-many distribution) can be viewed. Users can conveniently navigate and traverse down any cost assignment path and capture the contribution/distribution view of costs.

Deficient ABC/M tools usually have no reassignments. If a process-based planning tool claims ABC/M functionality, it is likely mix-blind and has no cost reassignment capabilities—only sequencing capabilities.

Process View Costing

In addition to an ABC/M system's popular capability to trace and reassign costs based on cause-and-effect relationships, it can also chain-link the same activity costs for a sequential cost build-up across time through business processes.

Deficient ABC/M tools may in fact only be tracing activity costs through business processes. But they are process-dedicated and incapable of reassigning costs to reflect and measure the diversity and variation of the mix of cost objects. They are mix-blind.

Capacity Measurements

ABC/M systems can accommodate the input measures of available capacities at very local detailed levels. Using those potential constraints, the ABC/M system can historically report the location and magnitude of unused or idle capacity costs. Advanced ABC/M systems, using reverse cost-flowing future projections, can perform rough-cut capacity planning (see the APICS definition) and alert users to capacity constraints.

Deficient ABC/M tools are capacity-insensitive. They assume infinite capacity in the historical view.

Yield Measurement

ABC/M systems allow for measurement and separation of off-spec and scrap produced at any activity. They integrate these measures with other operating systems.

Deficient ABC/M tools ignore measuring yield and relegate those measures to alternative systems.

Cost Dimensionality Viewing

Costs reassignments are linkages. By definition, there must be a contribution and a distribution view of any cost. When other attributes or categories (e.g., by sales region, by product family) are combined with the cost assignment network, there is an opportunity to perform multi-dimensional analysis. ABC/M systems leverage on-line analytical processing software (OLAP) to view costs.

Deficient ABC/M tools usually do not have cost objects, which are the more popular costs for multi-dimensional viewing.

Index

defining terminology, 314
demand, managing, 96
demand-driven costs, 236
diagramming software, 320
disaggregation, 118–119
dissatisfaction, with budgeting, 218–222
DoD. See U.S. Department of Defense
downsizing public employees, 17–19
driver types, 65
duplication of services, 125

E
e-commerce (B2B)
    consumer power, increase in, 153–155
    Internet, impact of, 153
    public sector, 156–157
    suppliers, impact upon, 155–156
    trading partner behavior, changing, 157
earned value management (EVM), 92,
    134–135
economic analysis software, 317
Economic Value Added (EVA), 134
EFQM. See European Foundation for Quality
    Management
EIS. See executive information systems
employees
    aligning behavior with strategy, 211–212
    downsizing, 17–19
    thoughts regarding ABC/M, 310–311
empowerment, 16–17
enterprise resource planning (ERP), 193
enterprise risk management (ERM), 247
European Foundation for Quality
    Management (EFQM), 203
EVA. See Economic Value Added
EVM. See earned value management
evolution of ABC, 330
executive information systems (EIS), 73, 174
Expanded ABC/M Cost Assignment Network,
    104
expenditures, restating as outputs, 4

F
Fabian, Alan, 276
FAIR. See Federal Activities Inventory Reform
    Act
FASAB. See Financial Accounting Standards
    Advisory Board
feature-based costing, 93

Federal Activities Inventory Reform Act (FAIR),
    120, 340
Federal Financial Management Improvement
    Act (FFMIA), 1996, 339
federal regulations, 337–340
fees for service, 15
FFMIA. See Federal Financial Management
    Improvement Act, 1996
final cost object profiling, rapid prototyping,
    264
final cost objectives, 71
Financial Accounting Standards Advisory
    Board (FASAB), 291, 305, 338
financial data collection, 90
financial information, need for, 23
financial perspective, balanced scorecard,
    202
financial reporting driven stage, cost
    management systems, 81–82
focus, performance management, 194
forecasting, 221
full-absorption cost recovery chargebacks,
    125
functional shiftability, 64
functions, excessive focus on, 3–4
fund accounting data, 115
future of ABC/M, 76–77
future of government
    ABC/M production systems, 329
    customer expectations, 325–326
    managerial economics, 327–331
    role of academics and universities,
        331–333
    understanding true costs, 326–327

G
GAO. See Government Accountability Office
general ledger, 53, 56, 93, 115
generic strategy map, 203
GMRA. See Government Management Results
    Act, 1994
goal non-congruency, 201
Government Accountability Office (GAO), 23
government entities, compared to commercial
    businesses, 32–34
Government Management Results Act
    (GMRA), 1994, 338
Government Performance and Results Act
    (GPRA), 20, 305–306, 337–338